Rocky Road

Rocky Road

The Legendary Life and Times of Billy Rancher

Bill Reader

*Patsy —
What's a nice person like you doing in the music business? Good luck with everything. Your swimming experience should help in the shark-infested water. It was great meeting you. Hope I see you again real soon.

Bill*

Copyright © 1996 by Bill Reader

All rights reserved. Printed in the United States of America. No part of this book may be reproduced in whole or in part, except for the quotation of brief passages in reviews, without prior permission from the publisher. Inquiries should be addressed to No Fate Publishing, 3800A Bridgeport Way West, Suite 492, University Place, Washington, 98466.

FIRST EDITION

Library of Congress Catalog Card Number: 96-92934

ISBN: 0-9655377-0-6

Every effort has been made to locate, identify and properly credit photographers. All photographs are copyrighted by the photographer credited, all rights reserved. In cases where the photographer is not known, the source that has supplied the photograph is listed. Any inadvertent omissions or errors will be corrected in future editions.

Designed by Greg Harris

Cover photo by Bart Danielson

Back photo by Mark Rabiner

*For my wife and best friend, Stephanie,
who makes everything possible.*

CONTENTS

Acknowledgments	ix
Introduction	xi
1. "You Know How Billy Is"	1
2. The Upstroke, and the Downstroke	4
3. So You Want to be a Rock 'n' Roll Star	15
4. Growin' Up	17
5. Ladies and Gentlemen, the Malchicks	25
6. Love at First Sight	36
7. "A Relationship Unlike Any Two Brothers"	39
8. The Unreal Gods	49
9. A Magic Summer	59
10. Billy and Karen	72
11. Playing the Paramount	78
12. The Shark Bite	81
13. Boom Chuck Rock Now!	85
14. Building the Legend	93
15. Europe	106
16. Boom Chucked by KGON	109
17. "Don't You Want to Root For a Guy Like That?"	115
18. New Jersey Shows Billy Who's Boss	122
19. Who Manages the Managers?	131
20. The Fast Life	141
21. Does God Have to Call Shotgun?	152
22. Let's Make a Deal Already	154
23. Welcome to Arista, Now Change Everything	158
24. Lost in LA	165
25. The End of the Unreal Gods	174
26. Helping One of Their Own	180
27. Flesh and Blood	183
28. Looking For a Miracle	194
29. A Close Call	196
30. Beating the Death Sentence	203
31. Another Way to Play	211
32. "They Can't Say the Ranch Never Tried"	219
33. The Show Must Go On	225
34. "I've Talked to God"	235
35. The End of Billy's Rocky Road	240
About the Author	247
Order Form	249

ACKNOWLEDGMENTS

This book wouldn't have been possible without the cooperation of two wonderful people, Billy Rancher's mother Astrid Hanke and her husband Jack. Thank you for your time, for sharing so many memories, and for your hospitality. Special thanks to Billy's brother and sister, Lenny Rancher and Ellen Willis, and to Billy's girlfriend Karen. I'm sure Billy would be very proud of all of you. The Unreal Gods — Dave Stricker, Jon DuFresne, Billy Flaxel and Alf Ryder — were open, and did their best to remember events that took place 15 years ago. Thank you. The first person I talked to, Steve Hettum, pointed me in all the right directions, and gave me videos, address books, newspaper and magazine clippings and posters. Joe Dreiling also provided boxes of materials, including photos that were used in this book. Speaking of photos, thanks, of course, to Bart Danielson and Mark Rabiner. Most of the photos that appear in this book were taken by Bart, who was a good friend to Billy. Other photos were supplied by Karen. Every effort was made to determine the identities of all the photographers, and their names appear with their photos. Keith Cox supplied tapes, posters and set lists. Thank you Buck Munger, for writing about Billy in nearly every edition of Two Louies from 1980 through 1986. Information was also obtained from stories that appeared in The Oregonian, as well as Multnomah, Scene and The Downtowner magazines. Thanks also to the following people, who were among those interviewed for this book: Glen Baggerly, Jan Baross, Jim Basnight, Houston Bolles, Mick Boyt, Earl Burks, Caroline Chern, Dana Coffee, Joe Delia, Tony DeMicoli, Candyce Dru, Jeff Erdman, Annie Farmer, Cheryl Hodgson, Todd Jensen, David Jester, Fritz Johnson, Pete Jorgusen, Stephen Kimberley, Jim Miller, Rebecca Orwoll, Attilio Panissidi III, Mo Stevenson and Ron Walp. Thanks to my friend Greg Harris who designed this book. I'd like to thank my parents, Tom and Sandra Reader, for their support and for teaching me many valuable lessons. Thanks to Bill Boie, Jim Smith and Ken Kohl, who have always been friends, and sources of inspiration. Last, but certainly not least, thank you to my wife, Stephanie, who was with me every step of the way on this project. If not for Steph's editing, encouragement and love, believe me, you wouldn't be holding this book right now.

INTRODUCTION

Corvallis, Oregon, 1982-83: During my senior year at Oregon State University, I lived with four great guys in a big house at the corner of 9th and Van Buren. I don't remember much about classes, football games or graduation. What I do remember is listening to Billy Rancher and the Unreal Gods' album, "Boom Chuck Rock Now!" day and night. The best feature of this house was a hot tub on the front porch. Because that's where we spent most of our time, the turntable was placed within arm's reach, just through the front window, so Billy's album could be played, flipped over, played, flipped over, and played again.

Salem, Oregon, 1993: After searching unsuccessfully for "Boom Chuck Rock Now!" for a year or so, my wife Stephanie found the album in a used record store. As her friend watched in disbelief, Steph jumped for joy, and immediately forked over $35 for her treasure, which she brought home to a grateful husband. After listening to the record, and looking it over for clues about Billy's life, we decided somebody should write a book about Billy. We decided, in fact, that I should write a book about Billy. Never mind that I'd never met Billy, seen him perform, or even known anyone who knew him. It took three years, working on vacations, weekends and late at night after long days at my real job, but here it is. This is for everyone who knew Billy and his music, and for those who should have been so lucky.

Bill Reader
Tacoma, Washington
October 1996

1 "You Know How Billy Is"

Steve Hettum couldn't believe his ears. "Five bucks? Are you nuts? Tony's gonna skin me."

Billy Rancher, rock star, laughed.

"Don't worry about it, Steve. Just go down there and tell Tony it's five bucks to get in, or we're not playing. We've got to make more money. We need new amps. We're movin', man. We're not gonna carry this rocket around in a wheelbarrow."

Most days, managing Billy Rancher and the Unreal Gods seemed more like a party than a job. But Steve wasn't looking forward to this meeting with Tony DeMicoli, the owner of Luis' La Bamba, the hippest rock 'n' roll club in town. Steve was a kid, just 24 years old, and he looked even younger with his curly brown hair and rosy cheeks. Tony was a mean-looking, mean-talking, Lucky Strikes-smoking tough guy from New York who always wore clothes as black as his thick moustache and frizzy hair. Black pants. Black sweater. Black shoes. Black, black, black. Tony DeMicoli had been in this business a long time, and he used guys like Steve Hettum for dental floss. And now all Steve had to do was march into Tony's club and explain that Billy Rancher wouldn't be playing this weekend unless the cover was raised to five dollars. Easy for Billy to say. Another thing Steve knew about his friend Billy Rancher, though: Once he made up his mind, there was no changing it. Billy was convinced he was worth five dollars. He was right, of course. Steve liked to tell people that Billy was egotistical, but in a cool way.

And it's true that in the summer of 1981, Billy Rancher and the Unreal Gods were "the hottest band in Portland, OreGONE," as Steve claimed when he introduced them on stage. But Steve wasn't sure Tony was going to go for this.

On his way downtown to La Bamba, all Steve could think about was one of the first conversations he had with Tony. "You say it, you do it," Tony had told him. "We don't need no contract. If you say something, you better fucking do it. That's the way it is."

"Tony, here's the way it is," Steve began, sitting tall in his chair in Tony DeMicoli's cramped office. "Billy says five bucks this weekend, or they're not playing."

Why isn't he saying anything, Steve wondered. *Scream at me, tell me to take a hike ... tie me to a big rock and toss me into the Willamette River, just do something.* Tony took a long, final drag on his unfiltered cigarette, exhaled, snuffed it out in a crowded ashtray, and lit another. "Steve, you gotta talk some sense into him. Tell him I'll charge four bucks, but that's already more than anyone else in town is getting."

Tony wanted to make sure his place was crowded with people who still had enough money in their pockets to buy drinks. He was putting up a fight, out of habit as much as anything, but he knew. He knew that Billy was going to fill his club, no matter what he charged.

"Tony, you know how Billy is," Hettum said. "It's five bucks, or he's not playing, and he means it."

"All right, fuck it. Five bucks. I hope somebody shows up."

That Friday night, Billy Rancher and the Unreal Gods played to a packed house at La Bamba, with fans lined up on the sidewalk outside the old stone building, pushing against the massive wooden doors, waiting for someone to leave so they could squeeze in. In other words, it was a typical Unreal Gods show. Those who made it to the dance floor, danced. Those who didn't jumped on top of tables, and they danced, too. Billy was wearing his leopard skin suit, and he was singing those songs that were so catchy you couldn't get them out of your head for days. He was playing his brown Fender Stratocaster, blond hair bouncing, sweat flying. The night ended much like many others that year at

La Bamba, with Tony DeMicoli pleading as closing time came and went: "Billy, get off the stage, we've got to get everybody out of here." Billy kept playing. Tony turned on the lights and told everyone to go home. They did, finally. They'd paid their five dollars, just like Billy said they would, and they'd gotten their money's worth.

2 The Upstroke, and the Downstroke

Billy Rancher invented boom chuck rock. It was rock 'n' roll, basically, guitars and drums mostly, but Billy was influenced by (and stole freely from) reggae, Motown, new wave. It was all fun, that's for sure. Billy wrote great pop songs, and then he and his new band played the hell out of them. In the summer of 1981, in Portland, Oregon, if you wanted to have a good time, all you had to do was find Billy Rancher and the Unreal Gods.

It was music that was full of energy. It wasn't simply music you could dance to, it was music you *had* to dance to. The Unreal Gods were the hottest band in the Northwest, the band you had to see, had to hear. The Portland media was relentless in its praise of Billy, and that was before anyone had actually seen the Unreal Gods play. Now, after a couple months of shows, the newspaper and magazine writers who slithered into Portland's funky downtown clubs and rock 'n' roll taverns to cover the city's exploding music scene would have been calling Billy the next Elvis, if only the King had been a little better showman. About the only ones who didn't get it were other musicians in town, jealous of Billy's success. Some said Billy wasn't all that talented — he wasn't a great guitar player, he wasn't a great singer. Maybe he wasn't, but while the Pink Floyd imitators were locked in their basements, noodling away, Billy

Billy Rancher, Portland's rock 'n' roll hero.
(Bart Danielson)

was singing his happy songs, and people were dancing. The punks called Billy a pretty boy, a sellout. Where was the anger, the attitude? You want an attitude? Here was Billy's: Fuck art, let's dance. Are we having fun? The answer, always, was yes.

Billy wasn't just having fun, he was having the time of his life. And why not? He was 24 years old, and he was a star. He was tall, and handsome, and rich didn't seem far off. He was in love with a beautiful girl. Besides, having fun was what Billy did. It's what he'd always done. But this had been a spectacular summer, even by Billy Rancher's standards.

The first Unreal Gods show was June 14th at Tipper's, a little bar in southeast Portland. The place was packed, thanks in part to a story a few days earlier in Portland's 300,000-plus circulation daily newspaper, The Oregonian. The article was written by John Wendeborn, a fan of Billy's work from the fall of 1979 through January of '81 with the Malchicks, a bluesy group that included Billy's little brother Lenny on lead guitar. The Tipper's show wasn't perfect technically, but there was a connection between the band and audience. Bass player Dave Stricker, the only Malchick Billy brought with him to the Unreal Gods, drove home that night with one thought running through his mind, over and over. This is going to be big. This is going to be so big.

From there, Billy moved into the downtown clubs. La Bamba, Tony DeMicoli's joint, became the Unreal Gods' home base. There was something magic about those shows that summer. Billy quickly attracted a large and loyal following. The shows became events, and "Where's Billy playing tonight?" became a popular question.

Billy's music was something new, something different. Other bands offered either heavy metal cliches, wimpy techno pop or unlistenable punk. Billy Rancher and the Unreal Gods were a rock 'n' roll guitar band that took Billy's simple, hook-heavy songs and played them with passion. Billy's fans packed the Portland clubs, and anyone not dancing was probably singing along. They were fun songs, boy meets girl stuff. Or girl leaves boy in the stereo area. Or boy and girl eat psychedelic mushrooms and go skiing. Every day, every breath he took, was a new song to Billy. The shows were crowded, and frenzied, and sweaty, and wonderful. Tony DeMicoli remembers. "He always seemed so comfortable on the stage. He was a natural. It's like he was born to be on stage, nowhere else."

Of course, there was more to it than the infectious music. You looked at Billy on stage, so handsome, so playful, and you wanted to like him. He wasn't surly, or in a drugged-out stupor like other rockers. He was 6-foot-4 and lean, like an athlete, which, in fact, he had been. And he had that made-for-MTV face. He was Portland's golden boy. He'd wear pajama tops for shirts and crazy, skin-tight pants. Or maybe his "legendary" leopard skin outfit. Legendary was one of Billy's favorite words, and there were many legendary nights that summer at La Bamba for Billy Rancher, Portland's rock 'n' roll hero.

One of Billy's biggest fans was Annie Farmer, who worked at the Paramount Theater in Portland. She was a few years older than Billy, and wasn't like the women who followed Billy home from shows, waiting in their cars, hoping he'd leave his girlfriend Karen long enough for them to get Billy's attention, maybe slip him their phone numbers. Annie liked Billy because he was polite. Annie Farmer grew up in New Orleans in an old money family. She's fond of quoting George Bernard Shaw. *There is no accomplishment so easy to acquire as politeness, and none so profitable.* She liked Billy because he was well-mannered; because, in her words, he had been brought up correctly.

Annie met Billy in 1980, when Tony DeMicoli invited her to come to a club he was running — the Long Goodbye on 10th and Everett in downtown Portland. He wanted Annie to see Billy's band, the Malchicks. They were a garage band, covering old Rolling Stones, Chuck Berry and Iggy Pop tunes, and playing some originals written by Billy and Lenny. The Malchicks were rough around the edges, but Annie loved the enthusiasm, the way the kids seemed to react to Billy and his band. She saw potential. Actually, she saw Billy's potential, and advised him to dump the rest of the group and start his own, playing just his songs.

The Malchicks did eventually split up, although that had a lot more to do with musical differences between Billy and Lenny than any advice from Annie Farmer. It had been several months since Annie had spoken with Billy when she got a phone call early in the summer of '81.

"Annie, I've got my own band now," Billy told her. "It's called Billy Rancher and the Unreal Gods. Come and hear us."

She did. "They were wonderful," Annie says. "Nothing Billy did was staged, it was inspired. Billy was doing something that came naturally to him."

Talking people into doing things for him also came naturally to

Billy. He talked Annie into convincing her boss, Michael McManus, to let the Unreal Gods open for reggae man Peter Tosh at the Paramount Theater on August 29th.

What Billy really liked to do was write songs and play them. That's all he was doing now. No more school. No more baseball. No more landscaping. Music, all day and all night. Billy Rancher and the Unreal Gods, eight days a week. Billy was living in a big two-story house at 0104 SW Lane Street, on the corner of Lane and Water in the hip southwest Portland Corbett district. The house, like all the others in the neighborhood, had been built early in the century, and was surrounded by huge oak trees. Billy lived there with guitarist Jon DuFresne and Jon's girlfriend Doreen, and Steve Hettum. Others stayed in the house from time to time, and it was always full, always buzzing. Every day, nothing but Unreal Gods business. Interviews. Making posters. Buying clothes. Writing songs. Rehearsals. Hettum remembers the phone ringing constantly. A few months earlier, he had been the one making the calls, trying to line up shows. Now the damn thing wouldn't quit ringing. "All of the sudden," Hettum says, "It was like, 'Jesus Christ, we're superstars.' "

Of course they were. Billy had been telling anyone who would listen that he would be. In the fall of 1979, when the Malchicks were just getting started, Billy informed a local musician named Joe Dreiling, "I'm going to be more famous than Mick Jagger. Come and see me." Joe did, and he couldn't believe what he saw. "The energy was unbelievable," Dreiling says. "They were such good-looking boys. Billy had tights on under his pants. He was in the middle of a song, and he started saying, 'Oh, it's so hot, it's so hot, I've got to take my clothes off.' So he did. The girls were going crazy, and I just thought, 'This guy will do anything.' I could see things were going to work. Billy was going to make it big." The next time Joe Dreiling saw the Malchicks play, he was managing the band.

Buck Munger is the editor of Two Louies, a Portland music magazine that got its start about the same time as the Malchicks. He remembers Billy Rancher knocking on his door. "He told me, 'OK, Buck, Johnny and the Distractions signed with A&M. Quarterflash signed with Geffen. Well, they're gone, and I'm here, and now it's my turn.' Billy Rancher was a kid who wanted to do this as a profession, as a commercial deal. 'Teach me about the business, teach me about publishing, teach me ...' And I wanted to help him, because he deserved it, because he was going to be a good influence on rock 'n' roll. He was not going to be some slimeball, puking, overdosing punk. If kids emulated him, they were going to be OK. Billy approached it like baseball. 'I'm with the guys, it's like a team, and I know about teams.' And he promoted his team."

He sure did. Billy had 10,000 posters made and he plastered them all over town. *Portland's premier world class rock 'n' roll show*. This was to promote the Unreal Gods' *first* show.

Billy decided his team needed to have weekly meetings, each Monday at the house before rehearsal. Monday, August 24th, wasn't a typical band meeting. For one thing, the Unreal Gods had never played in front of a crowd like they were going to see that Saturday at the Paramount. Another thing was unusual. Billy was late. Billy was a rehearsal fanatic, and he couldn't stand it when someone else was late. Everyone had gathered upstairs, waiting for Billy, talking about the Peter Tosh show. When Billy arrived, they'd split the money from the weekend's shows, talk business, then head down to the basement for rehearsal.

—

This much about the meeting was typical: Steve and Alf were arguing. Alf Ryder, the keyboard player, was 37 years old. (Of course, if there's any truth to the notion that you're only as old as the girls you sleep with, Alf would have been considerably younger). Alf scared the rest of the band by practicing primal therapy, screaming at the top of his lungs. Jon DuFresne wasn't sure what to make of Alf when he tried out for the band. "We went down to jam with Alf, and he had this funky old keyboard, and I was just thinking, 'Who is this guy? I hope he's not going to be in the band.' " But Alf spent $5,000 on an Oberheim keyboard, and Billy liked the sounds he could make with it, so Alf was in. Jon, and the rest of the band, overcame any fears they might have had about Alf, who proved eventually to be a valuable member of the Unreal Gods. But he was different than the rest of the guys, and not just because he was at least 10 years older and, on average, half a foot shorter than his bandmates. He was born Alfred Delia. He was a New Yorker. He had been in a band, The Brothers (with, yes, a few more Delias) back in the '60s. These things, Alf believed, certainly made him wiser than Hettum, who was the band's manager, near as Alf could tell, only because he was a friend of Billy's.

—

Actually, that is how Steve got the job. He'd met Billy in late 1979 down at Sack's Front Avenue, a club Billy played with the Malchicks.

Before they met, Steve had seen Billy playing basketball on a court outside Steve's dorm room window at Portland State University. He was impressed that Billy could dunk the ball with two hands, behind his head. Billy and Steve were Portland boys who were the same age, and shared similar interests: sports, girls, music and beer. When the Malchicks called it quits early in 1981, and the Unreal Gods were formed, Steve fell into his position as manager by setting up gigs, promoting shows and taking money at the door, doing whatever had to be done.

Another part of his job was helping Billy shop for clothes, usually at second hand stores. Pajamas were a staple of Billy's stage wardrobe, but anything Billy thought was different enough to shock someone had a chance of making it into an Unreal Gods show. (Buying clothes was sure easier, Billy's mother Astrid thought, back when he was a normal kid. After going to a Malchicks show and seeing Billy wearing plaid golf pants, a cumberbund and mascara, she gave up. Realizing the futility of shopping for Billy's clothes, and understanding that neither of her rock 'n' roll sons was going to have a typical 9-to-5 job, Astrid bought Billy and Lenny health insurance instead of clothes for Christmas in 1980). Billy was going for a look. He didn't want to simply stand on stage and play his songs. From the beginning, he wanted to present a real show, not just music. Unreal Gods gigs, owing in part to Billy's fascination with David Bowie, featured costume changes, stage props and a couple of go-go dancers who stood on the side of the stage and gyrated wildly as the band wailed away.

Recently, settling disputes between Billy and club owners had been added to Steve Hettum's list of responsibilities. Life at the Unreal Gods house was frantic, more so for Hettum than anyone else. A typical day for Steve could include answering the phone, making posters, dealing with clubs, setting up interviews, shopping for clothes with Billy and cooking, if there was any food in the house. And arguing with Alf.

—

Jon DuFresne's girlfriend Doreen was a hairdresser, a happy coincidence, since someone had to spike Jon's rock 'n' roll hair just right. Billy liked Jon's look, and his attitude, which is why he was in the band. That, and the fact he was the best guitar player in Portland. Billy and Jon made quite a striking pair at the center of the stage. Jon was tall, too, just an

Jon DuFresne's girlfriend Doreen applies makeup while the rest of the Unreal Gods – from left, Alf Ryder, Billy Rancher, Billy Flaxel and Dave Stricker – strike poses.
(Mark Rabiner)

inch or two shorter than Billy and handsome in a Rick Springfield kind of way.

Jon had been playing guitar in bands for about 10 years, since he was 15 years old, everything from country to Temptations-style Top 40 covers to punk. But he'd never had this much fun.

"It was just a rock 'n' roll fantasy," he says. "None of us were working at anything other than Billy Rancher and the Unreal Gods. We'd get up each day, and just start doing things that were related to the band. It was a very creative atmosphere. Me and Billy were hanging out together a lot, getting to know each other. It was the kind of feeling that made me think, 'Yeah, this is why I became a musician.'"

Dave Stricker was the only Unreal God who played with Billy in the Malchicks. He'd grown up in the same Portland neighborhood as Billy, and also went to Madison High School, a couple years ahead of Billy. Stricker taught himself how to play bass, and he'd played mostly country music before joining the Malchicks.

He was a typical bass player, content to stand in the shadows at the back of the stage and concentrate on playing the songs the best he could. Even though they were great friends, Billy had threatened to kick him out of the Malchicks if he didn't move more. The next set, when Billy looked back to check, Dave would tentatively stick one leg forward, then back. Then he'd smile at Billy. When the Malchicks split up, he had a choice to make. Billy or Lenny. Rock 'n' roll or reggae. Actually, it wasn't that tough. Billy wanted to put together a great band, kick Portland's ass and be a rock star. Lenny, who was only 19 years old when the Malchicks broke up, just wanted to play his guitar and have another 40-ounce Rainier Ale.

From the first days of rehearsal, Billy made it clear that this was a professional band. There would be a lot of rehearsing, a lot of meetings. There would be no hanging out, drinking beer with the audience. That was fine with Stricker. And he didn't mind that Billy was in charge. He'd watched the Malchicks fall apart because Billy and Lenny couldn't get along. Lenny was his friend, but he knew Billy was onto something big.

So Dave Stricker became the first Unreal God. Then DuFresne, Alf Ryder, and finally, drummer Billy Flaxel were added.

—

Flaxel, the youngest Unreal God at 23, joined just a few weeks before that first show at Tipper's. He replaced Mark Borden, who had the bad luck of breaking his arm in a motorcycle accident. Billy Rancher told him thanks, but no thanks. The Unreal Gods didn't have time to wait for him to heal.

Flaxel had been taking music classes at Mount Hood Community College in the spring of '81, but that was just an excuse to meet girls. He either didn't meet any, or, more likely, had already met them all, because he quit going to school. He'd been the drummer and lead singer in a group called Stratus that had just broken up. He wanted to be the leader of a band, but he needed to make some money. He wandered into a Portland music store and heard about a new band whose drummer had just broken his arm. A phone call and an audition later, and he was in. He was a solid drummer and he had a brown Chevy van, the Unrealmobile, which was used to haul band members and equipment to gigs. "I wasn't a great drummer, but I could rock your nuts off, you know."

He also had a rich father, Dr. John Flaxel, who became a financial supporter of the Unreal Gods. It was Dr. Flaxel, in fact, who paid for the band's time at Jack Barr's new High Tech Recording studio in Portland, where they were working on an album.

—

Finally, 15 minutes late for the band meeting, Billy arrived, striding through the front door with his long arm draped around Karen. Everyone's attention shifted to Billy, which is what usually happened when he entered a room. Not just because of his striking physical appearance, or because he was the leader of Portland's best band. There was something about Billy — his charisma — that made people listen to him, that made them believe every one of his crazy ideas would work. Most of them did, of course.

Buck Munger always thought that life seemed like a big cocktail party any time Billy was around.

On this day, though, something was different. Where was the smile, that big, toothy, silly grin? And why wasn't he going on about ideas for the band — new songs, a different stage set, a crazy outfit he was going to wear, anything. The band was going to play with Peter Tosh at the Paramount in five days, and everyone knew how much that meant to Billy.

"I've got to tell you guys something," Billy said, his voice trembling. "I went to the doctor, and I've got a lump in my groin. I've got to have some tests." Then he walked out of the room. Everyone looked to Karen.

Karen Sage was 19 years old. When she was 12, her family moved to an affluent Portland suburb, Lake Oswego, from the working class east Portland neighborhood the Rancher family had called home since 1970. Bill and Dorothy Sage would rather their daughter had fallen for a premed student, not some wild-eyed guitar player with big dreams in his head. And they certainly would have preferred that Karen had found someone her own age. Billy was five years older, and, let's say, wiser to the ways of the world. Eventually, Billy won over Karen's parents. He was a rascal, but he wasn't Keith Moon. You could invite him to your house and not be afraid he'd cuss at your grandma or puke at the dinner table. For the wild streak, he could thank his father, Joe. For the social skills — not to mention his blond hair and blue eyes — credit goes to his Swedish-born mother, Astrid. Karen and Billy met September 5th, 1980 in line for a midnight movie in Portland. By the time she left for the University of Oregon in Eugene, three weeks later, she was in love. Now, less than a year later, her boyfriend was sick, and she was left to explain it to the rest of the band.

She didn't know exactly how to say it, so she just said it: "Billy has cancer."

Karen Sage was just 18 years old when she fell for one of Billy's best lines: "Hi, I'm Billy Rancher."
(Bart Danielson)

3 So You Want to be a Rock 'n' Roll Star

Ron Walp wouldn't know a Fender Stratocaster if you smashed one over his head, but he knows what a baseball player looks like. Billy Rancher was an all-city shortstop at Madison High School in 1975, only a fair hitter but a brilliant, graceful fielder with good range, the softest hands you've ever seen and a feel for the game he picked up from his father Joe, a former minor leaguer. Walp, the coach at Mount Hood Community College in Portland, offered Billy a baseball scholarship, which suited Billy fine, because he wanted to keep playing baseball and start studying landscaping and coeds, and now he could do all of that and still live at home.

That fall, Billy ran into Pete Jorgusen, an old friend from Madison. They'd played basketball together in high school, but neither knew the other was going to Mount Hood. They played intramural hoops at college and started car pooling, usually in Billy's yellow Firebird. A radio ad caught Pete's attention one January afternoon on the way home from school. There was going to be a David Bowie lookalike contest, with the winner getting a couple of passes for an upcoming Bowie concert at Memorial Coliseum in Portland. Pete figured he'd just found a free ticket to the show. Oh, and one for Billy.

"Billy, you're a dead ringer, you've got to do it."

At first, Billy wasn't sure. "I don't know, man, I don't think I look that much like him."

"You do," Pete assured him. "We'll put some makeup on you, everybody will think it's really David Bowie. And then we get to see the show. For free."

About a dozen Bowie wannabes and assorted radio station and record store types were already gathered at the Holiday Inn when Billy and Pete walked in. "The place just got quiet," Pete remembers. "Everybody knew Billy was the winner."

The voting was a formality. The other Bowie lookalikes had simply painted their faces or bleached their hair strawberry blond. Billy didn't require much of a makeover, maybe a little eyeliner. He actually looked like Bowie, lean, with straight blond hair, but more than that, he acted like Bowie. He had an elegance, a style. Billy was a rock star, even before he was a rock star. The next morning, Billy's mother Astrid found a paper towel on her kitchen counter. With a purple felt pen, Billy had written:

I won!

I can't believe it's true. Over $180 in prize money and merchandise, free tickets, Rolls Royce chauffeur to the Coliseum, free T-shirts, $100 check coming in two weeks, plus much, much, more.

Tell you tomorrow!

Astrid wrapped the paper towel in plastic wrap and put it away for safe keeping.

On February 4th, the night of the show, Billy and Pete arrived at the Coliseum in a limo. When they got out, people waiting in line actually thought Billy was David Bowie. He did look a lot like Bowie. Billy couldn't believe the way the Bowie fans responded to him, the way they were treating him, as if he were royalty or something. *Imagine if he really was David Bowie.* Inside the Coliseum, Billy watched in amazement as 10,000 screaming fans went crazy when Bowie took the stage. He looked so cool, Billy thought.

Afterward, Billy and Pete tried to get backstage. They never made it, but they told the story for years that they had, and, in fact, had quite a nice talk with Bowie.

"He was star struck," Pete says. "He decided then and there that was the life for him."

4 Growin' Up

Not long after winning the David Bowie contest, Billy bought a guitar — a cheap Fender Telecaster knockoff — a chord book and a little amp, and started practicing. He learned to play a little, and discovered he could sing. Billy was still playing baseball at Mount Hood, but he had become more interested in being a rock star than a big league shortstop. Billy's father, Joe Rancher, nearly made it to the major leagues, and Joe always dreamed of having a son who would. In the spring of 1956, at the age of 37, Joe's playing days were long behind him when he married a pretty 20-year-old blonde named Astrid Svensson.

Astrid grew up on a huge farm near Sibbarp, on the west coast of Sweden, with four sisters and three brothers, and a bad case of what her mother called "America Fever." She wanted to see American movies, wear American clothes, learn all she could about this great country she read about. She asked her parents, Frans and Ellen, to let her go to America. One day, in 1954, Astrid was busy working at her job as a telephone operator when she got a call from her mother. "Are you still thinking about that America trip?" Ellen Svensson asked her 18-year-old daughter. "You better believe it," Astrid said excitedly. "Well, you can go, but only if you go with Arvid and Mabel." Arvid Carlson was a friend of the Svensson family. He was born in Sweden, but had lived in the United

States the past 25 years. He and his wife Mabel were visiting for the first time since they'd left Sweden, and they told Ellen they'd be happy to take Astrid with them to America, to live in Alexandria, Minnesota.

Astrid worked at the resort the Carlsons ran, and she made quite an impression on a visitor from Sioux Falls, South Dakota named Alan Egger, his wife and their two young children. The Egger children, who were 10 and 12 years old, were fascinated by Astrid, and her funny Swedish accent. "Can we take Astrid with us to Sioux Falls, mom and dad? She's fun."

Next stop, Sioux Falls. Astrid helped the Egger family any way she could, cooking and cleaning, but she wanted a real job. Alan Egger, the part-owner of a steel company, helped Astrid get work at a bank, and she moved into the brand new YWCA building. Her plan was to study English for two years, then return home. Instead, she stayed to study Joseph Rancher, a rugged, handsome ex-ballplayer. Joe maintained the baseball fields in Sioux Falls and taught kids how to play ball. Astrid couldn't understand why all the boys wore such funny-looking clothes when they played games.

Joe's parents were Lithuanian, and he was born in New Jersey. Baseball took him to Montreal, the Brooklyn Dodgers' Class AAA minor-league team, just one step from the majors. But World War II interrupted his career. Joe served with the 345th Squadron in Italy. After the war, he played some ball in Panama, but his shot at the big leagues was gone.

Joe wouldn't tell Astrid how old he was, so she didn't know he was 17 years older than her when they got married. Not that Astrid really cared. All she knew was that she was in love. Joe convinced Astrid that Los Angeles was the land of opportunity, so they moved there, and that's where Billy was born on February 28th, 1957. Turns out LA was the land of smog and crowded freeways, even back then, so they moved when Billy was three months old to Anchorage, Alaska. Two other kids came along — Ellen on March 6th, 1960 and Lenny on April 17th, 1961. Joe worked as a salesman, maintained fields and ballparks, and coached Billy's Little League team. He leased the concession rights from the city of Anchorage, and he and Astrid sold food and drinks at baseball games.

Anchorage in the '60s was a great place to be a kid. It wasn't much of a city yet, just 45,000 people or so, and spread out. It was the kind of place you had to get outside and make your own fun. The Rancher kids had no trouble doing that. Billy, Lenny and Ellen formed a bicycle gang, the Roughriders. It wasn't a gang, really, just three kids riding their bikes through the woods, but Billy thought it sounded a lot better if they called themselves a gang. As the Roughriders made their way over trails, along gravel roads and through their neighborhood, Billy would often tell Lenny and Ellen to stop, sure there was another bicycle gang in the area. "You stay here," he'd tell his younger brother and sister. "Don't be afraid. I'm going to scout ahead. Stay here, I'll be right back." Ellen doesn't remember actually ever seeing any other kids. "But we always believed Billy when he told us there were other gangs," she says. "We believed everything he said, believed in him totally, even if he got us in trouble. We were a bunch of banshees, and he was our leader."

Following Billy could be risky. Like the time he found an abandoned shack five miles into the woods from their house and decided that's where they'd play that day. They were having such a good time, swinging from a rope they'd tied around a tree, that they didn't even think about going home until nearly midnight. It was still light outside, one of those long Alaskan summer days. Astrid and Joe had been out looking for them for hours. The Rancher kids had just had the greatest day of their lives, thanks to Billy. And, thanks to Billy, they all got horrible spankings.

But having a leader meant having someone to take care of you, too. One day, the three Rancher kids were sledding down a snow-covered slope. Lenny crashed his sled, and he and Ellen were convinced they'd just discovered why it was called Killer's Hill. There was blood in the snow, and Lenny was sure he was going to die, or at least lose a leg. Ellen thought so, too, and she started to cry. Billy carefully picked up his little brother, put him on his sled, and pulled him up the hill. Then he dragged him down a rough logging road, toward their house. Ellen was running alongside Billy, as fast as her skinny little legs could go. "Oh God, he's going to die, he's going to die," she cried. Billy kept running and running, dragging Lenny. They got home, exhausted, and Astrid bandaged up Lenny's leg, and told him everything was going to be OK. It really paid to have a big brother sometimes.

On nights Joe and Astrid went out, Lenny and Ellen were left in the care of their older brother, their babysitter. Or so they thought. Once their parents were out the door, Billy liked to change into a character he called Bolly, a being from another planet. He was a convincing actor.

"Where's Billy?" Lenny would ask, close to tears. "Bring back my brother!"

"I took Billy off in the space ship," Bolly said in his best spaced-out, straight-faced monotone. "He won't be coming back for a while. If you don't do everything I say, I'm leaving, and I won't bring Billy back."

"That used to scare the piss out of me," Lenny says.

Anchorage celebrated its statehood in 1959 by building a beautiful baseball park. And during the summers, college players came to Alaska to play. Tom Seaver, Rick Monday, Bob Boone and many other future major leaguers came to Anchorage to play on fields manicured by Joe Rancher. Joe brought his kids to the field, and they'd hang out with the players. Billy usually managed to talk one of them into playing catch before the game.

In 1969, Joe moved his family to Oakland, California, where he got a job taking care of Oakland-Alameda County Coliseum, the home field of the Oakland Athletics. The Rancher kids went to the games. They got to meet all the players, then they'd sit in a section of the stands called Reggie's Regiment, and root for Reggie Jackson and the A's. But Joe and Astrid decided Oakland was not where they wanted to raise their kids. Astrid thought it was a "crazy place." So after just three months in Oakland, the Ranchers packed up and headed to Portland, Oregon.

They were halfway to Portland when they passed through Klamath Falls, a dusty little town in southern Oregon. Something caught Joe's attention: a baseball tournament. They still had a good six, seven hours of driving left, but that could wait. Joe pulled into the parking lot at the baseball field, and announced that they'd be spending the rest of the afternoon watching the American Legion tournament. In the stands, under a relentless sun, Astrid sat next to the mother of Rick Wise, a hotshot pitcher from Portland. (Rick Wise eventually won 188 games in the major leagues, mostly with the St. Louis Cardinals and Philadelphia Phillies, and was once traded for Hall of Famer Steve Carlton.) Mrs. Wise told Astrid that if they were moving to Portland, they should live in the Madison High School district, because Madison had a long tradition of good baseball teams.

So that's what they did. Joe and Astrid bought a house in northeast Portland, in the Madison school district. And Billy became quite a baseball player, an all-city shortstop. He told his teammates he wanted to play at Arizona State, where his hero Reggie Jackson had gone to school. He settled instead for a scholarship to play at Mount Hood

Community College in Portland.

Jeff Erdman was two years younger than Billy. He played played third base as a sophomore at Madison when Billy played shortstop. He remembers playing basketball on weekends, taking extra batting practice, going out for pizza. "He was just a great guy, the All-American boy. There were no negatives with Billy. He was a good student, polite to people, really a fun guy to be with."

Ron Walp, the baseball coach at Mount Hood, knew Billy and Joe. He always enjoyed talking with Joe at Skovone Field, where Joe worked for the city of Portland, keeping the fields in tip-top shape. "He was very meticulous, an expert on the care of a baseball field," Walp says of Joe Rancher. "He really liked to share his information with someone he knew was genuinely interested." Ron Walp was genuinely interested in Billy playing for him at Mount Hood. "He was the kind of kid you wanted to have on your side. He was a good fielder, real good at turning the double play. He was smart, he'd pick up signs. He'd been around a lot of people who knew baseball, you could tell that."

With Billy's first season at Mount Hood in 1976 came a new tradition at the school. Bat girls. Walp couldn't believe how many girls wanted to help out. What school spirit, he must have thought. "Man, good-looking women were always hanging around Billy. Like I said, he was a good guy to have on your side."

After a couple years at Mount Hood, Billy hadn't really done anything to make Joe think there was going to be a Rancher make the major leagues. Billy had proven to be an exceptional fielder, but he wasn't much of a hitter and was a slow runner. Joe was proud of Billy's accomplishments, though. He knew Billy had done his best, gone as far as he could. And, as far as the major leagues went, there was always Lenny. He was small, but showing a lot of promise at Madison. Although Billy didn't have big league scouts drooling, he did well enough at Mount Hood to have a chance to continue his baseball career at Portland State. Or did, until he heaved a big rock at some ducks and threw out his shoulder. He never played at Portland State, but that was OK with Billy. He realized he didn't have much of a baseball future, anyway. And he was playing the hell out of those 12 chords in his guitar book.

Billy and Pete Jorgusen had claimed the basement of Pete's parents' house, where they practiced with Greg Paul and Doug Pollock, a couple of rich kids from Parkrose High School. Sometimes Lenny would come

At the age of 18, Billy's passions were fishing and baseball.
(Ellen Rancher)

with Billy and watch practice, and Greg and Doug began teaching him how to play bass guitar. Lenny was becoming less interested in sports, and more fascinated by rock 'n' roll. Billy and Pete took him to see Rolling Stones and Led Zeppelin movies. Billy and Pete decided the rich kids didn't have the right attitude, so they kicked them out of their band. It wasn't so much a band as it was a couple guys learning to play their instruments in a basement. But, for the same reason Billy liked to call himself, Lenny and Ellen a bicycle gang when they were kids in Alaska, he figured anyone jamming in that basement with him was part of his band. With Greg Paul and Doug Pollock gone, Billy's band needed a guitar player. Lenny tossed aside his bass guitar and bought a six-string. Pete had noticed that Lenny had a natural rhythm, and in fact, might have some talent. Lenny caught on quickly, and was part of the band, such as it was.

They sat in the basement and butchered songs by Led Zeppelin and Tom Petty. Pete's sister Nancy would wear ear plugs while they flailed away at "Refugee," and "Breakdown," a couple of Petty songs. Finally, they decided to work on a few Chuck Berry tunes, something a little more their speed. They had a new bass player, Cary Carlstrom. Between band meetings, Lenny would practice in his bedroom, sometimes eight to 10 hours a day, wearing out Rolling Stones and Small Faces records, playing them over and over, practicing the licks until he had them just right. In fact, he was becoming a better guitar player than Billy, who was free to concentrate on playing rhythm parts and singing.

Billy and Lenny inherited their musical talents from their parents. Astrid learned how to play the organ at age 5. She could listen to songs on the radio, then play them. Joe, as it turns out, wasn't just a macho baseball player. He had a nice voice, and he loved to play the harmonica and dance. He was also a bit of a showoff. There were nights at home when Joe would entertain his family by playing his harmonica and singing, sitting in a chair in his underwear. He'd grab Astrid, who would scream for him to let her go, and he'd dance with her in the living room.

Despite his love of music, Joe was terribly disappointed when Lenny told him during the fall of 1978, his senior year at Madison, that he wasn't going to play baseball the next spring. Lenny was turned off by the jock crowd, and besides, baseball practice would have interfered with guitar practice. But Joe didn't want to hear Lenny's excuses. For weeks, they didn't talk. Billy had taken baseball as far as he could. But Joe would never understand why Lenny, such a good athlete, would give up on it, before his senior season, of all things. "Joe might not have admitted it," Lenny says, "but he wanted us to follow in his footsteps. He never let me explain why I couldn't play anymore, he just shut me off."

Slowly, Joe and Lenny tried to heal the wounds. They were talking at least. Nothing serious, just sports and small talk usually, but it was a start. Lenny felt like he was relating to his dad again, and that maybe someday he'd have a chance to explain this incredible feeling he got playing his guitar.

On Sunday, December 3rd, 1978, Lenny and Joe were in the living room, Lenny sitting in a chair, Joe on the couch, watching the Oakland Raiders play the Denver Broncos. It wasn't the kind of meaningful time he'd like to share with his father, but Lenny thought it was better than nothing. They could watch a football game together, at least. Ellen was in her bedroom. Astrid, who had been in the kitchen doing the dishes, was in the bathroom when Joe chased her out. "Pinhead (that's what he called Astrid when she had curlers in her hair), get out, I really need to go." Astrid went back to the kitchen. A few minutes later, Joe was back on the couch, complaining of a sore shoulder. He stood up and fell flat on his face, onto the living room carpet. Lenny laughed, assuming his dad was playing a joke on him. When Joe didn't move, Lenny got scared. "Dad, what are you doing?" he asked. "Oh boy." Astrid and Ellen ran into the room. Lenny didn't really know CPR, but he started pressing on Joe's chest. They all took turns, each of them pushing on Joe's chest, crying out in anguish, trying to bring him back. Astrid called Billy, who was living at Pete Jorgusen's house, and he rushed over.

Astrid, Billy, Lenny and Ellen piled into the family car and followed the ambulance to Woodland Park Hospital. "It's going to be all right," Astrid kept telling her kids as she drove. "It's going to be all right."

But she knew it wasn't. She saw that the ambulance's lights weren't flashing, and that the driver didn't seem to be in much of a hurry. She knew her husband was dead.

At the hospital, a doctor told them what Astrid already knew. Joe had suffered a massive heart attack. They'd done all they could to save him. But there was nothing anyone could have done.

Now Billy, at 21, was the man of the family. He had to take charge, make the funeral arrangements, so many things to think of. Lenny wished he'd have had a chance to really talk to his dad, to explain what music meant to him.

5 Ladies and Gentlemen, the Malchicks

Billy's band was getting better. Nancy Jorgusen, Pete's sister, would wander down to the basement once in a while to offer encouragement. "Hey, that one didn't sound too bad."

Billy, Lenny, Pete, Cary Carlstrom, and a new guitar player, Rod Bautista, were making noises that sounded remarkably similar to old songs by the Rolling Stones, Iggy Pop, Small Faces, Chuck Berry, Elvis, David Bowie and Bryan Ferry. And Billy and Lenny were writing songs. They'd played a few high school parties, and by the fall of 1979, decided they were ready for the stage.

Now they needed a name. Billy liked to take credit for coming up with the Malchicks, but Lenny is actually the one who suggested it after reading a magazine article that referred to the Rolling Stones as "Mick Jagger and the four hip Malchicks." The term is Russian slang for curfew breakers. It was perfect. Malchicks. Bad boys. The band had been formed in the image of the Rolling Stones, after all, both in the music they played and the life they were leading. They liked to drink, stay up late and play their music. They were behaving the way they thought rock 'n' roll bands were supposed to behave, which is to say, not at all, really. Lenny, who was 18 years old and had just graduated from high school, didn't smoke, but he'd stick a cigarette in his mouth and let it dangle from his lips, so he'd look like his heroes, Keith Richard and Ron Wood.

The local music scene in Portland was a little stale at the time. Seafood Mama (which became Quarterflash), Johnny and the Distractions, Upepo, Wheatfield and Sleazy Pieces played at the Last Hurrah, Sack's Front Avenue, the Earth Tavern, Euphoria Tavern. Every weekend, the same bands at the same clubs. They were safe bands. Seafood Mama's ticket was a female saxophone player and singer, Rindy Ross, and her husband and guitar player, Marv Ross. They wrote tight pop songs with the Top 40 in mind. Johnny Koonce was a hardworking, earnest Bruce Springsteen clone. Upepo was a salsa band, Wheatfield and Sleazy Pieces veteran rock groups that had been playing around

The Malchicks, from left: Billy Rancher, vocals/rhythm guitar; Dave Stricker, bass; Lenny Rancher, lead guitar; Pete Jorgusen, drums; Rod Bautista, rhythm guitar.
(Courtesy of Joe Dreiling)

Portland for most of the '70s. Only Tony DeMicoli was giving new bands a chance. DeMicoli was establishing a scene for punks and skinny tie new wavers at the Long Goodbye. He still remembers Billy, Lenny and the rest of the Malchicks coming in to see him for the first time. They walked into Tony's club and asked for a chance to play.

"I liked their style," DeMicoli says. "I recognized they weren't punks, but I liked their cockiness. I asked them what their name was. The Malchicks. OK, they can't be too far off. I told them we'd try it one time, see what they had, didn't even audition them."

So on October 7th, 1979, the Malchicks played their first club show, upstairs at the Long Goodbye. They ripped into their Rolling Stones and Chuck Berry covers, and played a few original tunes.

Tony DeMicoli was impressed by the band's showmanship. "These kids were just full of energy," he says. "They could have been singing the 'Star-Spangled Banner', and people would have gotten excited. It was entertaining. They wore costumes, there were these shenanigans on stage."

There were nights at the Long Goodbye that didn't go so well, nights a punk crowd would show up and taunt the Malchicks, nearly booing them off the stage. The punks were more interested in seeing bands like the Wipers, fronted by Greg Sage, a true punk pioneer. The Malchicks never did completely win over the hardcore punks, but they began to attract a different crowd to the Long Goodbye, outdrawing all the other bands. Then they set out to play other Portland clubs.

In January of 1980, "Wrong Number," written by Billy, was the best song played in any of the local clubs, according to Positively Entertainment, a Portland magazine. Billy was writing a lot of songs, Lenny added a few, and those tunes began to replace covers during their shows. Fans were drawn by the raw power and energy of bluesy, Stones-like songs such as "Too Straight for the New Wave," "Go Go Boots Are Coming Back," "She's So Cool," "Two Girls" and "What Do I Do?" They also enjoyed the shows, and the fact that no one knew from one night to the next what Billy and Lenny might do on stage.

Billy threw beer on the audience, swung from rafters, knocked over video games and amps, and insulted local club owners and radio stations for the fun of it. Lenny lurched around the stage, drunk on cheap beer, but playing guitar like nobody's business. And Billy and Lenny fought, both on stage and off.

The fights usually started over musical differences that were already dividing the Malchicks. Lenny wanted to jam, to keep the music as close to their Rolling Stones roots as possible. Billy was writing new songs that had more of a catchy pop quality to them. The fights were real, although those in the audience probably mistook them for part of the Malchicks' manic show. Fights would start during sets, when Billy and Lenny wouldn't agree on which songs to play. Lenny would pout, Billy would kick Lenny's amp over. Between sets, fans could hear screaming, cussing and glasses breaking. Other band members would have to separate Billy and Lenny. Many times Billy took the stage again without

Lenny, who would join the band in mid-set.

"The fights were almost always musical, our tastes in music and the ways to present it," Lenny says. "Billy wanted the Malchicks to turn into more of a pop group. Synthesizers were in, and that's what Billy wanted to do, and I just wouldn't go for it. I was into bluesy rock, and reggae. I went the other way, concentrating on my instrument and trying to get better. Billy was just concentrating on writing these pop songs."

Some of the fights were so intense they carried over from the stage. The fights had always been pushing, shoving and screaming at each other, until one night it boiled over. They were on their way to play a show, Lenny driving a pickup truck, Pete Jorgusen sitting in the middle and Billy riding shotgun. "They were always threatening to kick each other's ass," Pete remembers.

After several minutes of arguing, Billy had heard about all he wanted from his little brother. "Let's do it right here, right now," he yelled at Lenny. Billy reached over when the truck was stopped, yanked the keys out of the ignition and threw them out the window. They jumped out of the pickup and Lenny punched Billy right in the face. They began trading blows, and eventually Billy, who had three or four inches and 30 pounds on his younger brother, pinned Lenny to the ground and pummeled his face. Still, Lenny viewed it as a coming of age ritual. It had been their first real fight, and he was pleased that he'd gotten in the first shot, a punch that had shaken Billy. Lenny got the worst of it in the end, but he'd never given up. They played that night, Lenny's face bruised. That night, it was a great show. It would be like that sometimes, a great show after a day they'd argued or fought. But other nights they couldn't hide it, not talking or even looking at each other for entire sets.

As the band evolved, Billy was clearly the leader, the great showman, and the Malchicks reflected his vision, not Lenny's. Pete was content just to play his drums, not really choosing sides, but he began hanging out more with Lenny. Pete and Lenny were perfecting their rock 'n' roll buddies, us-against-the-world routine, drinking, playing shows, then drinking some more. It got them into trouble one night as they left a Portland club called Peters Inn. It had been a normal evening for Lenny and Pete. They had their arms around each other and were drinking and carrying on like a couple of sailors on leave. Two very large bodybuilders, both about 6-foot-4 with muscles chiseled by hours of work in the weight room, thought Lenny and Pete looked like "a couple of faggots," and told them so. Lenny and Pete tried to leave. They had a room reserved at the Hilton, and the plan had been to meet a couple girls, go back to the hotel to party. They barely made it to the hotel at all. The bodybuilders pounded Lenny and Pete, might have killed them, in fact, if their girlfriends hadn't pulled them off. All Lenny could do was cover his face and wait for it to be over. Lenny and Pete helped each other up, then walked to the hotel, bleeding and bruised. So much for their big night.

The Malchicks' other guitar player, Rod Bautista, was basically a stage prop. He looked like a Malchick, and could play a few chords. He was a young, handsome kid, all the better to draw good-looking girls to the shows. If his guitar got out of tune, everything came to a halt while Lenny tuned it for him. His amp was usually turned down, but he didn't know it. Rod was just busy filling in around Lenny's leads and smiling at the girls in the audience, trying to pick out the one he'd go home with that night.

Cary Carlstrom, the original bass player, was a good Malchick, but he wasn't much of a player, either. With Lenny playing lead guitar, and getting quite good at it, and Billy becoming an adequate rhythm player, it was no problem carrying Rod Bautista. But it would sure be nice to have a guy who could actually play bass. Enter Dave Stricker.

Stricker was three years older than Billy and didn't really know the Rancher brothers, even though they'd all gone to Madison High School. Stricker heard about the Malchicks, and that they were looking for someone. Stricker taught himself to play bass so he could play with his father, Andy Stricker, in a country outfit. He hadn't played much rock 'n' roll, but he figured he could learn.

Stricker met the Malchicks in their practice haven, Pete Jorgusen's basement. He liked their sound, their energy, although he thought it was funny that he had to tell them what chords they were playing. But he knew the Malchicks, and Billy in particular, had something. He couldn't wait to get started. Billy, Lenny and Pete all thought Stricker was kind of a hick, but they knew he could play. That was good enough for them.

Stricker called his friend Joe Dreiling, a guitar player who lined up music at the time for a Portland club called Sack's Front Avenue. "Joe, I'm telling you, this is it. You've got to meet Billy Rancher, we've got to do this."

Joe Dreiling had met Billy for the first time at an after-hours party at

Sack's early in 1980. They sat around a table drinking. Jim Pepper, who had been the headliner that night, was there. So was his girlfriend, Karen Knight, who played in a band called Slow Train. Karen couldn't keep her eyes of Billy, this tall, blond, cocky kid. Billy told Joe he needed to come and see the Malchicks, if he really wanted to hear some good music.

Joe Dreiling, the Malchicks' manager, had his hands full with Billy and Lenny. "It was like trying to train puppies," he says.
(Courtesy of Joe Dreiling)

Now Dave Stricker was telling Joe the same thing, so he went with Stricker to see the Malchicks play in the Long Goodbye basement. Billy and Lenny had just returned from a trip to Sweden, and they'd come home with funny haircuts, the kind you might get by handing the scissors to your kid sister and telling her to do the best she could. Billy sang, girls screamed. Joe Dreiling decided to quit his job at Sack's and manage the band, and Dave Stricker replaced Cary Carlstrom.

Actually, Joe didn't like the word manager, and preferred to think of the Malchicks as a group — Billy, Lenny, Pete, Dave and Rod, Joe, and a couple of roadies they'd picked up, Mick Boyt and Keith Cox. Joe had some connections in town, and knew a thing or two about getting a band gigs, and how to promote them. He had publicity photos taken and made business cards advertising the Malchicks, "rhythm and blue wave." He plastered Malchicks posters all over town on telephone poles and handled all the band's advertising and bookings. He helped make up goofy names for each of the band members. Billy was Billy T. Kidd, Lenny was Leonard Bamboo, Rod was Rodney Sperming, Pete was Pete Cheeks and Dave went by David Tutor. Joe tried to promote the band, and he tried to teach Billy and Lenny about being professional. It wasn't easy.

"They were always late. I started putting clocks on the stage, trying to get them to start sets on time. I tried to tell them, 'This is what works, this is what doesn't work.' There just wasn't any control, though. I used to thank the Lord for a good night, because it meant another night we'd gotten through without any disasters. One of the biggest problems was that Billy and Lenny really indulged themselves in being brothers. They were always fighting. It was like trying to train puppies."

But Dreiling persisted. He knew that Billy was worth it. "I always knew that Billy was going to make it big. I knew that the first time I saw him."

Joe thought it would be good practice for the boys to play a country set one night. He sent them to a country and western joint called Tony's with a list of songs. It was open mike night, and the idea was for the band to take the stage together and play some country tunes. They jumped on stage, tossed away Joe's play list and launched into a set of raunchy, rollicking Malchicks songs. The redneck crowd was patient at first, perhaps mistaking the first song or two for some new kind of country rock. When it became apparent that wasn't the case, it got ugly. Billy pressed on. Joe wasn't thrilled, but he realized that's the way it was going to be with Billy. "I wouldn't say that night worked," Joe says. "But I didn't mind that about Billy. He was always testing the limits, always willing to try things."

Billy was gaining confidence, making a reputation for himself as a performer. He wore makeup. He dressed in pajamas. He talked to the crowd between songs. The rest of the band just concentrated on playing. Lenny was getting better every day. Pete and Dave formed a solid rhythm section, and that was plenty for them. Rod tried hard, and he kept smiling for the girls.

Of course, Billy was the main attraction where the opposite sex was concerned. Joe Dreiling handed out Malchicks business cards at each show, with a list of upcoming performances and an address to write to the band. Most of the mail he got was from girls who wanted a more personal audience with Billy. Typical of the fan letters was a note from a couple of girls who wanted Billy to come back to Eugene, Oregon to "play with us." It was signed "much love, admiration and sexual fantasies, Suzy and Chris." Most of the letters, including the one from Suzy and Chris, never made it to Billy. Joe Dreiling had more important things for his star to worry about. Besides, there were plenty of girls at each show, another reason the punk bands and their followers were jealous of the Malchicks. "Girls were just attracted to Billy and Lenny," says Pete Jorgusen. "We had girls lined up each night, had our pick of which one we wanted to go home with."

Girls were just part of the Malchicks lifestyle. It was girls, beer and music. Most importantly, the music. The Malchicks lived out this perfect rock 'n' roll life on stage in Portland clubs and the rest of the time in the band's shrine to decadence, Malchick Manor.

Malchick Manor was a dilapidated two-story shell of a house at 3435 SW Curry Street in the Corbett neighborhood. From the fall of 1979 to early 1981, it was home to the Malchicks. Billy and Lenny were permanent residents, but at one time or another everyone in the band, plus Mick Boyt, Keith Cox, Joe Dreiling, Steve Hettum and assorted girlfriends and Malchick wannabes bedded down at Malchick Manor. Whoever was around when the rent came due dug into their pocket to keep the landlord away for another month. The house was usually cold, since they couldn't afford to turn the heat up, or sometimes, even to pay the electric bill.

Malchick Manor became known as the kind of place party hoppers would drop by any time, day or night. You didn't need to know who lived there, you just knew there was a good chance there'd be a party in progress. There was a basement downstairs, where the band practiced. The house was sparsely decorated, if, indeed, you could call bean bag chairs, grungy old mattresses, guitars and amps, duct tape and an empty refrigerator decorating. And then there was Wade Varner.

Billy and Mick Boyt wandered into a Portland restaurant and bar called Thatchers one day and saw Wade, who went about 6-foot-4 and anywhere from 280 to 320 pounds, depending on how much food money he had that week. Billy remembered Wade from Madison High School, not that they were buddies. He invited Wade to a show. Wade went, and decided that he, too, would be a Malchick.

The first time Wade invited himself to the house was to make stew for the band.

"You puppies are too thin," he told them. "Too damn skinny. I'm comin' over to make stew for you puppies."

Wade volunteered to lug the Malchicks' gear, and became a combination roadie/bodyguard for the band. Truth is, Wade was kind of a bully, but Billy made him feel wanted. Billy had a talent for that, for making an outsider like Wade Varner feel like he was important. At Wade's best, inspired by Billy's kindness and attention, he was like a big, slobbering Saint Bernard, loyal and protective of those he thought were his pals. But even among friends, Wade had a quick temper and a habit of gulping down handfuls of amphetamines, which made him an unpredictable individual, even by Malchick Manor standards. Wade got especially pissed if anyone took his food out of the refrigerator. Not that Wade had to buy the food, or put it there himself. Once it was in the fridge, the way Wade saw it, it was his food. Wade inspired the Malchick Manor habit of decorating with duct tape. If you wanted to keep something, your best bet was to duct tape it, preferably out of Wade's sight. Doors were duct taped to keep Wade out.

Wade didn't really have a room, just part of the hall with a bean bag chair and a little TV. Wade spent a good deal of his time watching Three Stooges reruns and hacking into a special spit box he'd set up in the hallway. Wade had some sort of saliva problem. Too much of it, actually, was the problem. This created a wet and rather disgusting obstacle course for anyone trying to step past Wade and into the bathroom. One day, Lenny and Pete decided to play a little joke on Wade. He'd just bought some bologna, put it in the refrigerator and told everyone to keep their grubby little hands off it. After Wade retired to his bean bag, the bologna was duct taped to the kitchen ceiling. Sure enough, Wade got up to make a sandwich, couldn't find his bologna and went into a rage. He stormed through the house. "Jorgusen!!!" he screamed at Pete. "Where's my bologna?" Convinced that Pete didn't know, he headed upstairs. He grabbed Lenny and threw him out of his bedroom, onto — and nearly over — the balcony. Then he spotted Joe Dreiling. He held Joe against the wall by his neck. "Where's my bologna, you sonofabitch?" Unable to choke a confession out of Joe, he careened back into the kitchen. Just then, Billy walked through the door. Wade grabbed a steak knife and tossed it at Billy, just missing. By then, everyone had gathered in the kitchen. "We were making a fool out of him, because he did so much shit to us," Lenny says. "After that, I avoided him. I felt sorry for Wade, but I just said, 'Hey, let's get this guy out of here.' We tried to get him out, but Wade would always point at the biggest amp and say, 'Who's going to carry that for you?' Wade never did leave."

Billy and Lenny's sister Ellen worked up the courage to visit Malchick Manor occasionally. She was amused by her brothers' efforts to live up to their Malchicks rock 'n' roll image. Ellen was working at a Portland music store, and liked hanging around the local scene. She used her fake ID to get into the Long Goodbye and watch her brothers play. She was proud of them, and she liked that Billy made a fuss over her at the clubs, and that he wrote about her in "Too Straight for the New Wave."

> *My sister is a charmer, she is a real doll*
> *She's always been a winner, I've never seen her crawl*
> *She's always got a smile, she's always got a kiss*
> *All these things go by, but nothing that she'll miss*
> *She's only been around since one-nine-six-oh,*
> *but she's got more taste than you and me will ever know*
> *She's too straight for the new wave*
> *She's too straight for the new wave*
> *She's too straight ... she don't relate to the new wave*

"I was too cool for the new wave," Ellen says. "I would sit there, sipping sodas, analyzing them. I was the ultimate critic. I thought they had enormous talent, but that bad boys image didn't impress me a bit. I thought they were trying to be like the Rolling Stones a little too much. I told them they had to be themselves."

In the spring of 1980, Ellen met Steve Pearson, a guitar player and singer for the Heats, a popular Seattle band. On July 29th that summer she married Pearson and moved to Seattle. Billy and Lenny were happy for their sister, but sorry to lose their biggest fan.

The Malchicks, meanwhile, were popular enough that Billy could give up his day job. Billy had studied horticulture at Clackamas Community College in Portland. He never earned a degree, but between what he'd learned in school and helping his dad, he knew enough to put together a landscaping company with a high school buddy, Terry

Quinn. Lenny, Pete, Mick Boyt and Steve Hettum were all recruited at one time or another to help. By the time the Malchicks started playing, Billy was almost out of the landscaping business, just the occasional job to make a little extra money. And there was the work Billy and Lenny did for Astrid at her home on Fremont Drive. The yard needed a little help, and Joe wasn't around any more. No problem. Billy and Lenny edged the lawn in the shape of two breasts.

Steve Hettum was working a job one day with Billy. Hiring on with Billy, as Lenny and Pete had discovered, usually meant you'd be laying sod while Billy drank lemonade with the owner and ran around town picking up supplies. "Mr. Logistics," Lenny called him. By now, the Malchicks had experienced some success and, well, Mick Jagger probably never had to haul barkdust.

"Fuck this," Billy told Steve. "I quit. I'm going home to play my guitar. I'm done landscaping."

"Come on, Billy, it's just one more job," Hettum pleaded. "Let's finish this, then we'll go home. We're just trying to pay the rent."

"Don't worry, Steve. Rock 'n' roll's gonna pay my rent."

Billy's mother Astrid asked her sons to do a little landscaping work. Billy and Lenny edged her lawn in the shape of breasts. No charge, mom!
(Stephanie Reader)

6 Love at First Sight

Meeting girls was not a problem for Billy during the early Malchicks days. Girls screamed when he sang, and they elbowed their way to the front of the crowd, where they hoped to catch his eye. On September 5th, 1980, all that changed. He met *the* girl. *His* girl.

Karen Marie Sage had just graduated from high school in Lake Oswego, a suburb just a few minutes southwest of Portland. Karen's parents — Bill and Dorothy Sage — had made a nice life for themselves, Karen and her older brother. They had a house by the lake. They were respected, and successful, and now they were sending their daughter off to college, to the University of Oregon in Eugene, so she could become successful. That's what people who lived in Lake Oswego did, they became successful. On a Friday night, Karen and several friends, about 10 in all, decided to take in a midnight movie at Fifth Avenue Cinema in Portland. The movie was "Performance," starring Mick Jagger. As they walked toward the back of a long line, Karen noticed three jokers who seemed to be having a better time than everyone else. Billy was doing most of the talking, Lenny and Pete listening, then bursting into laughter. Billy was wearing jeans, a T-shirt and a denim jacket. Kind of cute, Karen thought. And Billy noticed her. It was hard not to, actually. She was the kind of girl who stood out in a crowd. She had bright, brown eyes, a dazzling smile and, Billy couldn't help but notice, a trim, athletic body. "Are you a model?" would have been an appropriate pickup line. But Billy just smiled, and used the one that had always worked before. "Hi, I'm Billy Rancher."

He took Karen's smile as a sign she was interested. He was right.

"Want cuts?" Billy asked her.

Half of Karen's group were guys, and they were already in line, waiting for Karen and the other girls. It wasn't a date really, but still, she had come to meet them, and thought she should stay with the group. "No thanks."

They talked for a few minutes. Even as Karen and her girlfriends talked

Karen was going to school at the University of Oregon in Eugene, but made the two-hour trip home almost every weekend to be with Billy.
(Bart Danielson)

to Billy, Lenny and Pete, she had a feeling she'd seen Billy before, but where? Then she remembered. The previous weekend, Karen had gone to an all-ages club to watch a friend's brother play. After his band came a loud, obnoxious group playing what Karen considered raunchy music. The Malchicks. Karen and her friends had made fun of the Malchicks. She thought they were a bunch of punks. Maybe he deserved another chance, though. Karen told Billy she'd seen him the previous weekend. They exchanged phone numbers, and as Karen and her friends headed to the back of the line, she wondered if Billy would call her. She hoped he would. Karen was just 18 years old, a "young 18," she says, and she believed in love at first sight.

A week later, Billy called Karen at her parents' home. At 2 a.m. In the background, she could hear Lenny, drunk, throwing milk on Billy. At first she thought it was a joke, maybe one of her friends she had gone to the movie with, pretending to be Billy Rancher, the bigshot rock star. But it was Billy.

Their next meeting was at the Long Goodbye, where Billy snuck Karen in the back door to see a Malchicks show. Karen noticed writing on the 10th Street sidewalk. Billy T. Kidd.

A few days later, they had their first real date. Billy and Karen met at Elmer's Pancake House on 82nd Street near Astrid's house, then went out for pizza and a movie. They finished the evening drinking champagne at the airport, watching planes land and take off. The next day they went water skiing. Billy and Karen were together every day for the rest of the week, until she had to leave for school in Eugene.

That fall, Karen came home every weekend to see Billy, driving the brown Volkswagen Rabbit her parents had given her. After a while, she decided Friday classes weren't all that important. And, well, she could skip some Monday classes, too. She ended up spending as much time in Portland, with Billy, as she did in her dorm room in Eugene.

Billy wrote to Karen nearly every day, sometimes long, passionate, romantic letters, other times just a silly note to let her know he was thinking of her.

The Malchicks, with Billy front and center, didn't always win over the punk audiences, but had no trouble attracting female fans.
(Dave Theobald)

7 "A Relationship Unlike Any Two Brothers"

Tony DeMicoli remembers that when the Malchicks first came to him, and in their early shows, it wasn't always clear who the leader was, or if they really had one. Just five kids on his stage at the Long Goodbye, playing music, chugging beer, and tossing what they couldn't drink on their audience, hah, hah, hah. Now, a year later, there was no doubt who was in charge. Billy was writing songs the way most people scribble down shopping lists, and he was serious about making a career out of this. He'd seen the power his music had. The crowds. The girls. The praise from the local media. And he liked it.

All this was fine with Lenny. Billy could have all the attention, he could be the boss. Billy was moving, but one thing became clear: He wasn't going to be able to take Lenny with him. They were fighting more than ever. They fought over the music, and sometimes, just because they were brothers. And there were philosophical differences. Billy wanted to be the leader of a great band. Lenny wanted to play his guitar and drink beer.

But, for all their problems, the Malchicks had become one of the hottest bands in Portland. Greg Sage still was king of the punk scene with his band, the Wipers. But the Malchicks were bringing in a new crowd to the Long Goodbye, fans who were tired of the green-haired, needle-through-the-nose, mad-at-the-world punks. The Malchicks were loud, and rude, but it was rock 'n' roll. And gosh, they looked like such nice young boys up there on stage.

The Malchicks had expanded their territory, playing as far away as Seattle, and anywhere in Portland they felt like plugging in their guitars. The Earth Tavern, and the Euphoria — clubs that preferred to stick to the tried (and tired) and true — decided the Malchicks had established enough of a following to allow them to play on their stages. The Last Hurrah, Silversmith, the Getaway, the Orange Peel and the Copper Penny all welcomed the Malchicks. So did Urban NOIZE at 6th and Stark, not to be confused with another favorite Malchicks hotspot, Urban Noise, an all-ages joint located below a whorehouse on Northeast Union. The Malchicks played, and packed, all the best Portland clubs. They couldn't even get themselves kicked out of Sack's Front Avenue.

Billy and Lenny didn't care for Tom Ohling, the tall, long-haired rocker who ran Sack's. During one of the few covers they were still doing, an Iggy Pop song called "I'm Bored," Billy swung from the rafters, microphone in hand. Lenny, still playing his guitar, had to duck each time Billy passed by. Billy landed, then ran over to the video games. "I'm bored with Asteroids," he yelled, and toppled the machine. Ohling said the Malchicks would never play Sack's again. They were back a couple weeks later. In the music business, the ability to draw a large crowd evidently makes up for a momentary lapse of good manners.

Between club owners forced to live with their antics and Portland musicians jealous of their success, the Malchicks were gathering a small army of enemies. Then Billy and Lenny added another to the list — their brother-in-law, Steve Pearson.

Pearson, who married Ellen Rancher on July 29th, 1980 and took her to Seattle, was the lead singer and guitarist for a popular Seattle band, the Heats. The Malchicks were about to open for the Heats in a little club called the Fourth Avenue Tavern in Olympia, Washington. *Isn't this nice, Ellen thought. My brothers and my husband playing together. One big, happy family. They can play together all the time, they'll come up to Seattle to see us, this is great.* Steve told Billy and Lenny they could use the Heats' amps, then changed his mind. Making Billy mad before he went on stage — where he had access to a microphone — wasn't a very good idea. By the time Billy had finished telling everyone in

Olympia what he thought about the Heats in general, and Steve Pearson in particular, Ellen knew that happy Christmas gathering she'd planned wasn't going to come off quite as she'd hoped.

"Your brothers are assholes," Steve told Ellen.

She thought he was joking. "You don't really hate my brothers, do you? Steve?"

Turns out Steve didn't have much of a sense of humor about Billy's comments. From that time on, the Rancher brothers had a strained relationship, at best, with Steve Pearson.

Billy and Lenny wouldn't have cared, of course, except that they didn't like to see their sister unhappy. Billy and Lenny may have fought, but they could agree on one thing: Steve Pearson was a jerk. And the fact is, they never thought much of him, or his pretentious little band in the first place.

The Heats were small potatoes. The Malchicks were too, really, but Billy knew that wasn't for long. And he always made a point of watching the popular bands of the day, and meeting them when they came through Portland on tour. One of the Malchicks' favorite tricks was to stake out the Portland Motor Inn, the hotel where all the rock 'n' roll bands stayed when they were in town. There were meetings with the Cars, the Stray Cats, Bob Geldof's band, the Boomtown Rats. Lenny remembers sitting in a hotel room, partying, in awe of the Cars' left-handed guitar player, Elliot Easton.

By now, Billy had written dozens of songs, and he figured it was time to go into the studio and record a few of them. He was right about that. The Malchicks had taken all their different influences and created a unique sound and interesting songs. For all the sources they had stolen from — the Rolling Stones, David Bowie, the Beatles, Buddy Holly, punk and a little reggae thrown in — the Malchicks had their own identity. You couldn't listen to them and say they sounded like anyone else. On December 8th, 1980, the Malchicks were working at Recording Associates, putting the finishing touches on a six-song cassette.

The first song was a frantic cover of "Louie, Louie" that they did because, well, because they were a Northwest band, and all Northwest bands are required to learn the song. The second song was one of the Malchicks' best, "Two Girls," sung by Lenny. Lenny was more than a capable singer, and didn't mind singing in the studio. He'd even sing on stage occasionally, but he wasn't the least bit interested in being a frontman. That was Billy's job, and he was welcome to it. Practice was making nearly perfect for Lenny, who was content to stay in his bedroom for hours, playing those albums again and again, copying solos by Ron Wood and Keith Richard. "What Do I Do?" was next, and it showcased Lenny's guitar playing. The song has a heavy, almost punk feel, broken up by fast, clean guitar solos by Lenny.

The next two songs — "She's So Cool," and "Go Go Boots" — show the direction Billy was headed. The songs were more fun, more playful than earlier Malchicks tunes. You get a taste of Billy's style of writing lyrics, which was often to drink lots of beer and write the first goofy thing that popped into his head. Billy was writing songs every day. Everything that happened to him, every day, could end up in a song. A sample from "She's So Cool":

My baby's on the football rally squad
Yeah, my little baby is ultra mod
She's envied by 15 other girls
Because she's so cool

And from "Go Go Boots":

Go Go Boots are coming back, don't throw yours away
Go Go Boots are coming back, they'll be here to stay
And mini skirts, are coming back too
Go Go Boots are coming back, don't throw yours away

The fact that Billy and Lenny were headed in opposite directions was obvious, even on the same song. On "Go Go Boots," for instance, Billy's lyrics didn't mesh with the sound the band, driven by Lenny's guitar, seemed to be going for.

The last song on the cassette was "Do Nothing Til You Hear From Me," which offered even more evidence of Lenny's phenomenal guitar ability and growing confidence. He may have learned his style from listening to those old albums in his room, but he wasn't simply copying Richard and Wood.

The Malchicks had been in the studio for six hours that night when they heard the terrible news: John Lennon was dead, shot down outside his apartment in New York. The band packed up its gear and headed back to Malchick Manor to learn some Beatles songs. The Malchicks had listened to the Beatles, of course, and that influence could certainly be heard in the kinds of songs Billy was writing now. They weren't necessarily huge fans, but they all loved John Lennon, for his attitude as much as his music.

On their way back to the house, someone stopped by a grocery store to shoplift some bread and tuna. It was going to be a long night, and they were getting hungry. Even in the early days, when as much as 75 percent of their playlist was covers, the Malchicks had never done any Beatles tunes. But as December 8th turned into the early morning of December 9th, they worked out passable versions of a couple of Beatles songs, including "Twist and Shout," and a Lennon song, "Happy XMas (War is Over)." There wasn't a dry eye at Malchick Manor as they rehearsed that one. About 6 a.m. they headed out into the cold to honor John Lennon.

The boys drove to downtown Portland and set up to play. A generator, plugged in at an Arctic Circle burger joint across the street, provided power. At 6:30 a.m., with the temperature in the low 20s, the Malchicks started playing John Lennon songs. They were all bundled up. Lenny wore a heavy coat and ear muffs. Billy was dressed in jeans, a couple of shirts and a suit coat he'd bought at a thrift store — he liked to call it his rock 'n' roll jacket. A white, knit muffler was wrapped around his neck. Still, his face turned pink in the cold, and his fingers grew numb as they slid up and down his Stratocaster.

Businessmen and lawyers were startled when they arrived to begin what they thought would be another day at the office. It *was* just another day, except for all the people who had gathered to listen, and all the damn noise. "We blew people away, we were so loud," Lenny remembers.

It wasn't long after the leaders of the Portland business community had settled into their chairs that the Portland police were summoned.

"Who the hell's in charge here?" one of the cops asked.

Joe Dreiling stepped forward. The cop had noticed the John Lennon sign the band had placed in front of its makeshift stage, so he knew what was going on, even if he wasn't thrilled about all the commotion they were making. "I'm in charge, officer."

"Well, I can't kick you out of here. Yet. Come with me."

The cop led Joe to his car, then made a call to one of his superiors. "OK, we're going to see Mildred Schwab."

Mildred Schwab was a Multnomah County commissioner. And if

The Malchicks make like their heroes, the Rolling Stones, in front of a mural in downtown Portland.
(Dave Theobald)

the Malchicks were going to keep playing, they were going to need a noise permit OK'd by one Mildred Schwab. Outside, the cops had shut down the Malchicks.

Joe explained to her that they were just trying to play a tribute to John Lennon. To his surprise, Mildred Schwab was completely agreeable, and sent Joe on his way to pick up the permit. Must be a Beatles fan, he thought.

Noise permit in hand, the Malchicks were back in business. The early morning show downtown turned out to be the first of several Lennon benefits all over Portland that day. The Malchicks played at three different sites around town. A photo of Billy and Lenny playing outside in downtown Portland — with flowers and a picture of Lennon hanging from a tree near the stage — appeared on the cover of The Oregonian newspaper the next morning.

Billy and Lenny had been able to make peace for one night at least, to show their respect for the dead, but after the Lennon tributes ended, the Malchicks went back to their normal routine. By this time, that meant Billy and Lenny were fighting. If they could have gotten along, and worked together, Billy and Lenny probably would have discovered they were good for each other, like McCartney and Lennon. Billy was Paul McCartney — tight, pretty songs — to Lenny's John Lennon — a rougher edge, a desire to stretch out a little. And on stage, Lenny kept getting better as a guitar player. And he was happy to be just that, the guitar player. Billy was becoming a decent rhythm player, but mainly, he loved the attention that writing the songs, and singing them, provided. He thrived on being in charge, and being in the spotlight, the things that Lenny was so uncomfortable with. In fact, he needed it.

There were arguments as they wrote songs.

"C'mon Billy, why does everything have to be so planned out," Lenny would say. "Why can't we have some space for the band to take off?"

Billy would have none of it. "No, it has to be just like this, and we're going to keep playing it, the same way, until we get it right."

Lenny had a more emotional involvement with the music than Billy. "I can get sadder, or happier, than hell just by listening to a certain song, even a certain guitar note," Lenny says. "With Billy, he was always on an even keel. His one driving force was to be in the spotlight. There was always a motive behind everything he did. He was just driven.

That was good, in a way, because he had his vision. I just had a different one."

Some of the lessons Joe Dreiling was trying to pound into their heads were sticking with Billy. He was beginning to grasp the business aspect of rock 'n' roll. Lenny still was more interested in partying, in living up to that bad boys Malchicks image he was creating for himself. Lenny enjoyed the same things he had when the band was just getting started. Manic nights at the Long Goodbye, drinking, playing, people dancing on tables. The nights went by, whoosh, from 9:30 to 1:30. Then the after-hours parties. More drinking. Girls, if he wasn't too drunk. Lenny was living the lifestyle that had been glamorized by his heroes, and having a good time doing it.

By January of 1981, Joe Dreiling knew he probably needed to act fast if he was going to save the Malchicks from what looked like an inevitable collapse. He managed to arrange for a meeting with Peter Burke, whose father, Sonny Burke, produced many of Frank Sinatra's records. Peter Burke was an independent music publisher with ties to Portland. He'd played in a band in the '60s with Buck Munger, who eventually moved to Portland in 1970, and later started Two Louies magazine. In 1980, Munger sent J. Isaac, the manager of the Portland band Seafood Mama, to see Peter Burke. Peter eventually helped the band, which changed its name to Quarterflash, sign with Geffen Records. And now Joe Dreiling was looking for a deal for the Malchicks.

Joe sold his 10-speed bike and a guitar amp to buy a round-trip plane ticket to Los Angeles. He met with Peter Burke at Peter's father's home in Santa Barbara. Joe helped make the Malchicks big news in Portland, but he'd never done anything like this before, and Peter Burke wasn't impressed by Joe's amateurish presentation. He was impressed, however, by Joe's sincerity about his band, what he heard of a Malchicks tape, and some killer Oregon marijuana Joe brought along for the occasion. Burke offered to produce a Malchicks record, but said he wanted 100 percent of the publishing rights. Joe may have been dumb, but he wasn't stupid. He didn't know much yet about the recording business, but he knew that wasn't a good deal, and he was sure he had a band that was going to be worth millions. Eventually, Burke told Dreiling he'd produce three Malchicks albums and take 50 percent of the publishing. That sounded good to Joe, and he headed back to Portland with the good news.

There was only one problem: Billy and Lenny weren't getting along.

Karen, who had been Billy's girlfriend for four months by now, recalls the end of the Malchicks as a difficult time for Billy. He didn't want to go on without his brother, but because of the musical differences, because of Lenny's inability to behave professionally, and because he didn't share Billy's vision of making the big time, he had no choice. They were still living together at Malchick Manor, but they weren't talking. Billy padlocked his bedroom door shut to keep Lenny out.

"It tore Billy apart," Karen says. "But there was just no way they could keep playing together."

And as much as Lenny pretended he didn't care, it hurt him, too. During the last days of the band, it dawned on him that, for the first time, he wasn't going to be able to count on his big brother. He'd be on his own. Billy had always been there. As kids in Alaska, then in Portland, playing together, going with their dad on landscaping jobs, then doing it on their own after Joe died. He remembered Billy buying his first guitar, watching Billy and Pete practice in Pete's basement, then joining the band himself and being swept away by music. And he remembered the time he felt closest to Billy.

It was August of 1976. Billy was 19 years old, and had just finished his freshman year at Mount Hood Community College. Lenny was 15. Billy had won the David Bowie contest earlier that year, but hadn't really made the conversion from jock to rock. Joe and Astrid dropped them off for a four-day, 70-mile hike on the Pacific Crest Trail around Mount Hood, east of Portland. Astrid wasn't sure she wanted Lenny to do this, but Billy talked her into it, convincing her that he'd take care of his little brother. The first two days were miserable. They wore tennis shoes, not hiking boots, and developed painful blisters on their feet. Then they ran out of water. The closest they came to a drink on Day Two was sticking their tongues under a trickle running off the side of a hill. They got more dirt than water. When they laid down to go to sleep that second night, they were tired, thirsty and sore. Those were the good times, as it turned out.

It hadn't rained for two and a half months, and it was August, after all, so they hadn't brought any rain gear and had only light coats. On Day Three, a storm came in. First it rained, as they made their way past Ramona Falls. Then, as they began a long climb, came the earliest snow ever recorded at Timberline Lodge. Billy, who was carrying the heaviest pack, was tiring. It was getting dark, and cold, and snowing so hard they could hardly see where they were going. They needed to get to the lodge, somehow. Billy kept stopping, saying he needed to take a break, but Lenny seemed to be getting stronger.

"Here, give me some of your stuff," he told Billy.

Usually, Billy insisted on being the hero. But he knew they were in trouble, and if Lenny could carry some of his gear, fine. He packed some into Lenny's bag, and they took another run at their long climb. The pack was heavy, but Lenny had no trouble. The idea that he was saving the day had given him a shot of adrenaline that propelled him straight up the hill. Finally, they made it, arriving at Timberline Lodge. It was a blizzard by now. They began to warm up as they sat in the ski lodge; everything was going to be OK. It seemed that way for about an hour, anyway, until lodge employees kicked them out into the parking lot, explaining that they couldn't sleep in the lodge overnight. They didn't have anywhere to go, Billy and Lenny said, pleading to stay inside. Tough luck, kids, beat it. So Billy and Lenny made camp, pitching their tent in the lodge parking lot, which was white, covered with snow. It was still snowing on Day Four, but Billy and Lenny made it to the end of the trail. Neither could remember being so happy to see Joe and Astrid.

As he sat in the back seat on the drive home, Lenny felt proud of himself. They'd been left on their own in the elements for four days, and survived, and it wasn't Billy who had been the hero this time. Lenny felt more like a brother, not a little brother, or a kid brother, just a brother.

Now, with the Malchicks breaking up, it felt a little bit like he didn't have a brother at all. Now, he really was on his own.

"Me and Billy had a relationship unlike any two brothers," Lenny says. "We'd get in fights, then go on stage. Deep down inside, we loved each other. We always wanted to see each other do the best we could. But sometimes, it was a down and out hatred. By the end of the Malchicks, we hated each other."

January of 1981 was, in fact, the end of the Malchicks.

8 The Unreal Gods

Buck Munger almost swallowed his tongue when Billy walked into the Two Louies office and told him the name of his new band.

"The Unreal Gods?" He tried it again, slower this time. "The Un ... Real ... Gods. Gods. Do I have that part right, Billy? The Un ... Real ... Fucking ... Gods. Billy, in the old days, you couldn't even say God, now you want to call yourselves Gods? What the hell is an Unreal God, anyway?"

Billy laughed. He knew it was the right name for this band. They'd kicked around a few others. Billy liked the New Bohemians, until he came up with Unreal Gods. That would be the name of his band. Billy Rancher and the Unreal Gods. Oh, and another thing. Let's put a couple of go go dancers on stage. The Goddesses A-Go-Go. This was not going to be an ordinary rock 'n' roll show, that's for sure.

In the spring of 1981, Buck Munger was a 40-year-old editor of Two Louies, a magazine he started in 1979 as a newsletter for the Portland music community. Buck had established his new magazine's credibility quickly by showing off his intimate knowledge of the local music scene. Buck went to the shows, he knew the club owners, he knew the musicians, and his writing in Two Louies reflected that, particularly his column, As the World Turntables. And Buck had been involved with rock 'n' roll one way or another most of his life.

He had been a drummer in high school, then with a band in the Marines. He quit a job as a Phoenix cop because a department rule against part-time work in bars didn't allow him to play with the band he'd put together. There was a short gig in LA as the drummer for the Standells ("Dirty Water") that included a guest spot on The Munsters TV show. Buck had been a record producer, started Recording Engineer and Producer magazine in LA, and worked for Billboard in Nashville. He was a bigshot with Sunn and Norlin musical equipment companies, providing gear for Jimi Hendrix, Buffalo Springfield, The Who, Cream, Tom Petty and ZZ Top, among others. He'd even spent some time on the road with Hendrix. When Norlin wanted Buck to move from Portland to Chicago, he said "Thanks, but no." Actually, that's probably not how Buck — a self-proclaimed "contentious motherfucker" — would have put it. Buck knew the music business from just about every angle. Clearly, this was someone Billy needed to know.

Billy was spending a lot of time at the Two Louies office (Buck's house) in an old northeast Portland neighborhood not far from where Billy had grown up. This wasn't the Malchicks anymore. Drinking beer and playing at the Long Goodbye might be fine for Lenny and Pete, but Billy had bigger plans.

"Billy was the first guy who ever came to me who wasn't just an artist," Buck says. "He had an artistic vision, but he wanted to do this as a profession, as a commercial deal. He was really focused. And I wanted to help him. You wanted him to have everything, because he deserved it."

Billy and Karen were spending as much time together as possible. Karen came to Portland on weekends, or Billy would jump into his Saab and drive to Eugene. Karen watched the Malchicks fall apart. She knew it was killing Billy that Lenny wouldn't be part of his new band. But Billy and Lenny just had different ideas about the music, and about the level of professionalism that was going to be required. When they couldn't be together, Billy wrote Karen letters. He told her about his new band, what he wanted it to be. First of all, the music would have to be tight, he told her. No more stopping in the middle of songs because something was fucked up, or waiting for Lenny and Rod to tune their guitars. And the Unreal Gods weren't going to hang out with the crowd and drink beer. They weren't going to be seen before or after shows, just on stage. They'd change set lists, there would be different shows every night, dramatic shows, with dancers and costumes and makeup, not just five guys playing their music. Professional entertainment, Billy told Karen. That's what the Unreal Gods were going to be about.

Now all he needed were some Unreal Gods.

Dave Stricker was with him all the way. Dave learned how to play the bass guitar after he graduated from Madison High School in 1972, playing with his dad, Andy Stricker, in country bands. In May of 1980, just a few months after Dave joined the Malchicks, Andy Stricker took off, without a word. Dave hasn't seen him, or spoken with him, since. He isn't sure, but says he thinks his dad might be in Portugal. If he's still alive. Billy and Dave grew close during the Malchicks days, especially at the end, when Lenny and Pete became one team, Billy and Dave another. There was never any doubt in Dave's mind who he would go with when Billy and Lenny split.

"It was an easy decision," Stricker says. "The reason I didn't play with Lenny is that he really didn't have a clue as to why the Malchicks were working, why it was such a cool thing. Lenny was a great player and a great songwriter, but Billy had a vision. It was a great opportunity. I knew the Unreal Gods were going to be great."

So Billy and Dave went one way. Lenny, Pete and Rod went another, adding bass player Lee Oser and singer Tom Garman and calling themselves Them Roosters. Pete was closer to Lenny than Billy in musical taste, but there was another reason he stayed with Lenny. It was easier. Billy had emerged as the leader of the Malchicks, and there were times he wasn't the easiest guy to get along with. He was the boss. For one thing, he expected everyone to show up on time for practice and to be sober for rehearsals and shows.

Tom Garman had the right look for Lenny's new band, and a rough, Rod Stewart voice. His only problem was that he couldn't always sing in tune. Lenny would have been better, but he didn't have the confidence to step to the front. "I wasn't ready, because of my drinking, to lead a band and be an example. Billy was the kind of guy who could drink all night, then the next day have his shit together. I just wasn't ready to do what Billy was doing, to take that kind of responsibility."

The first version of the Unreal Gods — before they had come up with the name, in fact — was Billy, Dave, guitarist Danny Ross, Ross' friend

Attilio Panissidi III on keyboards and drummer Mark Borden. Danny was flamboyant, and he could play guitar like no one Billy had ever heard. Billy was intrigued by Danny's musical experience. He was a steel guitar wizard, and he'd been in the business forever, including a stop in Nashville. Most recently, he'd been in a popular Portland band called Sand, with Jack Muesdorffer, who changed his stage name to Jack Charles and joined Marv and Rindy Ross in Quarterflash. But Danny was 10 years older than Billy, and they weren't hitting it off. Billy learned a lot from Danny, but he wasn't interested in making this a partnership. It was going to be Billy's band, not Billy and Danny's band. When Danny Ross started to get too pushy, Billy bounced him.

The previous November, Billy had met a guitar player named Jon DuFresne. His band, Casey Nova, was playing at the Long Goodbye. Between sets, Billy told Jon he liked his guitar playing. They saw each other around the Portland circuit the next few months. Jon even sat in with the Malchicks once. He'd heard they were thinking about getting rid of one of their guitar players (Rod Bautista). They would have, except that the whole band fell apart first. Billy showed Jon some of the new songs he was writing, songs that became Unreal Gods tunes. Jon liked Billy immediately. He was impressed by Billy's attitude. He thought that Billy wasn't a cliche, like the fashionable new wavers, or the angry punks. He had a unique form of rebellion. A real attitude. Jon could dig that.

With Danny Ross gone, Billy needed a guitar player. He thought Jon had the right style, and the right look, for his new band. Billy called Jon and told him it hadn't worked out with Danny, and that they ought to get together to jam. For three nights Billy and Jon played together, running through the guitar parts to more than 20 of Billy's songs each session, plus a few covers. After the third rehearsal, Jon wanted to know where he stood. "Am I in, or what?" he asked. Billy apparently had considered the three meetings practices rather than auditions. "Oh, you're in. You're definitely in. You were in when I called you."

Jon grew up in the Portland suburb of Hillsboro, and had been playing in bands since he was 15 years old. He'd done a little of everything — top 40 cover bands, soul, country. He had just moved back to Portland in the summer of 1980 from Tulsa, Oklahoma. The explosion of the punk scene in the late '70s helped Jon realize what kind of music he wanted to play. He was tired of the dinosaur '70s acts, bands like

The Unreal Gods, from left: Jon DuFresne, lead guitar; Alf Ryder, keyboards; Billy Rancher, vocals/rhythm guitar; Billy Flaxel, drums; Dave Stricker, bass.
(Mark Rabiner)

Kansas and Styx and Journey. He wanted to play original music that was simpler, more basic, relying on different elements of all the styles he had played. Jon and Billy had the same musical ideas, the same attitudes. He *was* the Unreal Gods' lead guitarist.

It wasn't a job that Lenny wanted, even if he had been capable of adhering to Billy's crazy ideas about punctuality and sobriety.

"Jon was the perfect guitar player for the Unreal Gods," Lenny says. "There were always rumors that I was going to join the band. But I wasn't a believer in the Unreal Gods music. I knew they were going to be a great band, but it just wasn't my bag. I used to tell Jon, 'Hey, you don't have to worry about me, I'm not interested.' Besides, Billy didn't want me in the band."

So the brothers put their bands together, each still living at Malchick

Manor into the spring of '81. Even though they'd gone different ways musically, they still partied together, and there were times that Lenny got along fine with Billy, as long as they didn't have to play in the same band. Especially if there was a roll of duct tape handy.

Billy, Dave, Lenny and Pete Jorgusen went out barhopping one night that spring. Billy had a few too many beers, and was particularly rambunctious. In a bar parking lot, Dave, Lenny and Pete decided that something had to be done to shut him up. They held Billy down and duct taped him, from head to toe. "He was so out of it. We literally had to tape him up to keep him from hurting someone," Lenny says.

They tossed Billy into the back seat of Dave's car and began a leisurely drive around town.

"He was trying to fight out of it the whole time, but we just kept wrapping tape around him," Pete says. "He looked like a mummy."

Lenny and Pete taunted Billy as he struggled. Billy kept screaming and yelling, not that anyone could understand him, what with his mouth being taped shut. If his arms had been loose, he'd have punched someone, but all he could do was use his silver, duct-taped body as a weapon, lunging futilely at his tormentors.

As they headed up Burnside Street, Stricker was pulled over. "Officer," Lenny told the cop, pointing to Billy, "you're going to have to take this guy in. He's just too unruly."

Unwrapping Billy didn't do much to improve his mood, and he managed to give the cop enough trouble that he was taken downtown and given a private room for the night. Well, at least in jail a guy could get a decent night's sleep, which couldn't often be said for Malchick Manor.

Alf Ryder had auditioned with Billy, but never knew if he was in or out as long as Danny Ross was involved. Danny had his own keyboard player, Attilio. But once Danny Ross was out of the picture, Alf was called for another audition. Billy, Jon DuFresne, Dave Stricker and drummer Mark Borden played with Alf.

Billy liked the fact that Alf had some experience in the music business. Alf had been in a band with his brothers back East in the late '60s. One brother, Joe, was a record producer. Another brother, Frank, was directing videos. And another brother, Matti, was one of Bruce Springsteen's closest friends. And Alf was going to spend $5,000 on an Oberheim keyboard, an instrument that would play the synthesizer lines that Billy wanted for his new band.

The lineup was set until Mark Borden broke his arm in a motorcycle accident. Billy had several new songs he'd written, and with Jon and Alf aboard, the lineup was set. They'd been rehearsing, and now they were ready to go play. Then this. They needed a drummer, and they weren't all that interested in waiting for Mark Borden's arm to heal. They tried out a few, but there weren't that many drummers in Portland who were up to the standards Billy had set for his new band. Jon DuFresne wanted to bring in Sam Henery, who played with Greg Sage in the Wipers. Henery auditioned, but that didn't feel right. Too punk.

After abandoning Malchick Manor, Billy and Steve Hettum had moved into a house with Stricker. After practice one day in Stricker's garage, the phone rang. It was Billy Flaxel. A friend had told him the Unreal Gods were looking for a drummer, and he was available.

Actually, Billy Flaxel would rather not have to be a drummer in someone else's band. He played drums and sang in a metal band called Stratus, but they'd just broken up. He was going to school at Mount Hood Community College, but that was just an excuse to pick up girls. Billy Flaxel was a serious rock 'n' roller. He'd never had another job, and he didn't want one. The only careers he'd ever considered, in fact, were music and stunt snow skiing. What he really wanted, right now, was to be a lead singer, but he figured in the meantime he needed to make some money, so he called Stricker. The next day he auditioned. He was a hit. For one thing, he had a brown Chevy van and a nice drum set. Besides, he was a better drummer than Mark Borden. And he definitely had a rock 'n' roll attitude.

"All right, this is our drummer," Jon DuFresne thought as they ran through some of Billy's new songs with Flaxel.

Just two weeks after Flaxel's audition, Billy Rancher and the Unreal Gods packed up their gear, headed into Tom Robinson's Wave Studio in Portland and recorded two songs, "Go Go Boots," and "Rockabilly Queen."

Billy Flaxel couldn't believe how fast things were happening. They hadn't even had a chance to get music tight, but Billy was coming to rehearsal every day with new material. "This guy's an encyclopedia of music," Flaxel thought. Then Billy Rancher talked Tom Robinson into letting them use his studio.

"We were broke, we were young, we were fucking idiots, but we had

Unreal Gods guitarist Jon DuFresne and drummer Billy Flaxel. Steve Hettum (right) took care of business for Billy and the Unreal Gods in the early days. He was the first in a long line of managers for Billy.
(Bart Danielson)

a couple tunes, so he said come on in and record them. He let us do them for nothing," Flaxel says. "We'd only been together two weeks. We recorded them, and instantly, we had a sound. Those versions of those songs are great. They'll scare you. Very, very psychedelic and heavy. Very stark. It was so innocent, so uncontrived. I just walked out of there thinking, 'Wow, this is fucking fun. This is fucking great.' "

"Go Go Boots," which had been a Malchicks song, was recorded with a slow, haunting Velvet Underground vibe. "Rockabilly Queen" was the perfect vehicle for Jon DuFresne to show off a little.

Jon had found a house, just a few blocks from Malchick Manor, that he was going to rent with Mark Borden. But he blew off Borden, and invited the rest of the Unreal Gods to share the $300 a month rent. Billy and Hettum moved in with DuFresne and his girlfriend, Doreen. Alf eventually said he was moving in, although he really just needed a room to take girls. His apartment, because his girlfriend was usually there, wouldn't do. The house was a big dump, just like Malchick Manor, with a basement to practice in. It became known as The Unreal Gods House. Flaxel moved in with Stricker.

The team was almost set. Alf was the one who came up with the idea for the go go girls, although Billy liked to take credit for it. Alf's girlfriend, Mary Smith, had done some modeling, and was talked into being the first Goddess A-Go-Go. Mary called one of her modeling friends, Candyce

Dru, and recruited her.

Hettum would be the manager, setting up gigs and handling business. Billy Triplett, a big, gregarious sort who happened to be a genius at a mixing board, ran the sound. Mick Boyt, who had been with Billy since the early days of the Malchicks, was the No. 1 roadie, in charge of setting up the stage, repairing broken guitar strings, and basically taking care of anything that needed to be taken care of. For months, the band had been rehearsing. Mick was as eager as anyone to get started. "They just rehearsed and rehearsed," he remembers. "Billy had come up with a lot of new songs. He could write a couple of songs a day, all of them about real experiences. I could always tell what the story was behind each song. And there were some great stories."

The difference between the Unreal Gods and the Malchicks was obvious to Mick. "More organized from the get go," he says.

Keith Cox had done the lighting for the Malchicks' shows, but had been let go by Billy toward the end when the band was trying to cut expenses. It was a messy split. Keith had already gotten the boot when he agreed to do two last weekend shows in Eugene. He made the drive south on his own, and when he arrived on Friday, he was told Billy had already brought in someone else to do the lights. Keith went backstage, and got in an argument with Billy. They exchanged words, and as Keith left, Billy kicked the door on him. Keith came back through the door, and punched Billy in the eye. Billy went on stage that night with a shiner. Keith did the lights on Saturday, then told Billy he was through. He didn't expect to hear from him again, but several months later the phone rang one night, just as he was sitting down to dinner.

"Keith, this is Billy. I've got a new band. Mick's already in, and I want you, too. Whatever happened in the past, let's just forget it." Keith told him he'd think about it.

Keith called Mick and wanted to know about the Unreal Gods. Mick had a job with a delivery company, and he told Keith he'd take him around the next day and they could listen to tapes of the Unreal Gods' rehearsals. While Mick made his deliveries, Keith sat in the van and listened. Sounded pretty good, he thought. "Count me in," he told Mick.

Billy had lined up the Unreal Gods' first gig, Sunday, June 14th at Tipper's. It wasn't downtown, but it was a decent-sized club, with room for about 600. That would do for their first show. Downtown Portland could wait. Not that it would have to wait long.

John Wendeborn, the music critic at The Oregonian, had been a big fan of the Malchicks. When Billy told him about his new band, he was only too happy to write an article advancing the Unreal Gods' debut. The story, and photo of the band, ran a few days before the show at Tipper's. Wendeborn, on the basis of the Malchicks' music and Billy's personality, predicted great success for the Unreal Gods.

Billy had done everything he could think of. He'd hand-picked his new band, and promoted the hell out of their first show, with posters and interviews. Now it was put up or shut up time for Billy Rancher and the Unreal Gods.

9 A Magic Summer

Tony DeMicoli's new downtown Portland club, Luis' La Bamba, was scheduled to open in May of 1981. Headlining on opening night, of course, would be Billy Rancher and the Unreal Gods. No one had actually confirmed this with Billy, but it seemed only natural to him. Tony owed him, after all, for those nights the Malchicks had filled his old club, the Long Goodbye. Billy hadn't taken into account Tony's desire to go with a safer act, say a band that had actually played together in public. Tony chose to open La Bamba with Johnny and the Distractions, a Portland group fronted by Springsteen soundalike Johnny Koonce. Johnny and the D's, as they were known, were a regional success based on their busy club schedule, a really cool T-shirt and the release of a hard-rocking independent album. Actually, there was no reason for Tony not to choose Johnny and the Distractions. They packed La Bamba that first night, and shortly thereafter were the subject of a favorable story in Rolling Stone, then signed by A&M, which re-released their album. Still, Billy viewed Tony's decision as a slap in the face, and set out to show him how wrong he was.

Billy Rancher and the Unreal Gods opened June 14th away from the buzz of downtown, at a bar in southeast Portland modestly named for its 26-year-old owner, Tip Hanzlik. Tipper's was a regular stop on the Portland club circuit. The Malchicks had played there a few times late in 1980. It wasn't downtown, but Billy knew he'd get there soon enough.

The Unreal Gods gathered that afternoon at Dave Stricker's house. They were nervous, but Billy was joking around, keeping everyone loose. Stricker made a tape the band would play during breaks, everything from "Yakety Yak," by the Coasters, to Iggy Pop songs.

When the band arrived, Tipper's was filled, thanks largely to John Wendeborn's story and the posters stapled all over town. Opening night was a success, even if they didn't get all the songs perfect. The energy, the excitement the band created, was unmistakable.

One of the next shows was at a little bar called the Orange Peel in a shopping mall in the Hillsdale neighborhood of southwest Portland. With no story in the local papers or magazines to hype the show, and playing in unfamiliar territory, there were few Unreal Gods fans in the audience. The Orange Peel was the kind of place groups of buddies went after work to play pool and see who could down the most shots of Jack Daniels. The fact they were about to hear some music was merely a coincidence. It certainly wasn't the reason they were there. And no one knew what to make of the guy setting up the video equipment.

David Jester had been videotaping bands in Portland for a couple of years. It hadn't turned into a money-making proposition yet, but he did it for the fun of it, to dance and to be a part of the hip Portland music scene. Billy Rancher asked Jester to tape his new band, offering $25 to cover the cost of a two-hour tape. "And free beer?" Jester asked. "Free beer," Billy assured him, sealing the deal. David Jester had officially become Billy Rancher and the Unreal Gods' Video Guy. His first tape of the Unreal Gods was made at the Orange Peel show.

He didn't get off to a great start with the band, arguing with Mick Boyt about the lighting. "If I can't have the lighting the way I want it, I'm taking my camera and going home," he told Mick. The only thing worse than bad lighting, Mick reasoned, would be Billy getting pissed because he blew the band's video debut, so he made sure the lights were set up the way Jester wanted them. That problem solved, David Jester turned on his camera to capture what Billy had assured him would be the greatest rock 'n' roll footage since Jimi Hendrix set his guitar on fire at Monterey.

David Jester wasn't ready for what happened next. *Hmmm. Why are they booing?* During the first couple of songs, the crowd acted as if it were upset that Billy was making it hard to concentrate on games of pool and pinball. By the end of the first set, though, the crowd had come around, some even paying attention to what was going on on stage. What they saw, what they heard, was hard to ignore. It was rock 'n' roll, but this band didn't look or sound like any other this crowd, or David Jester, had seen. In a way, the songs were simple, catchy pop tunes, but this wasn't wimpy top 40 stuff, not the way Jon DuFresne's guitar solos worked with Billy's rhythm playing to slash through the melodies.

Jester couldn't describe exactly what he was hearing, but he knew what he was seeing, and he'd never seen an audience make this kind of turnaround. By the second set, Billy had everyone's attention. Billy and the Unreal Gods raced through their sweaty third and final set with their shirts off, delivering their best songs to the wild cheers of the delirious Billy Rancher Fans for Life who had crowded to the front of the stage. The pool tables were not being used, the pinball machines were quiet. After what Jester had been told would be the last song, he rewound his tape. The crowd cheered and stomped for five minutes, until Billy came back to play some more. Jester just put his tape back in, covering the first songs from what seemed now like a different show with a raucous 10-minute encore.

"Told you it'd be great," Billy said, helping a dazed David Jester load his video equipment.

The band, crew and several friends started a tradition that night by going to Jester's house to party and watch the tape of the show. Later that summer, Jester's house, located next to a golf course in Lake Oswego, became the site of several more video parties. They'd rent a big screen TV, buy some beer and watch the show again. Some parties drew hundreds of people, and lasted until noon the next day. "It was so much fun I even started paying for the tape myself," Jester says. He felt like Billy Rancher was his best friend in the world. "He was a charmer. He had a way of making you feel important, and he was very sincere about it. He cared about people."

If the band wasn't at Jester's house, or playing, that meant they were at the band house. Billy threw a bed in the middle of the front room downstairs, turning that into his bedroom. It was decorated with a fishing pole and an old baseball glove of his dad's hanging from a nail in the wall. It wasn't much of a castle, but Billy was the king. "Even in

Billy and the Unreal Gods quickly became the hottest band in the thriving Portland club scene.
(Bart Danielson)

that spartan living scene, Billy always had a kind of grace," Steve Hettum says. "It didn't matter to him where he was living, he knew there were going to be bigger and better things ahead. He was so open, never uptight, such a beautiful person. You were never able to rattle him, never catch him at an inopportune time, or on a bad day. Graceful is the word you'd have to use."

The house was buzzing, all day and night, with band members, roadies, girlfriends. There were rehearsals, of course, and Hettum on the phone lining up shows. Billy was constantly writing new songs, and there were posters to make and slap on telephone poles all over town. Billy Rancher and the Unreal Gods, 24 hours a day. The band wouldn't have it any other way.

"That summer, it was like every day was your birthday, Christmas and New Year's Eve rolled into one," Jon DuFresne says.

There was an all-for-one, one-for-all feeling among the band. They were out to conquer the world, or at least Portland. And doing a good job of it, so far.

"When we were on stage, we were five guys as one, and there was a ring of fire up there that you couldn't believe," says Alf Ryder. "I'd look out and see people screaming and cheering, standing on the tables at 2:30 in the morning. We all knew how big this was, how great this thing we had was."

At the center of all the activity, of course, was Billy. There really weren't enough hours in the day for everything he had to do — writing songs, taking care of business, talking to the media, shopping for new clothes, making posters, phone calls. And spending time with Karen, who was home that summer after her first year at the University of Oregon.

The band grew tighter, personally and musically, during that summer. With all the shows, and the constant rehearsals, everyone was getting their parts down just the way Billy wanted them. But all the musical expertise wouldn't have meant anything if they didn't have great songs to play, and Billy made sure there was never a shortage of new material. He'd sit in the basement, strumming his guitar, making up new songs every day. Everything Billy saw, or heard, or learned about, had a chance of becoming a song. He knew Steve Hettum had taken several literature classes in college, and studied Shakespeare. Billy walked into Hettum's bedroom late one night. "Steve, tell me about Hamlet, I've got to write some more songs."

What Billy wrote were incredibly melodic pop songs, with silly lyrics. Musically, the songs were driven by Jon DuFresne's lead guitar work. Lyrically, well, by whatever popped into Billy's head. Songs like "Girlfriend's Drawers" (I found the key to life/Inside my girlfriend's drawers/You don't open mine/I won't mess with yours) and "Rude Buddy Holly" (Buddy, it was so rude for you to leave/Oh, rude Buddy Holly you made my heart beat — sung by Billy in his best Buddy Holly hiccup, of course) would start out jokes by Billy, then, with each passing beer, start to sound more and more like real songs. "When the World Came Crashing Down," an early Unreal Gods staple, was usually dedicated at shows to the Malchicks. The song takes a poke at Billy's former bandmates (We nearly made the big time/'til the world came crashing down/you're living in the old days/and the world came crashing down). In "Upstroke Down" Billy had his eye on the future (Got a little record/I want to show around/Hey, you Hollywood producers/I got the Upstroke Down).

Then there were the songs about Karen. "Psylocybin Doll Face Child," was written after Billy picked Karen up at college and took her away for a ski trip where they swooshed down the slopes after eating a few mushrooms (Pool sized eyes and a smile/the girls stayed with me awhile/and all the dudes were so young/and running away/caution me all the time/the mushrooms on my mind/and the Psylocybin Doll Face Child/she had so much to say).

Even Joe Rancher, who died in 1978, provided inspiration to Billy for a song called "Somethin' New" (If Daddy was alive today/what do you think Daddy would say?/maybe somethin' new).

And if all else failed, he'd just make something up, like the story of the hard-luck Romeo in "Rocky Road," probably Billy's best song. (You never even noticed my name/I think that's such a crying shame/I'm walking down a Rocky Road for you/that's all that you have left me to).

But the song that defined the Unreal Gods' early sound was "Boom Chuck Rock." It was the name of one song, but also the name Billy used to describe the indescribable rock/ska/new wave/rockabilly sounds his new band was making.

"That was the coolest thing about Billy Rancher and the Unreal Gods," says Billy Flaxel. "We invented a sound, we named it, and we played it. We just had a style that set us apart from everybody else."

Billy referred to boom chuck as "a broad, general, humorous term," that can mean anything from a drum beat ("the bass is the boom, the snare

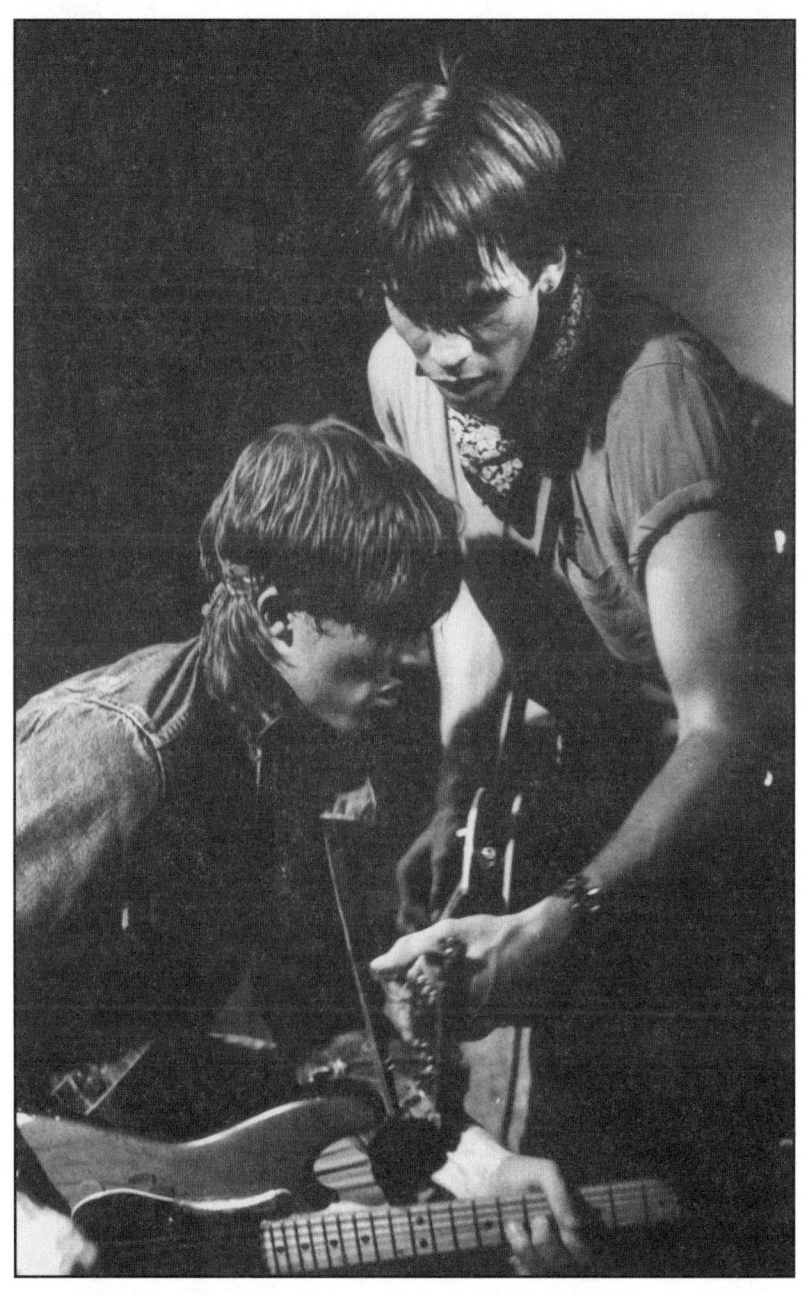

Jon DuFresne, right, with Billy, couldn't imagine being anything other than an Unreal God. "It was like every day was your birthday, Christmas and New Year's Eve rolled into one."
(Bart Danielson)

is the chuck. Boom chuck") to a heartbeat ("thump thump, thump thump, boom chuck, boom chuck") to a "back to basics reference to music."

He gives some of the credit for inventing the term to an eccentric Portland musician who called himself The Incredible John Davis. Billy had befriended The Incredible, which was no easy feat. Billy admired Davis' guitar-playing ability, his style. In the months that he was putting together the Unreal Gods, Billy spent several nights watching Davis play, then talking with him. Davis, who was in his thirties, could be a nice enough guy one minute, then the most violent, rude, disgusting individual you could imagine the next. He enjoyed playing just long enough to attract a crowd, then stopping in mid-song to scream, "What the fuck are you idiots looking at? Get a fucking life." A punk with an acoustic guitar.

Billy says he developed boom chuck after "rapping boom chuck" with Davis. No one else involved with the Unreal Gods could stand to be around him, but they had to tolerate him because he was Billy's friend. Billy let Davis open Unreal Gods shows. By then, no one else would have let him on stage. (The Incredible John Davis was busted a few years later for growing pot and given a cell in the Oregon State Penitentiary, thus becoming The Incarcerated John Davis. By then, though, he'd come and gone in Billy's life, having made his contribution to Billy's success.)

"Boom Chuck Rock," like most of the Unreal Gods' songs, was a rollicking good time with a DuFresne guitar solo thrown into the middle.

The boom chuck rock ain't no heavy sound
the boom chuck rock is just the up and down
They call it boom chuck, it's just a boom chuck, go
the boom chuck rock is just the only kind of rock I know

Well, everywhere you go you hear the boom chuck sound
in the cowboy halls, and in the punk rock town
They call it boom chuck, it's just the same thing twice
the boom chuck rock, yeah it sounds so nice

Roadie Keith Cox noticed the crowds getting bigger and bigger, with lines forming outside the clubs to see Billy Rancher and the Unreal Gods. And he noticed how perfect the music was, and what a charismatic showman Billy had become.

"I'm not a very emotional person, but I remember once at the Copper

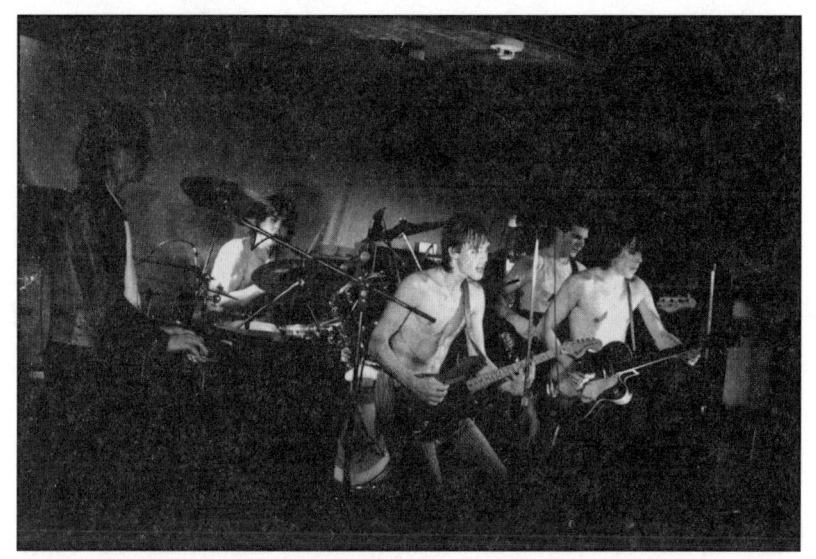

The Unreal Gods burned up the Portland clubs. "There was a ring of fire up there that you couldn't believe," says Alf Ryder.
(Bart Danielson)

Penny they sounded so good it brought tears to my eyes," Cox says. "I remember this feeling of pride just welling up inside of me. When they were on — and they were almost always on — they were the best."

They played as often as they could, several nights a week, and quickly established themselves as the best band in Portland. They played at La Bamba the week after debuting at Tipper's, then several more times that summer, becoming Tony DeMicoli's hottest ticket.

Before DeMicoli turned it into La Bamba, the place was a restaurant called The Medieval Inn. Tony kept the medieval decor. The two big wooden front doors looked like the entrance to a castle. It was cool and dark inside, with the stage on the main level and a Mexican restaurant downstairs. At the beginning of a typical Unreal Gods night at La Bamba, Billy's fans gathered early and sat around the long wooden tables, drinking beer, waiting for the band. When the music started, they spilled onto the dance floor, or just jumped up on a table and danced, or sang along.

"Wherever we were was the place to be in Portland," Billy Flaxel says. "Everyone would look forward to where the Unreal Gods were. We got the college crowd into it, everyone who was looking for something to happen. Downtown Portland was a fun, live place. We were a downtown band. It was just unbelievable, a very exciting time."

The only Portlanders who weren't fans of the band, it seemed, were other bands. The story in The Oregonian before Billy and the Unreal Gods had played a show didn't sit very well with veteran groups that had struggled for years without getting that kind of attention. But they were missing the point. It wasn't just the music that John Wendeborn was writing about. It was Billy. Wendeborn had something to go on, having seen Billy with the Malchicks, so he had an idea what the music would sound like, and what kind of a show Billy would put on. But he also liked Billy, and he knew Portland's clubgoers and eventually the record-buying public would, too. Wendeborn was tired of the punks. Here was someone he could root for, so he did.

And Billy didn't care, quite frankly, what other Portland bands thought about him, his band, or his image. All he knew was that it was working for him. People were coming to see him, the media was writing about him. Besides, he didn't know how else to act. It wasn't Billy's fault he wasn't a punk with a shitty attitude. He really was tall, and blond, and handsome, and talented, and charismatic, and happy, and in love with a beautiful girl. So sue me, OK?

One of Billy's rivals in 1981 was a band led by Darrell Strong called the Confidentials.

"They were the Rolling Stones to Billy's Sgt. Pepper Beatles," says Buck Munger. "But it was obvious to everyone the competition existed only in terms of door draw, because the songs weren't there for the Confidentials. Darrell Strong just didn't have the songs, and he wasn't as charismatic as Billy. With Billy, the material was there. You can't do anything in music without the material, and Billy had it. He had it from day one."

What Billy had, in addition to the ability to write great songs, was a feel for how to put on a show and the courage to follow his artistic vision. Not to mention good timing.

If Billy had received any local competition, it would have come from Quarterflash or Johnny and the Distractions. But both those bands were in LA recording albums, Quarterflash for Geffen and Johnny and the D's for A&M. And on the national scene, it was about time to kill off some of those old '70s ghosts.

"Music was changing, and we were a local band with a new sound," Jon DuFresne says. "But we were acceptable. The Portland punk scene was very aggressive. We had as much energy, or more, than the punks, but all kinds of different people could get into our music."

This was also a time when the Portland music scene was more happening than Seattle's. The Unreal Gods played Seattle that summer, and became more popular at Astor Park and the Hall of Fame than Seattle's top club acts, like the Cowboys and the Heats (led by Billy's new brother-in-law, Steve Pearson).

One Portland band that wasn't a major threat was Them Roosters, Lenny's new group. Them Roosters could be included among the bands that were jealous of the Unreal Gods.

"We'd go to their shows and then tell ourselves that if we had Billy's equipment, we'd be better than them," Pete Jorgusen says. "We blamed it on our equipment."

"Rainier Ale dreams," Lenny says. "Cocaine dreams."

Lenny didn't dig the Unreal Gods sound, but he watched them play several times. Once in a while he'd bring his guitar along, just in case.

"I remember standing at the side of the stage at the Last Hurrah, because I knew they were going to play 'Love in Vain,' and I wanted to play slide with them," Lenny says. "Some times, Billy would ask me up on stage. Other times I was too drunk, and he wouldn't let me play."

Not that Lenny wanted to be an Unreal God. He told DuFresne more than once that his job was safe, despite any rumors he might have heard about Lenny wanting to join the band. It wasn't the kind of music Lenny wanted to play, and he wouldn't have had a clue about the kind of shows Billy was doing.

For starters, there were the go go dancers. The Goddesses A-Go-Go. Candyce Dru was one of the original dancers.

"The first couple of shows, there was no real choreography, we were just kind of bopping around, doing some basic go go steps," she says. "Then we started putting the movements to the music, giving it more of a theatrical look. Then we put in lots of different costume changes. I'd go over the set list with Billy before shows, and he'd ask me how much time we needed between songs, and we'd kind of shape the set around the dancing and the costumes."

Candyce was in her thirties, older than everyone in the band except Alf. She did a lot of partying and a lot of running into the guitar player. A rule was finally made: Candyce figures out which side of the stage Jon DuFresne is on, then goes to the other. This kept her from stumbling into Jon, but it didn't mean fans were safe from her on-stage convulsions. One

Billy and Candyce Dru, one of the original Goddesses A-Go-Go, before a show.
(Bart Danielson)

poor guy got a little too close and Candyce kicked him right in the face, dislocating his jaw. For better or worse, the Goddesses A-Go-Go helped set Billy apart.

Also, it's a safe bet there weren't many bands using makeup in 1981 in Portland. Most bands were either punk (the Wipers), hard rock (Sequel), skinny tie new wave (the Dots), or macho working-class rock 'n' roll (Johnny and the Distractions). But Billy — perhaps owing to his fondness of David Bowie and Mick Jagger — wasn't afraid to use a little eyeliner and blush to highlight his best features.

"He was always coming over to me with a makeup pencil in the dressing room, saying, 'Do me, do me,' " Candyce says.

One of Billy's favorite costumes was a leopard-skin suit, but he had many different looks on stage. Pajama tops were a favorite shirt choice. The pants were usually colorful, and often skin-tight.

But there was more to the show than the makeup, the costumes, the dancers. There was a comfortableness in his style, the way he delivered the music, talked between songs, directed his band, and generally controlled the situation and everyone in the room.

Billy was a natural on stage.

"He was really a unique person, a great performer," Jon DuFresne says. "He had a real love for people, and he shared that. He didn't hold anything back. And we were out to set the world on its ear. Anything any other band did, we wouldn't do. We wouldn't even go hang out in the clubs. Billy didn't want us to be seen before shows, didn't want us to go have a beer with the crowd after the shows. So we were just this mysterious band. We were on stage, then we were gone. Billy told us we were stars, and that's how we should act."

In one brilliant summer, Billy Rancher and the Unreal Gods had become the kings of Portland rock 'n' roll, playing at the hottest clubs, partying and even starting to record their first album.

Steve Hettum knew he had a tiger by the tail. "There's just no way to describe the energy, the momentum, the firepower we had that first summer."

Billy Rancher was a rock star, even before the rest of the world knew it.
(Bart Danielson)

10 Billy and Karen

If anyone was having a better summer than Billy, it was Karen Sage. Billy and Karen had kept their romance going through her first year of college, with letters, phone calls and visits every weekend. Now she was home to spend three months with Billy. And the Unreal Gods.

She was still just 19 years old, so Billy had to sneak her into most of the shows. But that wasn't much of a problem when you were the star's girlfriend. It was a position, she discovered, with plenty of applicants.

If Karen had any doubt about that, it was erased when she noticed women following her and Billy home from shows, or when she saw the party girls brazenly throwing themselves at Billy, even as he had a long arm wrapped around her shoulder.

"After the shows he'd always want to go to parties and unwind," Karen remembers. "Girls were all over the place. I mean he was pretty gregarious, he really enjoyed the attention. If I wasn't at a party with him, I'd always think, 'Oh, I should be there.' If I wasn't there, what was going to happen to him?"

Steve Hettum marveled at the way Billy turned away girls. "He had a real cool way of saying no to a girl," Steve says. "He'd say something nice to her, and she'd leave feeling good about it. And he had plenty of

Karen and Billy quench their thirst after a show.
(Mark Rabiner)

chances to say no. Girls approached him all the time, but he wasn't a user. Billy wasn't an angel, but he loved Karen."

Glen Baggerly, an old baseball buddy of Billy's from Mount Hood, couldn't believe the girls at the shows. Or what they'd do to try to get Billy's attention. "He had a pretty good-looking following," Baggerly says. "I'd ask him about it, I'd say, 'Jesus, man, you can have anybody you want.' But he was so focused. He'd say, 'Glen, all I want to do is play my music and make people happy. I don't give a shit about these women. They're everywhere, they're always everywhere.' Besides, he had Karen. She was really good for him. He needed her."

Baggerly thought it was funny to watch Billy and Karen together. Billy was always kissing and hugging Karen, who was more reserved in public. "It was comical," he says. "He was always all over her, and she would just be looking like this little puppy. I'd always be telling him, 'Give her a chance to breathe, man.' He was very loving."

And Karen was good for Billy, and for Billy's music.

"Billy was completely in love and devoted to Karen. He could have had anyone he wanted, but being that happy and that satisfied gives you a lot of time to concentrate on other things besides trying to get your dick out," says Billy Flaxel, who hadn't reached a similar level of contentment and, alas, had to turn elsewhere for fulfillment. "Billy took all those energies and put them into his music, because he already had what he wanted."

Karen may not have been crazy about the parties, and all the other girls, but she loved the Portland rock 'n' roll scene that was swirling around Billy.

Billy and Karen would critique the performances together into the early morning hours. "He always wanted to discuss the shows," she says. "I always loved that part of it, especially if there wasn't a party that night, and it would just be the two of us, talking about the shows. We'd talk for hours about new ideas. I usually thought most of Billy's ideas were crazy, but they always seemed to work."

Karen was often with Billy as he wrote songs. She enjoyed watching him write, especially if the songs were about her. "I loved that," she says. "I mean, I never asked him to write songs about me, but when he did ... I would just think, 'My God, this is great.' "

Karen's parents, Bill and Dorothy Sage, might not have agreed, especially if they knew what "Psylocybin Doll Face Child" was about.

Billy's outgoing personality eventually won over the Sages, but they were never totally comfortable with their daughter dating this rock star. "I'm sure they were scared, but they never really voiced it with me. They liked Billy."

Billy and Karen were together constantly that summer. Most of the time, of course, it was Unreal Gods business. But they managed to find some time to jump into Bill and Dorothy Sage's boat and water ski on Lake Oswego. The way Buck Munger saw it, having a respectable girlfriend like Karen was another difference between Billy and other Portland musicians.

"Billy's love affair with Karen was wonderful," Munger says. "She was a beautiful, quality girl in a backstage, sleazy environment. I liked Karen. I liked seeing Billy and Karen together. It was another no-sleazy difference between Billy Rancher and these other punk, asshole kids who were so proud of being uncommercial. Billy was so commercial, so image-correct. Billy and Karen would walk into the room, hey, it's a cocktail party."

The cocktail party ended on Sunday, August 23rd.

Billy's testicles were sore. He thought maybe he'd hurt them during a playful wrestling match with Lenny, or perhaps had a hernia. Bill Sage called his doctor, David Paull. Dr. Paull asked Billy to come to his house for an exam. Dr. Paull delivered the bad news: Billy had a tumor, and it had to come out. Karen couldn't believe what she was hearing. "He's so young, just 24 years old, so healthy," she thought. "How can he have cancer? Why is this happening?" Surgery was scheduled for the next day at Providence Hospital in Portland.

Before he went to the hospital, Billy had to tell the rest of the band. Monday afternoon, they were gathered at the band house for the weekly Monday meeting and a rehearsal. It was a big week for Billy Rancher and the Unreal Gods. On Saturday, they would be playing at the Paramount Theater, opening for reggae star Peter Tosh.

No one knew better than Billy just how big an opportunity the Tosh show was. In fact, he had made it clear to Dr. Paull, and to Karen, and to Astrid, that he was not going to miss that show. He'd have the surgery, but he was going to be on the Paramount stage on Saturday night. Now, how to tell the band. He didn't really have any plan as he walked into the house with Karen. "Um... I've got something I've got to tell you guys," he began. Everyone knew it was something serious, because for once he wasn't joking around, or enthusiastically describing a new song, or talking about an upcoming gig. "They found something unusual in my testicles. There's a lump there. I need to go back in for some more tests." Then he walked out of the room. Everyone looked at Karen. What the hell was going on? "Billy has cancer," she told them. "He's going in for surgery."

Billy Flaxel remembers how he felt after hearing the news. "We were shocked, but we all thought, 'Billy's young, this is no problem. This is curable. He'll be OK.' "

"There was a feeling like it was no big deal," Karen says. "It was traumatic, but we were sure it wasn't a life-threatening situation."

The surgery went well, or as well as the removal of a testicle can go. Dr. Paull said a second surgery to remove lymph nodes would be required. His suggestion had been to do it the same day as the removal of the testicle. "How long will I have to be in the hospital?" Billy asked. "Probably a week, maybe more," Dr. Paull answered. Billy didn't hesitate. "Can't do it, doc. I've got a show Saturday." Billy agreed to come back in for the second surgery the day after the Peter Tosh show.

Steve Hettum went to the hospital on Tuesday to see Billy. He told Billy that the band would understand if he couldn't play Saturday. "Steve, this is the biggest show of my life, and I'm going to be there," Billy told him.

"Really, Billy you don't ... " Hettum never finished the sentence.

"Steve, don't get your tits in a bind. I'll be there. Everything's OK. We're doing the show, then I'm coming back here for another operation. Don't worry, man."

On Wednesday, Billy was released from Providence Hospital. He couldn't get back to the band house fast enough. Just a couple days to rehearse.

Karen believed everything would be OK, because Billy told her it would. He'd always been right before. But she was scared. Billy had just had one testicle removed, and was going to be cut open in a few days to remove lymph nodes and check for more tumors. And all he could talk about was the show at the Paramount.

The rest of the band was worried about Billy. And worried more, maybe, about Karen. She'd earned their respect. She wasn't just one of the girls hanging around the Unreal Gods shows and parties. She was Billy's girl, and this seemed like an awful lot for her to handle.

"Everybody loved Karen," Alf Ryder says. "We loved her more than Billy. She was easier to love."

11 Playing the Paramount

A few days before the Tosh show, Billy had talked his way into the Paramount for a rehearsal. Karen approached roadie Keith Cox, who was in charge of lighting, and asked him for a favor.

"Keith, he's going to want to drink, but he just got out of the hospital," she told him. "Please, don't let him have anything. Please?"

"OK, OK, no problem," Cox said.

During the rehearsal, Billy would pop open a beer, only to have it taken away by Keith as soon as he sat it down. After this happened three or four times, Billy caught on. Now it was his turn to take Keith aside.

"Hey, Karen's just worried about me," Billy told him. "Isn't she great? Listen, don't worry about it, I'm just going to have a beer or two."

Keith liked Karen, but Billy was the boss, so ... well, what could a few beers hurt?

Rehearsal was painful for Billy, but a small problem like cancer and the removal of a testicle wasn't going to keep him from playing Saturday. Besides, the practice had confirmed what he had hoped: Billy Rancher and the Unreal Gods were ready.

Unfortunately, 3,000 Peter Tosh fans weren't ready for them. First of all, people don't go to reggae concerts because there's nothing better to do that night. Reggae fans take their music seriously. It's a spiritual experience, not just a show. And they wanted to see Peter Tosh, not these white boys playing their amped-up rock 'n' roll. And, as usual, when given a chance to throw gas on a fire, Billy couldn't resist.

If the reggae fans were going to put up with Billy Rancher and the Unreal Gods, the least they expected the band to do was to show the proper reverence for the evening's proceedings. Fat chance. For one thing, the name Unreal Gods probably didn't make them any new friends that night. Then Billy took the stage smoking a huge papier mache joint. Now, maybe this was Billy's tip of the cap to the reggae culture, but the fans at the Paramount that night took it as an insult. Billy tossed the fake joint into the audience, only to have it come flying back at him.

Billy decided that if two go go dancers were good, four would be even better, this being such a big show. Turns out that was a little too Vegas for the reggae crowd. They also weren't thrilled with the song, "Black Man," which they may have interpreted as racist, even though the lyrics weren't. Billy finally ruined any chance he had of winning over the crowd by choosing a song called "Over Easy." (Buy yourself a gun/and get it over easy). At the end of the song, Billy shot each member of the band with a fake gun, and celebrated as they took turns dropping dead. Someone apparently forgot to mention to Billy that reggae crowds don't appreciate violence.

It's too bad Billy lost the crowd early, because the Unreal Gods put on a very energetic, tight 50-minute set that would have gone over just fine at La Bamba, or the Copper Penny. All the crowd knew, though, was that it didn't like these loud, smart ass rock 'n' rollers. And they let them know it. Boos easily drowned out the cheers of the few Unreal Gods fans. Not that Billy and the band cared, really.

"We were being very Rolling Stones-ish about the whole thing," Jon DuFresne says. "We didn't give a shit. We knew it was the right thing to do. We were shaking people up, but we knew we had to, because the Portland music scene was pretty staid at that time. We were trying to upset everything, just because it had to be done."

It was another one of Billy's calculated controversies. From the beginning, Billy had done everything he could to make sure people were going to hear all about his new band. Every show, every gimmick, every stage antic, everything was done for a purpose: to make Billy Rancher and the Unreal Gods stars.

After their set, they were shown to their seats to watch Peter Tosh. The band had been treated like, well, like an opening act, all night long by people at the Paramount, which wasn't doing Billy's frame of mind any good. Their seats were located in the balcony, behind the stage.

Depending on who's telling the story, Billy threw a canteloupe or popped a champagne cork, hitting a fan who had been harassing him, or Peter Tosh's road manager. Either way, it was enough to get the band thrown out.

"We were just bored," DuFresne says. "It was time to go, anyway."

Back at the band house, Billy held court. It had been the first negative reaction the Unreal Gods had received. "Don't worry about it," he told everyone. "It's not our fault a bunch of stoned reggae fans don't recognize a good show when they see one."

Of course, it was easy for Billy to be philosophical. He was tired, and sore. But no one was going to ruin the moment for him. He'd played the Paramount. He was happy, content to savor the moment. And so what if a few people booed him? That didn't seem like such a big deal when he thought about returning to Providence Hospital for more surgery.

12 The Shark Bite

With Billy's tumorous testicle removed, Dr. Paull needed to check to see if the cancer had spread. He would rather have done this on Monday, when he did the first surgery, but he gave in to Billy's insistence that Part Two had to wait until after Saturday's show at the Paramount. "Don't worry," Billy told him. "I'll be back the day after the show." The day after was here.

This was a much more complicated surgery, an eight-hour procedure to remove 63 lymph nodes from Billy's lungs, kidney, arteries and intestines. A lung had to be collapsed during the operation, and a tube inserted so he could get enough oxygen. Karen, Astrid and Ellen waited for what seemed like days. Finally, Dr. Paull emerged and told them the surgery had gone well. Later, biopsies of the tissues showed no cancer. The doctors got all of it when the testicle had been removed.

"Billy was really relieved," Karen says. "We had this feeling that this wasn't that big a deal. The doctors were confident it hadn't spread. It never crossed our minds that he could die, we never thought how grave cancer can be. We were young, immortal."

Doctors told Billy he had been extremely lucky, but that he shouldn't push it. Don't plan on doing much for a couple of months, they said.

Billy listened, and shook his head solemnly in agreement. But he had a different timetable. The rules the doctors were laying out were for someone who was going to be a "panty-waist" about it, Billy told Karen, someone who was going to be feeble, and negative. He thought it was funny when a reverend came into his room to brace him for the tough times he would face, the times he would break down and cry. A nice gesture, but the reverend's time might have been better spent bracing Portland for Billy's return.

Billy was pronounced healthy, and released on September 6th, a week after the surgery. He took home a thick, red scar that started just under his right armpit and curved down his side, across his flat stomach, under his belly button, ending at his left hip.

Billy hanging out in downtown Portland.
(Bart Danielson)

"He called it a shark bite," Karen says. "He told people he'd been in a surfing accident."

Shows had to be canceled, of course, until Billy was ready to play again. No problem, Steve Hettum thought. What kind of an asshole could possibly object to a cancer patient taking a couple weeks off? There was one catch, though. Only his family, closest friends and a tight circle around the Unreal Gods knew Billy had the surgeries. He didn't want anyone else to know about the cancer, for now, at least. Hettum's job, then, was to cancel all these shows without telling the club owners why. First stop, La Bamba.

"Tony, Billy's not going to be able to play for a few weeks," Hettum told Tony DeMicoli..

"Why the fuck not?"

"Listen, you've just got to trust me on this. He'll be back soon. Tony, we've had a good relationship, and I'm not jerking you around here, neither is Billy. This is important, and he'll be back pretty soon. OK?"

And so it went for Hettum, one club after another, convincing owners that Billy needed a little time off, that he'd be back soon. Hettum hoped he was right.

Jon DuFresne couldn't believe what was happening. But he felt better after visiting Billy in the hospital after the operation.

"I'd never had to deal with anyone around me being sick," he says. "I mean, we were just getting the band going, and we were flying, then 'Oh no, Billy has cancer.' It was devastating. But then the surgery was a success, and when I talked to Billy, I knew he was going to conquer it. It seemed to just make him better, like there was no way he was going to let this get him down. He was really positive. He kept talking about how lucky he'd been, how much we had going. He was really excited about getting out of the hospital, getting back on stage and back into the studio to finish our album. He said he had a lot to be thankful for. He said he felt really lucky."

The day after Billy's second surgery, DuFresne and Steve Hettum were guests on AM Northwest, a Portland afternoon TV show that was examining Portland's new wave music craze. The topic was probably a good idea, but the program was hosted by the magnificently uninformed and unhip Jim Bosley and Margie Boulé, who really were Too Straight for the New Wave. When Bosley asked DuFresne a question, Jon didn't bother to answer, instead looking into the camera and telling his friend Billy Rancher, who was home sick, to get better. Billy was actually still in a hospital bed, but that was a secret. For a while, at least.

After the show, DuFresne left to visit his girlfriend Doreen, who had moved to Boston. He assumed the Unreal Gods were going to have a lengthy break. He called every few days to see how Billy was doing. During one call, he was told Billy was resting, getting better. The next call, he was told Billy was writing songs, that he was ready to start rehearsing again, and that Jon better get his ass back to Portland.

"He was just going at it with a vengeance," DuFresne says. "I got back, and there were like 10 or 15 new songs to learn."

By late September, the band house was busy, and neighbors were once again treated to late night rehearsals. Billy felt fine. He'd beaten cancer, which came as no great surprise to Billy or anyone who knew him. He'd always won at everything else in life. To the Unreal Gods, to his family and friends, it looked like Billy was back, better than ever, confident, happy and ready to take on the world. Only with Karen, late at night, after the rehearsals, after everyone had gone, did he express any fears. "Does my voice still sound the same?" he'd ask her. Billy was worried that the collapsed lung during the second surgery might affect his singing. Karen held Billy tight and told him his voice was as good as it had ever been. She told him his fans were still going to love him. She told him she would always love him.

On October 9th, Billy Rancher and the Unreal Gods returned to the stage at La Bamba. Billy looked and sounded great.

13 Boom Chuck Rock Now!

Billy's return to good health meant he could get back into the studio and finish the first Unreal Gods album.

In July, Jack Barr had agreed to let Billy and his band use his Portland studio, High Tech Recording. Barr had just opened the studio, and was eager to get local musicians in to record. The deal was $900 to record 12 songs. The band would be given unlimited time to record the album.

The money came from Dr. John Flaxel. "He was really excited about the band," Billy Flaxel says. "He thought it was a good, and unique band. He's a very hip man, and he knew we were on to something, that we had something very special. He was really excited about it. Billy's charisma just won him over."

Dr. Flaxel's main concern, of course, was Billy Flaxel's career, and his wagon was hitched tightly to Billy Rancher. But it wouldn't be fair to John Flaxel to say his only conern was for his son. He truly enjoyed and liked Billy Rancher, and he was a generous and caring man where the Unreal Gods were concerned. And while he had no experience in the music business to base this on, he honestly felt the Unreal Gods (and their excellent drummer, Billy Flaxel) were going to be stars. And, it didn't hurt Dr. Flaxel's ego any to be part of the Billy Rancher and the Unreal

Billy had written more than 100 songs by the time he took the Unreal Gods into the studio to record their first album.
(Mark Rabiner)

Gods scene.

Now that they were in the studio, there was the matter of picking 12 songs. Billy had written more than 100 by then, so that wasn't as easy as it might sound. Billy was a prolific writer, capable of pounding out several songs a week. In fact, he was probably a little too prolific. Billy's songwriting style had evolved some from the Malchicks days, when his method was to get extremely drunk, write down the first words that came into his head, then develop a nice little Chuck Berry riff. Presto! A song. Now, a more mature Billy sometimes wrote songs when he wasn't drunk, and the first words that were creeping into his head usually had something to do with Karen.

Both lyrically and musically, the songs were more complex than those he wrote for the Malchicks. But still, these were not political songs, these were party songs. Songs, as Billy said, about "what's going on in a young boy's mind." He was simply trying to write songs that made people dance, and would make him famous. The result, then, was a formula for constructing nice boy meets girl pop songs. Lots of them. This was a very creative time for Billy, and he was cranking out a lot of good tunes. But most of them could have used a little editing, perhaps more thought given to each song. But Billy didn't work that way. He couldn't help it. Songs just kept coming to him. "He wrote great songs," Billy Flaxel says. "They were simple songs, but always with a twist to them, like using a lot of ska beats."

And once Billy was finished with one song, and another idea had ahold of him, it was time to move on. Still, it was hard to argue with his success. Fans who were dancing to sets of 30 to 40 original songs a night certainly didn't have any complaints.

In picking cuts for the album, "Boom Chuck Rock" — the song that defined the sound Billy was going for — was a no-brainer. That song, more than any other, typified the Unreal Gods style: a strong, driving backbeat, a rockabilly guitar solo by Jon DuFresne and Billy's quirky lyrics.

A couple other live favorites — "Rocky Road" and "Upstroke Down" — would have to be included. "Rocky Road" starts slowly, the different players coming in one at a time, and builds dramatically. It's also, among the early songs, the best example of Billy's sensitive side, featuring a restrained, emotional vocal performance. In "Upstroke Down," Billy confidently forecasts a trip to Hollywood to show off his record.

Some of the band members considered "Girlfriend's Drawers," "Psylocybin Doll Face Child" and "Rude Buddy Holly" to be silly, lightweight songs, but they were songs the club audiences liked. Besides, they were three of Billy's favorites, and this wasn't exactly a democracy. "Girlfriend's Drawers" *is* a silly, lightweight song, based on a sophomoric double entendre. "Psylocybin Doll Face Child" is an interesting song, appropriately trippy, considering the inspiration. In "Rude Buddy Holly," Billy pays tribute to Buddy, while chastising him for dying so young.

"Go Go Boots" has a feeling of drama that is wasted on silly lyrics. "Rockabilly Queen" is a manic stomp featuring a nice Jon DuFresne guitar solo. Both songs are survivors from the Malchicks era, and were the two songs the Unreal Gods had recorded in the spring of 1981 just two weeks after Billy Flaxel had come aboard. The versions of the songs on the new album aren't as stark as the spare versions done at Tom Robinson's studio.

"Uptown," has a slow, dreamy, tremolo guitar feel. "English Boy" and "Somethin' New" are showcases for Alf's keyboards. "Symmetry in My Play," one of the Unreal Gods' best live songs, is one of Billy's most developed songs, with a subtlety not found on many others. The song has a reggae beat, and a simple, clean guitar line thrown into the middle.

There were other songs that were considered, some that probably should have been included, but those are the 12 Billy decided on for the album. "Don't Be Sad," "World Came Crashing Down," "Too Straight for the New Wave," and "Even Your Nightmares Come True," were all big hits in the clubs that wouldn't have been out of place on the album. But with more than 100 songs to choose from, something had to give.

Jack Barr thought Billy would be out of his studio in a couple weeks. The Unreal Gods finished recording in February of 1982, seven months after they started.

At shows, Billy kept telling fans the album was going to be out "in a couple of weeks." Months rolled by.

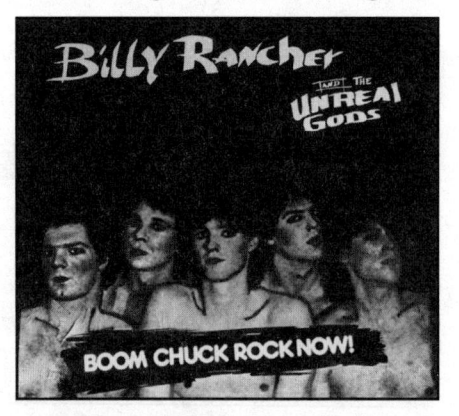

Jon DuFresne hated the look of the album, but Billy had no such concerns. "He seemed determined to enjoy things," says Dana Coffee, the Portland artist who photographed and designed the "Boom Chuck Rock Now!" cover.

"None of us had any experience in a recording studio," Jon DuFresne says. "We were just figuring it out as we went along."

Billy Flaxel: "We spent our money in one day, but we made this guy just go on, and on, and on."

Finally, the 12 songs were recorded. Billy Triplett, who had been the Unreal Gods' sound man for their live shows, worked with Barr to engineer and mix the recordings. Billy Rancher had made it clear to everyone he didn't want the album to sound "too slick." He wanted it to capture the feel of an Unreal Gods' performance, but what he got was a collection of good songs that, in some cases, lacked the energy of the live shows. The band wasn't thrilled with the way the recordings turned out.

"They sounded so good live, that I just didn't think the album captured the excitement of what Billy Rancher and the Unreal Gods were all about," says roadie Keith Cox. "I remember the band didn't like it. They thought Jack Barr added some really spacy sounds to it. People who were Billy's fans liked it, it was a novelty — Billy's first album. But it wasn't the same as they were live."

Jon DuFresne said he was disappointed by what he heard. "Listening to it today, I like about half of it," he says. "There are certain things I thought we should have done differently. I thought we were a little overproduced. But that's the record business — you have to make concessions."

DuFresne learned that lesson when it came to the cover for the new album.

Alf Ryder and his girlfriend Mary Smith (who had been an original go go dancer but quit after just a few shows) visited Billy in the hospital after the second surgery. They brought him some artwork by Dana Coffee, a Portland artist they admired. Billy liked what he saw, and wanted to meet the artist to talk about an album cover idea.

Coffee watched a couple of Unreal Gods shows and talked to Billy about his idea.

"He wanted kind of a super hero look," she says.

Coffee photographed the band, shirtless, wearing heavy glam makeup. That photo was then doctored to look less like a photo and more like a crude drawing of the band.

"I was going for the look they had described, but the longer I worked on it, the less they wanted to look effeminate," she remembers. "Here they were, slathering on makeup, and telling me they wanted to look more macho."

The final result could not be desribed as macho, but the photo did achieve an unreal quality.

"I hated that picture," DuFresne says. "I remember going, 'Why are we using this picture, it's so stupid.' The band had a really cool image, and I don't think that did us justice. I just thought it was a little gay. I don't know why Billy was so tied to doing that. I thought it was suicide. That was my first record, so I was pretty serious about every detail."

Billy and the band splashed around in the fountain at a "black-tie" event at the Civic Auditorium.
(Bart Danielson)

Coffee remembers that Billy had no such worries.

"They were kind of young and feckless, really," she says. "Well, Alf wasn't that young, but they were definitely very feckless. Billy was different, though. He seemed to have a little more sense of his mortality. He seemed determined to enjoy things. There was kind of a genial goodheartedness about him."

It looked fine to Billy Flaxel. "I loved the idea, myself," he says. "I know Jon had a big problem with it. It was just another one of Billy's crazy ideas that worked. Billy was tight with Will Vinton, the claymation guy in Portland who did the California Raisins. He wanted to do stuff for us for free, just to get it out there. We all thought it was stupid, but Billy believed in it heart and soul. We just couldn't see it. But Billy was hot on this dude, he told us this was going to be big, that claymation was going to be huge. How the hell did he know that?"

There was no controversy on the photos to be used inside on the lyric sheet. Bart Danielson put together a collage of more than 60 photos he had taken in just a few months as the Unreal Gods' unofficial photographer.

Bart met Billy at La Bamba, on a hot summer night in the middle of a 30-hour guitar-playing marathon by The Incredible John Davis. Billy was wearing his leopard skin outfit, which made it easy for Bart to pick him out of the crowd. Bart was about the same height and age as Billy, which seemed like enough in common to start a conversation. "Hey, dude, that's kind of a wild suit you've got on."

As they talked, Bart mentioned that he grew up in Lake Oswego. "Maybe you know my girlfriend, then," Billy said. "Karen Sage."

Their parents' houses were both on Lake Oswego, not far apart at all. Bart was a few years older than Karen, but he knew she was good friends with several of his friends and his sisters.

When Bart said photography was a hobby of his, that's all Billy needed to hear.

"He asked me to shoot him, see if we could put something together. He liked what I did, and it was fun for me to help him out."

Billy had a new friend, and a new photographer. And the more Bart hung around, the more he saw how good Karen was for Billy.

"She kept his feet on the ground," he says. "She was the conservative lake brat. You had to always maintain in front of Karen. You just didn't say anything negative to her. She wasn't used to hearing anything like that. Other people, Billy would tell them what he thought, tell them to go to hell. You just don't say something like that to a person like Karen. What a tight bond they had. They were both very lucky people."

Billy and Bart were like little kids together. Most of Billy's other friends were musicians, or wished they were. Being with Bart reminded Billy of a simpler time. This was more like riding sleds with Lenny and Ellen.

"I was basically the most normal guy he knew," Danielson says. "And we just had a blast together, just being together, talking. The comedian in him was unreal. We'd literally laugh so hard we'd have to hold our wieners. We were just a couple of kids, you know, 'Don't try to drink any milk, 'cause it's going through your nose.' We'd just have to go into different rooms sometimes. We couldn't look at each other, because all we'd be able to do was laugh."

Billy liked to call Bart "Bartkowski," or "Scoutski," or usually, just "Scout." His relationship with Bart also rekindled his interest in sports. The former baseball player had never lost his interest, it's just that most of his pasty-faced, skinny rock 'n' roll friends weren't up to touch football, or softball, or one-on-one basketball, or tennis, like Bart was.

"He was so aggressive, so competitive," Danielson says. "Tennis was our big game. We'd go baseline to baseline. We'd play when it was 10 degrees. I never won a match, and I'm not shabby. We had some legendary matches."

When Billy and Bart weren't playing tennis or holding their wieners, they found time to shoot some photos. Billy, naturally, turned out to be a perfect subject.

"He was a total ham. He just loved it," Danielson says. "One time, on First Night in Portland, they were doing the play 'Annie' at the Civic Auditorium. There were people with black ties all over the place. Billy's got his shirt off, playing in the fountain as people were walking into the theater. I told him he kind of looked out of place. He pulls out a bow tie, and puts that on. Still no shirt, but now he's got a bow tie. 'How's this?' he asks. And the thing was, it wouldn't have even mattered if I had film in the camera. He had an eye for more than the music. It was incredible the kinds of things we'd come up with and try to shoot. He was just a lot of fun."

And the camera loved Billy. Just as there had been so many great songs that had to be narrowed down to the 12 that would make it on the album, there were hundreds of photos. And Billy didn't look bad in one of them. Finally, the photos, the music, the cover art, everything had come together on Billy's first album. It was scheduled for release in May of 1982.

14 Building the Legend

In the fall of 1981, Billy could take his band and play any club in Portland. But he was looking for something different. One day he showed Steve Hettum what he had in mind.

"Where are we going?" Hettum asked. They were heading down 82nd Street in Billy's green Saab. All Steve knew was that Billy was excited about something.

"You'll see," Billy said. "You're going to love it. I've got a way to keep the club owners in town honest. We can make big money at this place."

Billy pulled into what used to be the Mayflower Bowling Alley in east Portland, at the busy corner of 82nd and Division. It had become a Chinese restaurant called Lung Fung. Where the bowling lanes had been stood a huge room that the new owners (a Taiwanese couple, Peter and Caroline Chern) had turned into a lounge, the Dragon Room. It was a huge room, with garish red carpet everywhere and yellow lights. It definitely had that Chinese restaurant feel to it. There was a huge dance floor in the front of the room, surrounded by tables.

"This is where I want to play," Billy said. "No more stinky little bars. We could pack this place. What do you think?"

"I think it's a dump," Hettum said. "But it's a big dump." Hettum

Billy Rancher, king of Portland's night-time world.
(Bart Danielson)

looked around, guessed that the place could hold about 1,000 people and started calculating how much money the band could make by charging four or five bucks at the door.

"We're going to make this place famous," Billy said.

"So what's the deal?" Steve asked. "How much do we get for playing here?"

"Well, we're not exactly getting paid," Billy said, "not for the first show, anyway."

The only live music at Lung Fung to that point had been a Vietnamese cover band hired by Peter Chern. Billy convinced Peter to let the Unreal Gods play the Dragon Room, but they were going to have to pay him $500 for the privelege.

"Don't worry, man, we'll make that back at the door, easy," Billy told Steve. "And when they see what we can do here, they'll be begging us — and paying us — to play here."

"Let's do it," Hettum said.

Plans were made for the Unreal Gods' Lung Fung debut, a Christmas show, December 21st, 1981. Billy, who was proving to be a master at promotion, went to work. First, he made sure John Wendeborn at The Oregonian, Buck Munger at Two Louies and anyone else in town with any media clout knew about the show. Posters went up all over Portland. And Billy bought late-night TV advertising time. The ads ran at 2 and 3 in the morning on KPDX, Channel 49, a new station in town.

"He wasn't afraid to try anything," Hettum says. "He wasn't afraid of failure. He was telling me about the commercials, and I wasn't sure. He just said, 'Who cares if it doesn't work. Fuck it, we'll try something else. Nobody's going to shoot us if they don't like the commericals, are they?' "

That first show was the only time Peter Chern charged the Unreal Gods to play the Dragon Room. From then on, the band took the money at the door, Peter took the bar. Everybody made money, just like Billy said they would.

The Unreal Gods played weekends at Lung Fung, then started doing all-ages shows on Tuesdays and Sundays. After a month, Billy and the Unreal Gods were drawing close to 1,000 people to the Dragon Room. As far as Peter Chern was concerned, the Unreal Gods could play his place seven nights a week, as long as the drink-buying dancers kept showing up. Caroline Chern just liked to have Billy around. Billy always made a point of saying hello to her before the shows.

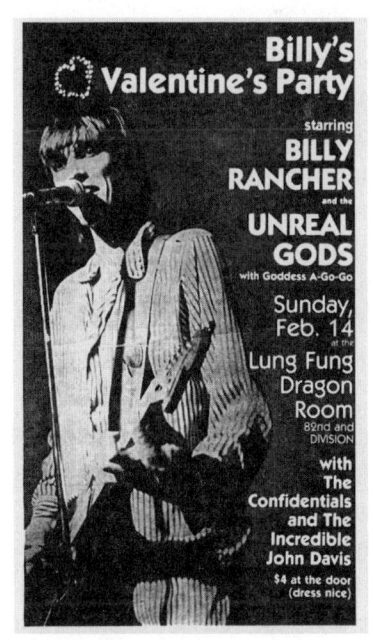

Billy had posters made to promote this 1982 show at the Lung Fung Dragon Room.
(Courtesy of Joe Dreiling)

"He was so polite, so intelligent," Caroline says. "A lot of young people would come in and say, 'Silly old Chinese woman.' But not Billy."

The all-ages shows at Lung Fung were giving the Unreal Gods a chance to expand their fan base to include those who couldn't get into the downtown clubs.

Houston Bolles, a junior at Lincoln High School, never missed an Unreal Gods show at Lung Fung. He was there one night when Billy invited Lenny on stage to play "Start Me Up," a Rolling Stones song. Houston had no way of knowing at the time of the tension between Billy and Lenny, but he noticed Lenny was uncomfortable on stage.

About a week later, Houston rolled past Lenny and Pete Jorgusen as he skateboarded down Sandy Boulevard. "Hey, that's the guy I saw jamming with Billy Rancher," Houston thought. He hit the skids, turned around, and went after them.

"Are you Lenny Rancher?" he asked.

Lenny looked at Pete and laughed, then turned his attention back to Houston. "Yeah." Houston told him that he'd seen him playing guitar with Billy. Lenny told Houston about the new band he was putting together with Pete, the Pipsqueaks.

Houston kept running into Lenny and Pete, who were always walking around town. "Don't you guys believe in cars, or buses?" Houston asked Lenny. "We just like walking," Lenny told him. The truth was, neither of them could afford a car. When they found out Houston had access to his dad's VW bus, he was recruited to haul the Pipsqueaks' gear. Thus began Houston's rock 'n' roll education. Lenny, who was just 20 himself at the time, was his professor. Lenny taught, Houston learned. How to play guitar. How to get drunk. How to pick up girls. All the important stuff. Houston made sure his Sunday nights were free, though, for Billy's shows at Lung Fung.

Another young fan of Billy's was Barbie Kelly, a Lincoln High School student who wrote a music column for Buck Munger's Two Louies. Well, it started out as a music column, at least. It quickly became a Billy Rancher Watch. Reviews of Billy's shows ("good-feelin', high-energy stuff"). Parties Billy and Karen attended. Upcoming gigs. Pleas for Billy to play at Lincoln High. She almost fainted the night at Lung Fung that Billy dedicated "Too Straight for the New Wave" to her.

Meanwhile, a teenager from Eugene, Oregon, an aspiring punk rocker named Courtney Love, made it to as many of the Unreal Gods shows as she could, developing a serious crush on Jon DuFresne.

From the kids like Houston Bolles and Barbie Kelly and Courtney Love to the affluent thirtysomething crowd that had decided Unreal Gods shows were the cool places to be seen, Billy had done a nice job of creating a following. The legend continued to grow, and so did the crowds at Lung Fung.

Two of the busiest dancers at the Lung Fung shows were Billy's mother Astrid, and her fiance, Jack Hanke. Billy would send a limo for Astrid and Jack, to deliver them to the door. "I guess he wanted to make sure I'd show up," Astrid says.

On February 14th, Billy hosted a little event he modestly called "Billy's Valentine's Party." After sets by The Incredible John Davis and the Confidentials, it was time for the main event, a rousing show by Billy and the Unreal Gods. Autographed photos of Billy were sold at the door.

Then came the infamous "Louie, Louie" incident.

The Unreal Gods and the Heats, Steve Pearson's band, were scheduled to play together Sunday, March 21st at Lung Fung. Two shows were scheduled, an early all-ages show, then an over-21 show. The Unreal Gods, Billy announced, would be closing both shows. Not so fast, said Pearson, whose ego was almost as big as Billy's. "We'll close the show," he said. Billy and the Unreal Gods were clearly the biggest draw in Portland at the time. The Heats were doing OK in Seattle, but they weren't exactly the fucking Beatles, the way Billy saw it, so they could open. Pearson was ready to go home, when a compromise was reached. Billy would close the first show, the Heats would close the over-21 show.

The all-ages show went fine. Both bands were well-received, but the hometown Unreal Gods were the favorites. Billy opened the second show by playing "Louie, Louie." And playing it, and playing it until he had cleared the building, which took about 45 minutes. Most of the over-21 crowd had come to see Billy, anyway, so they left when the last note of the marathon cover had been struck. Everyone else just left because they were pissed off. When the Heats took the stage, the crowd of 400 in the cavernous Dragon Room had shrunk to about a dozen.

"We'll see if he wants to fuck with me again," Billy told Hettum on the way out.

This wasn't going to help family reunions with Ellen. Another person who didn't appreciate the stunt was Alf Ryder.

"The only good thing about that was that we could say we did it," he says. "You had to be there to realize how uncomfortable it was to have people boo you, to have people walk out on you. Whatever his reasons were, they were unprofessional."

Next up was a battle of the bands with the Cowboys, another Seattle group trying to make a name for itself in Portland. The Cowboys, all in their mid-30s at the time, were a veteran, hard-rocking outfit that had grown tired of the stale Seattle scene. In the January 1982 Two Louies, singer Ian Fisher explained the band's strategy to Diane Hollen:

"Portland simply has a healthier bar scene than Seattle. Not only are the club owners reasonable to deal with, but the Portland audiences are more willing to accept original music. Portland is vibrant, and the bands here are lucky."

The Cowboys had been playing the bar circuit for 2½ years in Seattle. Seattle's music magazine, The Rocket, named the Cowboys the band with the best groupies. The Cowboys made the girls scream, and they made hard-driving, danceable music. But for all their success, they'd recently discovered how hard it was to get played on Northwest radio stations. A 45, "Rude Boy/She Makes Me Feel Small," didn't get any airplay in Seattle. So they came to Portland to try their luck. What better way to prove themselves, they thought, than knocking off Billy Rancher and the Unreal Gods.

The band took out an ad in Two Louies.

Billy was a popular subject for Portland photographers.
(Bart Danielson)

Hey, Billy Rancher and the Unreal Gods!
We hear you're pretty good. Care for a little action?
How 'bout a head to head dance off?
Two nights: You open one night ...
Yeah! And the Cowboys open the next?
Whaddya say?

Steve Hettum, with all the savvy of a seasoned boxing promoter, dismissed the Cowboys' challenge. "We don't want to work with them," Hettum told Buck Munger. "They just want to make a bunch of money off our draw."

But in the next Two Louies, Billy had an answer. Underneath of picture of Billy, holding a hammer:

In response to your dance-off challenge:
Even though you haven't changed your song order, or much of anything about your act since you first played Portland over a year ago, Billy Rancher and the Unreal Gods will agree to play a double-bill with you charming gents. Let's just say that, for all the months of going through the motions, I will give you credit for a danceable beat and a few good originals. How about: Saturday and Sunday, April 10 & 11 (two shows, 5 and 9), Lung Fung Dragon Room.
Yours truly,
(patiently waiting for new songs)
Billy Rancher

In the same issue, the Cowboys are photographed ripping up pictures of Billy. The battle of the bands was on.

The shows drew near-capacity crowds of 800 each night. The winners were Portland music fans, who were treated to two nights of the best music the Northwest had to offer. Billy, thanks in part to having a hometown crowd, received the better response, but the Cowboys also played tight, energetic sets.

Barbie Kelly reviewed the event for Two Louies, which is a little like asking Don King to judge a Mike Tyson fight.

"Both bands brought the dancers out," she wrote in the May edition of Two Louies. "And both bands drew a chorus of high-pitched screams when they left the stage before encores. (Not the foot-stomping, hand-clapping hoots and deep-throated calls for more that you hear in the bars, but screams, like you hear in those old movies of Beatles' concerts.) It was definitely a rare event for the underage crowd to hear two such bands on the same bill. Nevertheless, I'd give the gold to the Unreal Gods.

"I'll admit it. I'm biased. These are our hometown boys (and girls) and loyalty goes a long way. Still, there's something clean, almost hopeful about the music of the Unreal Gods. Good-feelin', high-energy stuff. Music on the light side of heavy."

Billy didn't just beat the Cowboys and the Heats on his turf. The Unreal Gods played many shows during that winter, and into the spring of 1982, in Seattle. They also looked to expand south, to other Oregon markets, specifically the university towns of Eugene and Corvallis.

Billy and the Unreal Gods were popular with the college crowd in Eugene, and it gave Billy a chance to see Karen. Actually, they saw each other every weekend anyway, but it was usually Karen who had to do the driving.

Billy's first show in Corvallis was November 21st, 1981 in a downtown club best known for its many different owners, and ever-changing name. For about a year, the place had gone by the name of the Crazy Horse Saloon, and was Corvallis' hottest live music club. Now, it should be explained that being the hottest live music club in Corvallis was no great accomplishment. But owner Rod Thomas was doing his best to bring original music to Corvallis, a town that had been happy dancing to Top 40 cover bands or records spun by DJs.

Billy played an amazing 40-plus song set that eventually won over the Corvallis crowd the way David Jester had watched him win a crowd at Portland's Orange Peel club a few months earlier. Corvallis is very white, very conservative and very image conscious, more than you would expect of a college town. A group of 15 or so Portlanders had come to watch Billy, and they noticed the stares of the locals, and the words they uttered. *Punk motherfuckers. Faggot bastards.* Billy's show, complete with Goddesses A-Go-Go, wasn't like anything the good people of Corvallis had seen before. But the tight, catchy music finally got them off their butts and onto the Crazy Horse's two dance floors, and had them humming Billy's songs as they walked out the door and back to their dorm rooms, or farms, or wherever they'd come from.

Thomas told a Portlander after the show, "I was happy to meet Billy Rancher and find out what a gentleman he was after all that nasty stuff I'd heard."

Apparently Billy's Malchicks bad boys act, or rumors he was difficult to work with, had preceded him to Corvallis. But Billy and the Unreal Gods did make some friends and fans that night in Corvallis, and played several more shows there, the audiences growing each time.

Billy had won again. Billy made audiences warm up to him, by playing with so much passion, so much energy they didn't have a choice. Audiences, actually, were easy. Billy was becoming more confident, both on and off the stage. And he was willing to take on anyone he felt had slighted him.

Billy assumed he was bigger than any radio stations, or writers, or booking agents, or club owners, or anyone else who pissed him off, and he was probably right. If you'd done something to get on Billy's bad side, there was a decent chance he'd let everyone know about it, over the mike during a show.

"Billy made a point of alienating every radio station in town," says Jon DuFresne.

In April of 1982, Two Louies ranked the most powerful people in the Portland music scene. KGON Radio program director Gloria Johnson was No. 1. KGON was Portland's most popular rock 'n' roll station, leaning toward a heavy, hard rock sound. Head banging dinosaurs like Van Halen, AC-DC, Rush, Tom Petty and Foreigner were the station's favorites. There wasn't room for anything lighter, or anything local. KGON was absolutely unwilling to take a chance with original local music. Quarterflash, a Portland band fronted by the husband and wife team of Marv and Rindy Ross, signed with Geffen Records in 1981. Prior to signing, they'd released an independent single, "Harden My Heart," when they still went by the name of Seafood Mama. KGON refused to play it. The single eventually went to No. 3 nationally, and the album into the top 10.

Billy hadn't made many friends at KGON. He either figured his first album, due out May 30th, was going to be so good Gloria Johnson wouldn't have any choice but to play it, or he didn't give a damn whether she did or not.

And when he was asked to play at one of KGON's weekly simulcasts from the Foghat, a Portland club, he wasn't sure it was such a great idea.

"Why are we going to do this?" he asked Steve Hettum. "Why do we want to kiss their ass? We're going to be bigger than all the shitty bands they play on that station anyway."

Once they arrived to set up, Billy didn't like the way he was being treated at the Foghat, the way the KGON disc jockeys were talking to him. Then the station asked him to play a certain style of songs. "Fuck that," he said. "I'll play whatever I want." By now, KGON executives, no doubt thinking this was the worst $92 they'd ever spent, decided to cut the Unreal Gods' set from 45 minutes to 20, hoping to minimize the damage. Nice try. "Fuck KGON," Billy said, over the air. "You guys fucked me around, and you're not going to do that again." Then, realizing the

Billy, looking suspiciously like Mick Jagger.
(Bart Danielson)

crowd was into heavy metal more than the Unreal Gods, he tossed beer on them. This was the last time the Unreal Gods did a KGON simulcast. And the last time they were ever heard on KGON, in fact.

It was an act Hettum had seen often.

"The reason Billy could get away with things like that, the reason he was so cocky, is that he had a belief that he was going to be bigger than any of those people, and they'd be begging him to play some day," Hettum says. "He really didn't give a shit what KGON thought about him."

KGON was far from Billy's only target.

"Anything that bothered Billy was fair game," Mick Boyt says. "He'd bring it up between songs, in the middle of songs. He'd lecture Lenny over the mike in front of a big crowd."

Poor Lenny. Billy, who liked to party as long and as hard as anyone, liked to remind Lenny that he shouldn't drink so much. The difference, the way Billy saw it, was that his drinking didn't affect his performance on stage. Lenny, who was putting together the Pipsqueaks, used to show up at Unreal Gods shows hoping to play a song or two, especially if they were going to do any Stones covers. Problem was, he was usually too drunk to plug in his guitar. If he was, he could expect to hear about it from Billy.

The last person Billy should have had a beef with was Buck Munger, who raved about him and the Unreal Gods each month in Two Louies. But Buck committed the unforgivable sin of publishing the January 1982 edition featuring a cover photo of the Unreal Gods in which Alf Ryder was partially obscured in the lower right corner. Somebody was going to have to pay for that!

After a show at Luis' La Bamba, Billy and Jon DuFresne spotted a stack of Two Louies, tossed them into the gas fireplace in the basement and walked upstairs. They were followed, a few minutes later, by billowing black smoke.

"Gotta go," Billy announced, and he and Jon bolted, leaving Mick Boyt and Billy Triplett to clean up the mess. It was light outside when they finally finished. Billy, meanwhile, had gone home and told Steve Hettum — who had taken a night off — that he was going to have to fix things with Tony DeMicoli.

"It was 2 o'clock, I was home sleeping, and Billy comes into my room and tells me I've got to go straighten this out with Tony, that Tony said we're not going to be able to play there any more," Hettum recalls.

"Just another part of my glamorous job."

The incident was quickly forgotten and forgiven. Billy played La Bamba again the next weekend, and Buck raved about him in the next month's Two Louies.

It was hard for Billy to do any wrong, even when he tried. Billy and the Unreal Gods were the best draw at any club they wanted to play in the Northwest. Billy kept cranking out songs, the band kept getting tighter, and the music kept sounding better. The Unreal Gods opened for national acts touring through Portland and Seattle — the Stray Cats, Bow Wow Wow, Marshall Crenshaw, John Cale, Adam Ant, the Tubes. The Unreal Gods had always been well-received, at times better than the headliners, except for the early Peter Tosh reggae night debacle. The opening gigs were fun, Billy told Hettum, but it wouldn't be necessary to schedule any more. Billy decided the Unreal Gods were going to be closing shows, not opening them.

Hettum, by now, had a job a lot of other people were suddenly interested in. Joe Dreiling, who had managed the Malchicks and was a true friend to Billy, offered his services. In January of 1982, Dreiling proposed starting a company, Deity Productions, that would represent Billy and the band. Billy wrote back:

Dear Joe,

Deity Productions is a name I choose not to use for representation for Billy Rancher and the Unreal Gods because I feel it would stress the God aspect too much. We're not Gods or Goddesses, we're Unreal Gods and Goddesses. Besides, it sounds too fuckin' smooth for my taste.

P.S. This doesn't mean I don't want to do business. I just want to have what I consider the best representation of the band. Keep up the hard work and it most likely will pay off.

For now, at least, Steve Hettum was still the manager of Billy Rancher and the Unreal Gods. Which is to say, they didn't really have a manager. That's not a criticism of Steve Hettum. He was young, he wasn't a lawyer, he didn't know anyone in the record business. What he was, was a great friend to Billy, and he worked hard to keep the band booked, get the posters up, keep things running smoothly, collect the money at the door and clean up after Billy and the band. But Billy was calling all the shots.

By now, everyone knew of the two surgeries Billy had in August and September of 1981. But his health was fine. Regular checkups revealed no trace of cancer. The huge scar was a constant reminder to Karen, but she, too, was convinced the negative tests meant Billy had beaten the cancer.

Billy was trying to convince Karen to quit school. They were crazy in love, and wanted to spend as much time together as they could. But Karen had no intention of giving up college.

"After I convinced him I wasn't leaving, he was very supportive, very into the fact I was going to finish school," Karen says. "I did tell him I'd take some time off to travel."

Karen took a break spring term of 1982 to go with Billy to Europe. The first part of the planned trip was to Sweden for Billy's grandfather's 90th birthday party. After that, Billy and Karen would bounce around Europe for a few more weeks, returning in time for the release of the "Boom Chuck Rock Now!" album.

The Unreal Gods played Friday and Saturday shows at La Bamba, April 16th and 17th, to overflow crowds. After the Saturday show, Roger North and Tye Tinsley, friends of the band, threw a bon voyage party at their house. Billy and Karen spent most of the time cuddling on the couch. They were relaxed, and happy, and ready for a vacation.

15 Europe

Billy was proud of his Swedish heritage, and he was proud of Karen, so this was perfect. He'd have a chance to show Sweden to Karen, and Karen to his Swedish family and friends.

This was about the 10th time Billy had been to Sweden. As kids, Billy, Lenny and Ellen had spent as much as five months at a time on their trips to southwestern Sweden to see Astrid's family. Each time, they played with their cousins, learned the language and got funny haircuts. The hair grew out, and the Swedish language was usually forgotten until the next trip.

Astrid and Jack Hanke were there, also, this time. Astrid, who left Sweden in 1954 at the age of 18, visited with her seven brothers and sisters. The 90th birthday party for Astrid's father Frans was attended by more than 200 Swedish relatives and friends. Frans had visited the United States for the first time in the fall of 1978, when he was 86 years old. He was afraid of flying, but he wanted to meet his son-in-law, Joe Rancher. He just made it. Joe suffered a heart attack and died December 3rd that year. When he returned to Sweden, Frans wrote a song about his exciting journey. He was glad, now, for the opportunity to meet Jack and Karen.

"The time we spent there with Billy's family was great," Karen says. "They were very close. Billy was cute, because I could tell he was very happy to be showing me off to them. It was fun."

Billy and Karen spent most of their time in a little cottage next to one of Billy's cousin's houses. The cousin, Birgitta, was a year younger than Billy. Her husband Jan was a musician, and had a band in Sweden. (No, not ABBA). He and Billy spent many of the nights jamming. Jan played guitar, and Billy would make up silly Swedish lyrics to blues songs.

Billy and Karen also spent some time with Astrid's brother, Lennart, and his wife Margareta. Lennart lived in the two-story house on the farm where Astrid had grown up.

After two weeks in Sweden, Billy and Karen decided it was time to move on, to see Europe.

They took a train to Italy, to see Glen Baggerly, Billy's old baseball buddy. Baggerly was in his third year of playing professionally there. He played in 1980 in Milan, and had spent the past two seasons with a team in Bologna. Billy watched Glen's team work out, and was talked into putting on a glove and taking some ground balls. Billy played softball for the fun of it, but it had been five years since he'd played baseball in what must have seemed like a different lifetime. But he fielded the grounders flawlessly.

Billy's habit of constantly sucking on popsicles amused the Italian players. "He loved popsicles, everywhere he went he had one in his mouth," Baggerly says. "They couldn't get over that."

The Italian players were also confused by Billy's light skin and blond hair. He didn't look at all like Baggerly, who had dark, curly hair and tanned, dark skin. "Is he American?" the Italian players would ask Baggerly. "He doesn't look like you."

"Listen," Baggerly told the Italian players, "in the United States, we've got it all."

After a few days in Bologna, it was time to move on. Next stop, France. Billy and Karen stayed in Nice, and took a 20-minute train ride one day to attend the Cannes Film Festival. At Cannes, Billy figured out a way to make sure Glen Baggerly wouldn't forget him.

Baggerly tells the story:

"There's a knock on my door, and it's this black girl, which is unusual, because there are no black girls in Bologna, Italy. The girl looks at me and says, 'Hi, I met Billy at the Cannes Film Festival and he said I could come and stay with you, and you wouldn't mind a bit.' She says this with a totally straight face. At first I thought it was a joke, but she was serious. She says she's from London and is headed back there, but needs to stay with me for a while.

"I look at my roommate, and he looks at me and says, 'What did he do?' You've got to understand, I'm one of the few Americans on this team, I'm representing my country, and my team is going to croak if they know I've got a black girl in here. I let her stay two or three days, then I had to tell her she had to go, because I couldn't explain this to anybody.

"Next time I talked to Rancher, he just said, 'Yeah, I thought you'd like that one.' "

Billy and Karen stayed a few days with Karen's aunt in Paris. One night Frank Zappa walked into a little club in Paris. "Billy was very excited being around him. He just loved Frank Zappa."

Later, Billy and Karen saw the Stray Cats play at the Marquis, a tiny club in London.

"The music we saw — and the culture — really influenced Billy," Karen says. "He couldn't wait to get back and put what he'd learned to use."

16 Boom Chucked by KGON

Billy returned to Portland just a few days before a very special show at Lung Fung. This was no ordinary Dragon Room gig. May 30th, 1982 was the "Boom Chuck Rock Now!" album release party, the confirmation that Billy Rancher was an honest to goodness rock 'n' roll star and Portland hero. Billy and the Unreal Gods played two sets that night, and sold the new album and Billy Rancher T-shirts and posters. Billy signed autographs. Maybe life could get better than this, but Billy didn't know how. He'd done it. He'd made a great record, and the Unreal Gods were packing in audiences wherever they played. Everybody loved Billy Rancher.

Well, maybe it seemed sometimes that Lenny didn't, but there were signs the strained relationship between the brothers was improving. Billy invited the Pipsqueaks, Lenny's new band, to make their debut by opening the album release party. Memories of the Malchicks' breakup had not been completely erased, but on this night, at least, there was peace. Everything was right with the world, as far as Billy was concerned.

The next day, Billy, Karen, Jon DuFresne and Bart Danielson celebrated by drinking champagne and taking pictures of each other in front of a "Boom Chuck Rock Now!" display in the window of a local music store.

Above: Jon and Billy outside a music store display for "Boom Chuck Rock Now!"
Right: Billy's album was played by stations from Seattle to Eugene, but not on Portland's KGON.
(Bart Danielson)

Jon ran up and down the sidewalk, hurdling parking meters. Billy and Karen sipped the bubbly and kissed. It was the happiest day any of them could remember.

Everywhere he went, Billy tuned his radio to KGON, waiting for the station to play his new album. "They have to play this," Billy told Karen.

Well, no they didn't. KGON might have been the best rock 'n' roll station in Portland — certainly it was the most listened to — but that status was not attained by playing local music. KGON claimed the recording of Billy's album wasn't up to their standards, from a production standpoint, and they might have been right. They weren't the kind of station that played independent records. The truth was, they didn't need to take any chances, and they weren't about to cut into their format to play Billy

Rancher, especially after all the shit they'd taken from him. He was good at pissing people off, Tony DeMicoli always said, and he'd worked especially hard at pissing off KGON.

Billy had no such problems in Seattle, where songs from the album were played by several stations, and fans lined up to see him. Billy and the Unreal Gods always did well in Seattle.

Trips to Seattle were made in the Unrealmobile, Billy Flaxel's brown Chevy van. They played Astor Park, the Hall of Fame, the Backstage, Michael J's — and drew just as well as when they were in Portland.

Earl Burks is a comedian who was telling jokes in clubs in the Seattle area at the time. He made a point of seeing Billy whenever the Unreal Gods came to Seattle. When he could get in, that is.

"There were always people lined up who could never get in the door," Burks remembers. "Everybody wanted to see Billy. He was way ahead of his time. Everybody else was just a musician, but he was way above that. He had a presence, like an angel or something. He just had this amazing aura."

The routine on the Seattle trips was usually the same. Billy and Steve Hettum would get up early and visit radio stations, newspapers, magazine offices, record stores — anywhere someone wanted to interview Billy, or just meet him and talk. He was a favorite, in fact, of The Rocket, Seattle's highly respected music magazine. Then it was off to thrift stores to shop for rock 'n' roll clothes. Billy was big on pajamas, bandanas, head bands and colorful pants (plaids and checkered patterns were his favorites). About the time Billy and Steve would return to whatever crappy little motel they'd had enough money for, the rest of the Unreal Gods would be waking up, ready to start the day. Aside from Billy, who didn't want to burn any daylight when he could be out promoting himself and the band, and Hettum, who did what Billy asked him to do, the rest of the Unreal Gods weren't what you'd call morning people. Their best chance of seeing 8 a.m. was a really good party that lasted a few hours longer than usual.

Billy liked to drop in on other shows, just to check out the competition. Especially if a Portland band, say Johnny and the Distractions, was playing Seattle. When those visits revealed what he'd hoped — that no one outdrew Billy Rancher and the Unreal Gods, not in Portland, Seattle or anywhere else — he'd head to the show, cockier, more sure of himself than ever. Then it was time to change into his stage clothes, maybe even the leopard skin suit if it was a special night. A little eyeliner, a little rouge on the cheeks, let's take the stage and kick some ass. 7-Eleven for some junk food, and back to the motel to party and talk about the show. It always took Billy hours to wind down from a show. Karen made most of the trips to Seattle, and how many beers Billy drank after a show was usually directly related to whether she was there. If she was, maybe it was a just a couple. Milk a beer or two, swallow some mint cod liver oil to soothe the vocal cords. If she wasn't? *How many hours until our next show? 19? Let's party.*

Billy always liked playing Seattle because it meant he'd have a chance to see his sister Ellen — even if it meant seeing Steve Pearson, too.

A great trip to Seattle for Billy was picking up a copy of The Rocket that mentioned the Unreal Gods favorably and panned the Heats, then stopping in to visit his sister and brother-in-law. "Seen the new Rocket?" he'd ask, casually tossing it down on the coffee table. Then he'd grin.

Ellen had worked hard to establish an image in Seattle, at the clubs. "I was always in the background, but this totally cool person," she says. Which is why it was risky for Ellen to go to Billy's shows.

He'd spot her in the crowd, sometimes before the show, sometimes after — what the hell, sometimes during, if he felt like it — and he'd grab Ellen and throw her over his shoulder. Billy loved to make a scene with Ellen. "Billy, put me down," she'd scream. "I'm going to kill you." Then she'd whisper in his ear, "You're blowing my image, put me down." Billy would throw her into the air, spin her around. Then he'd give her a kiss and put her back in her seat. Ellen would tell Billy again that she wished he wouldn't make such a fuss over her, just leave her alone, let her be cool. But she didn't mind, not really. She always had fun when Billy was in town. She'd act upset, but he made her laugh. Always. God, she loved her big brother.

Then it was back to Portland, where everybody loved Ellen's big brother. Except KGON, of course. And the feeling was mutual.

Billy didn't pass up a chance to take a shot at KGON, usually during his shows. A favorite target was disc jockey Bob Ancheta, who managed a popular Portland hard rock band called Sequel. Ancheta was quoted in Two Louies saying he'd never play "Boom Chuck Rock Now!" Later, Ancheta attempted to set the record straight by saying that he was misquoted. He hadn't said he wouldn't play the record, he claimed, he said he didn't like the record. That didn't go over too well with Billy, who was sure Ancheta didn't want to play the Unreal Gods at the expense of his band, Sequel. "Conflict of interest," became one of Billy's favorite phrases during the summer of '82.

Maybe the record really wasn't produced well enough to meet KGON's standards. Maybe Gloria Johnson and Bob Ancheta just didn't like it, or they didn't like Billy. Maybe a dispute the Unreal Gods and Sequel had over the use of lights at a gig in Seaside on the Oregon coast was still being held against Billy. Whatever the reasons, one thing was clear: KGON was not going to play "Boom Chuck Rock Now!" And just as clear was the fact that as long as Billy still had a microphone and a stage, he wasn't going to let them hear the end of it. This two-minute, mid-song message delivered to KGON during a version of "Too Straight for the New Wave" at a June, 1982 show at the Copper Penny was typical:

(Billy brings the band down. Over the thump-thump, thump-thump of Dave Stricker's bass guitar and a trance-like synthesizer line by Alf Ryder, Billy starts to ramble) …

Now I'd like to say,
I would like to thank everybody tonight for coming out to the Copper Penny.
But I realize you haven't heard these songs before, they're not on KGON.
Billy Rancher and the Unreal Gods play all their own music.
We're going to try to please everybody for the next 10 years,
and hopefully, we'll be a big band.
I know this is something new,
we've been playing downtown for about a year or so.
We played in Seattle, we're getting airplay with our album in Seattle on three stations now.
I'd like to ask everybody a question: What is communism?
How do you spell communism?
I don't like communism.
I'm very glad we have the United States of America, I am.
But … I want to make a very rude point.
This might make a lot of people mad.
I don't want to start any fights, but …
We've got airplay in Seattle, and we're having a tough time breaking into the airwaves of Portland.

We've got a few stations, Eugene and Corvallis, that are playing our songs. But there so happens to be a KGON album.

It's very strange that some of the bands on the KGON album happen to be managed by KGON DJ's — like Sequel — and they get airplay on the KGON album.

Now I don't want to make two plus two ...

where I come from, two plus two equals four, and I don't want two plus two to equal communism.

But I'd like to say, hey man

(Billy Flaxel comes crashing in on drums and Jon DuFresne begins hammering a staccato guitar line

Am I too straight for the new wave?
Or, maybe ... maybe I'm too late for the new wave
Or maybe you can tell me
Hey, what the fuck's the new wave?

(Guitars rave, drums pound. Fade).

"We're going to try to please everybody for the next 10 years, and hopefully, we'll be a big band."
(Bart Danielson)

17 "Don't You Want to Root For a Guy Like That?"

Portland's other media — newspapers, magazines, television — were much kinder to Billy than KGON had been. And no one worshipped Billy Rancher and the Unreal Gods like Barbie Kelly, the Lincoln High School student who wrote a column for Buck Munger's Two Louies. Every month, Barbie raved about the latest all-ages show Billy had played, told her readers they just HAD to go see Billy, and encouraged the Unreal Gods to play more all-ages shows and at more high schools.

One day, Billy decided he was going to make Barbie Kelly the most happening person to ever walk the halls of Lincoln High School. Billy went to Lincoln, marched down to the office and said he'd like to see Barbie Kelly, that he wanted to thank her in person.

"Sir, there is no Barbie Kelly here," an exasperated secretary told Billy.

He showed her the latest copy of Two Louies. "Then who is this?"

About that time, a thirtysomething English teacher named Gerry Foote walked into the office. She almost had a heart attack when she saw Billy.

"Can I help you?" she asked Billy.

"Yeah. I'm looking for Barbie Kelly."

Gerry Foote pulled Billy into the hallway. "There's no such person," she told him.

"Then who wrote this?" Billy asked, waving the folded magazine. Then Gerry Foote told Billy that she was Barbie Kelly.

Billy took a huge yellow and orange sucker out of the pocket of his jean jacket and handed it to Gerry. "Well, you write a great column, Barbie Kelly."

Buck Munger loves to tell the Barbie Kelly story.

"What a beautiful kid," he says. "So innocent. I mean he goes to Lincoln High School looking for Barbie Kelly. This kid is beautiful. I love this kid. Don't you want to root for a guy like that?"

Buck Munger and Gerry Foote weren't the only ones on Billy's side.

John Wendeborn was the first member of the Unreal Gods' bandwagon, writing a very favorable story before they'd even played a show. And Billy was a staple for all the Portland music or entertainment magazines that came and went — Two Louies, Positively Entertainment, Scene, Multnomah Magazine, the Downtowner, Black and White — as well as The Rocket in Seattle. Part of the reason is that Billy's music was too good to ignore. And even if they had been tempted to ignore Billy's music, they couldn't ignore Billy.

"Billy knocked on a lot of doors," Buck Munger says. "He was over here all the time, just to sit down and talk. Once Billy knew you were legitimate, that you had credibility, he wanted to make sure you knew who he was. He saw the magazine, he saw me, he said, 'OK, you're him, great, I'm Billy Rancher, I'm going to be a star, listen to my artistic vision.' And I never had a problem with Billy, when it was just him. He was very real."

Real, yes. Energetic, sincere, honest, yes. But not above telling a little white lie if it would help his cause. Billy's age was all over the place, depending on which magazine you were reading, but he usually liked to take a year or two off. The truth was, he was born on February 28th, 1957, which made him 25 years old during the summer of 1982, at the time of the release of the Unreal Gods' record. He told The Rocket in May of '82 that he was drafted by the Minnesota Twins and played a year of semipro baseball. Billy was an outstanding high school player, and had gone to Mount Hood Community College on a baseball scholarship, but he'd never been drafted and had played a couple summers of American Legion ball, not semipro. He always liked to tell people he and Pete

Jorgusen met David Bowie at the 1976 concert after he won the Bowie lookalike contest. Never happened, but it made a great story, the way Billy told it.

The Portland media was in love with Billy, and his music, and if it ever came down to choosing sides in a fight, they were always with Billy.

Bob Ancheta, the KGON disc jockey who managed Sequel, wrote to Two Louies to defend his right to be both a DJ and a manager, and to explain why his station wouldn't play Billy's album. The parting shot was a message to "keep your information straight. I don't have time to deal with people like you (Buck) and Billy Rancher." Buck responded by writing that he wasn't sure why other Portland stations weren't playing Billy's music, but he did recall that Bob Ancheta's reason was that he was upset about a show the Unreal Gods and Sequel played together July 3rd at the Seaside Convention Center. Sequel had paid $150 for lights, and Billy decided he'd use them for the Unreal Gods' show. Ancheta said Billy was warned twice to quit using the lights before he finally did. When Sequel took the stage, the lights didn't work. Billy's crew got the blame. "We'll never play with them again," said Ancheta, who also let it be known then that he wouldn't play Billy's album. Steve Hettum says Ancheta was just mad because half the crowd left after Billy played and before Sequel started.

"I just remember it was kind of a disaster," says Todd Jensen, Sequel's lead singer and bass player. "We were very young, and very competitive. Today, it seems like there's a camaraderie among bands, but at that time in Portland, there wasn't. It was like if you were in another band, you're not our friend. And Sequel and Billy's band were apples and oranges. We were both very popular in Portland, but playing different clubs and going for a different market. At the time, stylistically, I wasn't into what Billy was doing. But it was easy to see they were doing something a lot of people liked. In hindsight, it's obvious he was ahead of his time. He had some great ideas."

And Billy was an expert at spreading his word. To say Billy used the media would imply that he manipulated them. Actually, he was immensely likable, with an ability to convince people to help him and, it seemed, a lucky rabbit's foot in his pocket. The difference between Billy and Portland's other rock musicians — the ones who were so proud of themselves for not "selling out" — is that Billy simply understood what the media could do for him. He understood what making regular visits to

Billy wearing his "legendary" leopard skin suit at the height of the Unreal Gods' success.
(Mark Rabiner)

Buck Munger's house, sitting down for radio interviews or posing for pictures could mean. So he did it. And he really was someone the media wanted to help. He was charming. He was a great talker. He looked good on magazine covers, so young, and handsome, and engaging. And he had something to offer, some substance: his music.

By the summer of 1982, MTV had been playing music videos for a year. That's fine, Billy thought, at first. When I do my first album for a major label, we'll make some videos. But, as usual, Billy was in a hurry. And if a three-minute music video was good, a half-hour TV show was even better. And, as always, there were people ready to help Billy.

Tim Schafbuch was a fan. A fan whose father, Mick Schafbuch, happened to be the general manager of KOIN-TV, the CBS affiliate in Portland. Don Blank was a local producer who had taped a show a few years earlier with Seafood Mama. The show helped Seafood Mama sign its deal with Geffen Records, after which it changed its name to Quarterflash and sold a couple million albums.

The plan all made perfect sense to Billy. He talked Don Blank into opening up his studio, filling it with Billy Rancher fans who would dance while he played his best songs. Then he convinced Mick Schafbuch to clear a half-hour of KOIN-TV time later that fall to show it to Portland.

On the hot, humid night of August 31st, 1982, a couple hundred of Billy's lucky fans were led into Blank's northwest Portland studio, through a hallway into a large dark room that had been converted to a dance floor for the occasion. The lights were turned on, revealing a floor recently painted with silver circles and multi-colored stars. It was uncomfortable in the room, hot and stuffy, with the smell of fresh paint hanging in the air. There were no chairs, so the dancers just stood restlessly, waiting for Billy to jump onto the small stage that had been set up at one end of the room. Four cameramen took their places. A woman wearing a headset reminded the dancers to whoop it up at the beginning and end of each song. She didn't need to tell them. These were all Billy Rancher fans, and they'd been whooping it up every chance they'd had the past year or so. The dancers continued to sweat it out, while lights were set up and tested. It was so hot in there. Finally, Billy and the Unreal Gods were ready to come out and play.

They started with "Upstroke Down," a song off the Boom Chuck Rock album, one of the Unreal Gods' best songs. The crowd cheered at the end of the song, then waited for the next song, which was ... "Upstroke Down." Then long breaks between songs. Then three or four more songs, also played twice, sometimes three times. After a couple hours, everyone took a break, and the sweaty dancers bolted outside into the night for some fresh air, or into the bathroom to get a drink of water from the sink.

Back on the dance floor, they were treated to more of Billy's best songs — "Symmetry," "Uptown," and, of course, "Boom Chuck Rock." When they played Boom Chuck, a giant neon sign behind the stage alternately flashed Boom … Chuck … Boom .. Chuck … BoomChuck-BoomChuckBoomChuck. And again, all the songs were played over, to make sure they had it right. There was a lot of starting and stopping, which was frustrating for everyone — the dancers, the roadies running the lights and sound, Billy and the band. Even though the four hours spent in the studio lacked the excitement of a real show, there was something thrilling about what they were doing. Besides, by the time Don Blank got done editing it into a half-hour, it looked like everyone was having fun. Just another night with Billy Rancher.

Mick Schafbuch and Don Blank were just two more people joining what seemed like an all-out effort by the city of Portland to make Billy Rancher and the Unreal Gods bigger than the Beatles. Everyone had adopted Buck Munger's attitude about Billy. *Don't you want to root for a guy like that?*

"Billy Rancher didn't have a record deal, how the hell did he get this Don Blank show?" Munger asks. "I'll tell you how, the same way he got stories written about his new band in Two Louies, by coming over to see me like clockwork, by being real with people."

With "Boom Chuck Rock Now!" recorded, the Don Blank project in the bank, and the Unreal Gods firmly established as Portland's hottest act, Billy was ready to get back into the studio.

Lou Erlanger played guitar in the '70s for the New York-based rock band Mink DeVille, and was living in Seattle in 1982 when he met Billy. He told Billy he wanted to produce records, and he'd be happy to help the Unreal Gods in the studio.

"He told us he knew people in record companies, and he wanted to be a producer," Jon DuFresne recalls. "He produced some tracks for us in Seattle, but they didn't really come out that good."

Billy Flaxel remembers working with Erlanger.

"We were doing some really weird shit. Lou was freaking," Flaxel says. "We'd spend time recording opening cans of beer, but it reflected the personality of what was going on with the band."

There was talk of a new EP, tentatively titled "Uptown Variety," that would include new versions of "Upstroke Down" and "Uptown," as well as a couple of new songs, "The Police Tol' Me" and "High School Degree." Billy also talked about doing a complete album by Christmas. He already had the title for that one, too — "In Tremolo."

Billy was writing songs like a madman when the band wasn't playing. In an Oregonian story that ran July 30th, he told John Wendeborn he'd written 20 songs in a recent three-week stretch, including five in one night. "I just get these ideas and write them down," Billy said. "The words come out, and pretty soon we work out a melody."

Nothing ever came from their brief association with Lou Erlanger, at least in terms of recording any new music. But that connection did spawn an idea — a trip to New York. Erlanger told the band he'd set up an East Coast tour. And when Billy found out Lou's sister, an editor at Rolling Stone, was getting married and had planned a big party at a Manhattan nightclub, he talked Lou into scheduling the Unreal Gods as the band.

So it was set. Billy and the Unreal Gods would play at a New York hotspot in front of a bunch of Rolling Stone magazine executives, then hit the road for an East Coast tour.

18 New Jersey Shows Billy Who's Boss

By the time he was supposed to be lining up shows for Billy back East, Lou Erlanger had just about had his fill of Billy Rancher and the Unreal Gods. In fact, he told Billy, line up your own fucking shows.

The idea, when he started working with the band that summer, was for Erlanger to record a few songs in Seattle, then help Billy get a major record deal. But he became frustrated trying to exert any control over Billy during the recordings. Billy, and the band, were both inexperienced and arrogant when it came to making records. That's a bad combination, as far as most producers are concerned. Billy's songs sounded great live, but needed some refinement in the studio, or at least that's what Lou Erlanger was trying to get across. Soon, it became clear that the relationship between Lou and the Unreal Gods was going to be neither long, nor prosperous.

"He got his feelings hurt, to the point he was really mad," Jon DuFresne recalls. "So when it came time to go to New York, we were on our own."

So what if there was no tour? So what if there was no party for Rolling Stone editors. Nothing was going to stop Billy from going to New York. Besides, it had already been in all the papers.

"They'd just been saying all summer they were going to New York, then we saw stories that we were going to New York, then even after it all fell apart, I think Billy felt like he was committed to going," says roadie Keith Cox. "When it came right down to it, I don't think Billy really had much of a plan."

That's OK, Alf did. Everybody would stay with the Delias, Alf's family in New Jersey, they'd play some clubs, maybe do some recording. Alf's brother Matti owned a bar, On Broadway, in Westwood, New Jersey. The band could stay with Matti, and store the equipment and rehearse in Matti's auto repair shop. One of Alf's other brothers, Joey Delia, was a bigshot producer and session musician. Maybe he could help them meet some people. Another brother, Frank Delia, directed and produced music videos in LA. The roadies, the go go dancers, Steve Hettum, Annie Farmer and anyone else who was coming could find a bed with one of Alf's relatives. Sounded good to Billy. "Let's go to New York."

Billy, Karen, Jon and his girlfriend Doreen drove from Portland to Los Angeles in Billy's Saab, then stayed with Frank Delia at his house in the Hollywood hills for a few days before leaving for New York. Billy wanted to check out LA, get the lay of the land. He'd take over Hollywood as soon as he got back from New York.

Money for the New York trip came from a familiar source — Dr. John Flaxel. He agreed to pay to get everyone back east. Now the only problem was getting the equipment there. Mick Boyt called to make train reservations for the roadies and the go go dancers, Candyce Dru and Alaina Pereira. He mentioned they'd be bringing some carry-ons, and was told the limit was two per person. They showed up at the train station with amps, guitars and a drum kit. "Here's our carry-ons," Mick announced. It wasn't easy, but by the time he finished his song and dance, all the gear was loaded on the train. "They were pissed," he remembers.

Mick, Keith, Billy Triplett and the dancers spent three and a half days on the train, finally joining the rest of the band in Westwood. "We talked the conductor into letting us take a shower," Keith says. "That was about the highlight of the train trip."

The roadies were then shuttled to yet another Delia brother's house to spend the first night. "He had some mental problems or something," Keith says. "We said, 'Hey, we ain't staying here anymore.' " So they joined the party at Matti's house.

Annie Farmer wasn't so lucky. Annie worked at the Paramount Theater in Portland, and had helped Billy get the gig opening for Peter Tosh the previous summer. She volunteered to make the New York trip to introduce Billy and Steve Hettum to some entertainment lawyers and agents she knew in New York, and to arrange a meeting for Billy at Columbia Records. Her only request of Hettum before making the trip was that she'd need to have a hotel room. Don't worry about it, Hettum assured her, Alf has figured out the accomodations. For Annie and Candyce and Alaina, that meant staying with Alf's parents, separated from everyone else, with no transportation.

Hanging with Alf's crazy family wasn't exactly what Billy had in mind when he'd planned a trip to the Big Apple, but that's what the Unreal Gods did for the better part of six weeks.

Matti's ranch style house was located in a middle class Westwood neighborhood, a few miles from his garage and bar. He was the leader of the Delia brothers, a short, tough-talking caricature of an Al Pacino movie character.

"The whole family were your typical East Coast Italian guys," Jon DuFresne says. "They weren't the kind of guys you fucked around with, I remember that."

Roadie Mick Boyt and sound man Billy Triplett celebrate after a show with Karen.
(Bart Danielson)

While the band members sat around and drank beer, Keith Cox and Mick Boyt spent most of their time at Matti's shop, working on cars. Matti told Billy they could use a van that was parked at the shop, if anyone could get it running. "Great," Billy said. "Keith, see what you can do." Keith was working on the van one day with Mick when Matti and a friend came into the garage.

Mick pulled his head out from under the hood when he saw Matti come in. "Mick," Matti said, "I'd like you to meet Bruce."

"I'd shake your hand, but it's dirty," Mick said.

"That's all right," Bruce said, laughing and grabbing Mick's hand.

After Matti and his friend left, Mick turned his attention back to the van.

"Do you know who that was?" Billy Triplett asked Mick.

"Sure. That was Bruce."

Billy Triplett looked at Keith Cox, and they both laughed. "That was fucking Bruce Springsteen."

Matti's claim to fame, as it turns out, was not owning an auto repair shop and a dumpy little club next door, but being good friends with Bruce Springsteen. Maybe that didn't mean much to Mick Boyt, or other members of the Unreal Gods' party. (Jon DuFresne's first reaction to seeing Springsteen was that he was much shorter than he imagined he would be. Karen thought he was "very nice, very polite. He had a cute butt.") But in New Jersey, Bruce Springsteen was God, and Matti was one of God's best friends.

The trip had been mostly a waste of time the first couple of weeks, but Matti had a plan to change that. "I'm going to bring Bruce by the club the next time you guys are playing," he told Billy. "You ask him up on stage."

The Unreal Gods had played On Broadway a couple of times, and were beginning to attract a crowd. But playing with Bruce Springsteen, Alf told Billy, guaranteed they'd be in every newspaper in New York and New Jersey. "You can't buy that kind of publicity," he said. Alf worried that Billy didn't seem very excited about it, but assumed everything would be OK once Bruce came to the club.

One night Bruce showed up, ready to play. He sat in the audience, and waited for Billy to ask him up on stage. And waited. And waited. Billy finished the set and the band walked backstage, wondering what was going on.

"Bruce comes into the dressing room and said we were real good, that we had a shot at it," DuFresne remembers. "Then he leaves, and we're going, 'Oh, OK, Bruce Springsteen. Cool.' Then later Matti starts screaming at Billy. 'Why the fuck didn't you ask him up there?' Billy just didn't want to. He said something like, 'Well, what song would we have played?' Who cares? Chuck Berry, anything. But if there was something Billy didn't want to do, there was no way you were going to talk him into it. I mean, I just thought the whole thing was being handled. We had a certain kind of protocol, you know. I'm not the leader of the band."

No, Billy is The Boss of the Unreal Gods. And Billy Flaxel says he understands Billy's reasons for not having Bruce join him on stage.

"The Unreal Gods did our own shit," he says. "We weren't a jam band, we didn't play blues, we didn't play cover songs. We did our own things. Out of respect, it would have been fun to have him come up, but the way Billy looked at it was, 'Why have Bruce come up here? We're better than Bruce Springsteen.' That was kind of our feeling at the time. We had a sound. We had a thing going, and we were pretty confident about it."

Alf and Jon felt like Billy had blown it.

"It was sad. Billy just wimped out," Alf says. "There's only one version of the way this happened: Matti asked, 'Is it OK for Bruce to come up?' And Billy said, 'No way, forget it.' I have no idea why you would turn down that chance, but it wasn't unusual. It was always one step forward, two steps back with Billy. That doesn't mean I don't think he was great — he was. He was incredibly talented and charismatic. I think he just didn't want to feel like he owed it to anyone."

Jon remembers thinking it was odd that Billy, usually so savvy when publicity opportunities presented themselves, would turn this one down. But if he'd learned anything about Billy by then, it was that he was as stubborn as he was talented.

"Even if something was a good career move, he was only going to do what he wanted to do," Jon says. "We'd see that a lot, but we were having so much success, it was hard to argue with him. We always had the feeling that Billy could screw some things up if we let him, but he's the goose that laid the golden egg, so what could we do?"

In other words, when Jon, or Alf, or Dave, or Billy Flaxel had their own band, they could invite Bruce Springsteen up on stage.

Over the years, it has been mistakenly reported in Springsteen biographies that Bruce played one song with the Unreal Gods on September 29th, 1982 at On Broadway in Westwood, New Jersey. It never happened, but it should have.

Meanwhile, there still wasn't much to do except the occasional show at Matti's club. Steve Hettum called Tony DeMicoli back in Portland to see if he knew anyone, anybody who could help them get a gig in New York. No luck.

Billy and one of the dancers, Alaina, were sick. Steve Hettum gave Alaina his plane ticket and sent her home. Billy had a terrible cold. Keith Cox went home a month into the six-week trip to tend to personal business in Portland. Mick Boyt was so upset about what he viewed as a big waste of time that he quit, although he was rehired as soon as the band got back to Portland. Nothing seemed to be going right.

"We were just sitting around the house all day going crazy," DuFresne says. "We'd come off this stretch of more than a year where we're playing non-stop, being really active, and now there's nothing to do. Billy's coughing all the time, he's really sick. It was like, 'What the fuck's going on here? What are we doing?' We're all just sitting around drinking beer. We were all broke. The money had run out after a couple of weeks."

Finally, it looked like the band might get a break. Annie Farmer had arranged for a New York City corporate music lawyer to watch the band play. He did, then he invited Annie and Steve Hettum to his Manhattan office. He told Annie and Steve that he loved the band. He advised them against signing a contract with a Portland company. "Don't sign this deal," he told Hettum. "This is a small-time shark looking for a big-time fish." He told Annie he could get the Unreal Gods a gig at the Peppermint Club in Manhattan. And, he could arrange for Billy to meet with Columbia Records executives. Steve couldn't wait to call Billy and give him the good news. He was talking to Billy when Alf picked up another phone.

"Steve you don't have the authority to do this any more," Alf told him. "Matti's going to manage the band."

Steve hung up, and told Annie Farmer what had just happened. They headed back to Matti's house to talk it over.

Annie Farmer wasn't impressed by the fact that Matti was a friend of Bruce Springsteen's. "Billy, he runs a god damned repair shop," she told him. "I know people who want to talk with you. I've got a meeting set up for you at CBS."

"Sorry, Annie, I'm going to go with Matti," Billy told her.

"You're going to blow off CBS?" she asked. Annie knew she wasn't getting anywhere with Billy.

"I was very, very hurt, and I was hurt for Billy, because I knew he was blowing a big chance," Annie says. "I was really surprised, because I felt like Billy was choosing loyalty to Alf over integrity when he did that. That wasn't like him."

Annie and Steve went back to Portland. Steve took Alaina's train ticket he had traded her. He was told to go back to Portland and start setting up shows for when the band returned in late October. It was a long train ride.

"I realized my limitations after meeting the lawyers in New York," Hettum said. "Those guys eat cement and come up chewing. They were talking about things I didn't understand. I was young. I was good at taking care of business in Portland. There was nothing else I could do for them in New York. What Alf said to me was hard to take, but I knew they needed someone else."

He just wasn't sure Alf's family should be handling the Unreal Gods' business.

Matti, as it turned out, managed the band only briefly. Another brother, Joe, made a far more important contribution.

A combination of factors — Joe's connections in the music business, the dropping of Bruce Springsteen's name, the conversations Annie Farmer had with Columbia Records, and $20,000 of John Flaxel's money — bought the Unreal Gods a couple days at the legendary Power Station recording studio in New York.

Working with engineer Larry Alexander, who had worked with David Bowie and John Lennon, and with Joe Delia overseeing the project, Billy and the Unreal Gods recorded five songs — "Rocky Road," "Uptown," and three new tunes, "The Police Tol' Me," "Happy Santa Claus," and "Made in Hong Kong."

Recording five songs in two days was quite a bit different for the Unreal Gods than their first studio experience, when they were left to their own devices for several meandering months in Jack Barr's studio, putting together "Boom Chuck Rock Now!" This was different, professional. The difference in the quality of the two recordings was obvious.

"I'm really proud of those songs," Jon DuFresne says. "That was the best thing we'd ever recorded. We knocked those songs out in no time flat. We didn't even think about it. We didn't even think that we should be nervous being in the Power Station."

The sessions went just as he'd hoped, Joe Delia said.

"Time was really tightly budgeted," he says. "There was so much time for setup, so much for recording the tracks, everything was budgeted, down to the vocals and the mixing. It was all pretty well planned out, but I'm sure we spent every cent we had."

Actually, they barely squeezed in "Happy Santa Claus."

"We had four songs done, and Billy was saying, 'Come on, let's do Santa Claus,' " Billy Flaxel says. "We wanted to stop. I mean, we were in the fucking Power Station. We didn't even know the song 'Happy Santa Claus,' but we just wing it, and it's a really cool song. It came out great."

I'm a happy Santa Claus
when I think of you
'Cause when I think of you
I feel like jelly inside

I'm a happy Santa Claus
when there is some snow
'cause when there is some snow
it's a wild sleigh ride

"Some time I'll tell you what that song really means," Flaxel says. Or, we could just take a look at the last verse:

I'm a happy Santa Claus
when there is some snow
'cause when we do some snow
I get high ...

OK, maybe the trip to New York hadn't gone exactly as Billy had planned. He'd been sick for much of the six weeks. There was no tour, no showcase for Rolling Stone editors, just a couple shows in Matti's crummy little club. Billy threw away a chance most bands would kill for when he snubbed Bruce Springsteen. And an opportunity for a deal with a major label was lost when Billy turned down a meeting with Columbia Records. He needed to mend some fences with his roadies, and with Steve Hettum and Annie Farmer. Still, Billy managed to land on his feet, as usual. He'd learned a little about the big time, and come away with an excellent five-song tape that he planned to shop around. He'd get that record deal soon enough. Now, all he wanted to do was go back home to Portland and play at Luis' La Bamba.

19 Who Manages the Managers?

Everybody wanted Steve Hettum's job all of the sudden. There was no doubt Billy was going to get a major record deal soon, it was just a question of with who, and when. After returning from New York, Alf and his brothers seemed to be calling most of the shots, but they would soon learn a couple of lessons the hard way. Just because you're Billy's manager today doesn't mean you're going to be Billy's manager tomorrow. And even if you *were* Billy's manager, that didn't mean he was going to listen to you.

Steve Hettum was Billy's friend before he was the Unreal Gods' manager. He had been more than capable of setting up local gigs, handling promotion and distributing 3,000 copies of the indepenedent "Boom Chuck Rock Now!" album. But he realized Billy was about to go big-time, and was going to need lawyers, managers and agents who knew more about the business than he did. Hettum was willing to step aside. He didn't plan on getting stepped *on*, though. He returned from New York and started booking the Unreal Gods through the end of 1982, including $5,000 worth of shows October 29th through 31st at La Bamba.

"At that time, we were all supposed to be on salary," Hettum says. "I was supposed to get $150 a week, but I hadn't gotten paid in 10 weeks. I talked to some of the lawyers who told me all the money was going to be tied up until Billy got signed, nothing was going out. I said, 'OK, fine, I'll be a booking agent.' The standard was 10 percent, but they thought that was too much, so I said I'd take five percent. And five percent of $5,000 was $250, and I wanted my money. This didn't have so much to do with Billy, but Alfred wanted his brother Matti to manage the band. So Alf says, 'Give Steve a hundred bucks and tell him to fuck off.' I nearly strangled him to death. I said, 'That's not what you told me, that's not what you promised.' Alf sees how much money is coming in, then decides I can have $100."

Hettum booked the Unreal Gods for three shows at Astor Park in Seattle, November 11th through 13th, for $3,500.

"Alf says, 'There was only $750 left after expenses, so here's forty bucks,' " Hettum says. "So right then I just said, 'OK, listen, I've had a good time, the shows are booked through the end of the year, good luck.' That's when I fell out."

And when everyone lined up to take his place.

Joe Dreiling, who had managed the Malchicks, offered his services. Joe says he never "got legal" with Billy, but he was there as a friend and to help book local shows. Tony DeMicoli was also an unofficial adviser to Billy and the band. Alf started taking care of a lot of the business, and had his brothers Matti, Joe and Frank lined up to get into the act. A Delia family friend, William Gladstone, a 40ish LA yuppie who was in the jewelry business, eventually became Billy's official manager. There were other Portland lawyers and music business wannabes who took runs at working with Billy. The money was still coming from Dr. John Flaxel, and from a new source, a rich Portland businessman named Fritz Johnson.

"Billy was such a big-hearted man, he just didn't know how to say no," DeMicoli says. "And he ended up with a lot of managers."

Karen remembered how simple it was at first. Just the band and girlfriends hanging out at the house, playing shows, writing songs. Now things were getting complicated.

"Billy wanted a manager desperately, but some of the people he picked were poorly chosen," she says. "He wanted a manager so he could stick to songwriting. He was constantly frustrated by things that he didn't want to have to deal with. Billy was open to anybody, and these strange people started coming into our lives. He wanted to turn some of that control over to other people, but he didn't have the knowledge himself about how to hire someone. You have to be objective, but he did it all on a personal level, hiring friends that he partied with. So many flaky people would approach him, and they all wanted a shot."

What the Delias, and many others learned, however, was that Billy was used to doing things his way, and wasn't the easiest person in the world to manage.

"He'd hire these people, but then when they started doing it, they weren't doing it the way he wanted," Karen says.

"Billy knew I worked with Jon Koonce (Johnny and the Distractions)," Buck Munger says. "He'd say, 'Hey, why don't you be my manager?' And I'd say, 'Because I'm the 34th guy you've said that to since 4 o'clock this afternoon.' We were all hip to that. But I'd watched this guy take his show on the road, all without any real management, and, of course, I thought, 'This kid needs a manager.' A real manager, someone he could trust, someone he'd listen to."

"We had videos and recordings that were killer, all marketable stuff if they had been handled by the right people," Alf Ryder says. "That was Billy's fatal flaw, he tried to manage himself. When it got down to it, he couldn't. And he believed in Hollywood. He believed everything would be OK because he had talent. I know tons of kids that believe in Hollywood, and they're all going to go down there and get their balls cut off."

Annie Farmer had been stung by the way she was treated in New York. She didn't believe Alf or any of his brothers or friends were any help to Billy.

"Billy was just too trusting," she says. "I cautioned him against that, so did Joe Dreiling, Steve Hettum. Alf suckered Billy into letting his brother manage him, and he fucked him over for his chance in New York. Alf is vindictive, mean and petty. There were people around Billy who were very jealous. He was just light years ahead of anybody else in his band, because of his soul. And everybody was trying to use Billy for their benefit. In New York, Steve and I were crushed, not from an ego level, but because we knew what was best for Billy's career. Steve knew that instinctively, and I knew it from a business perspective. We knew he was going to be fucked, and Alf Ryder is the one who fucked him, because of his own ego."

Alf wanted to keep his brother Joe Delia involved. Joe had produced the Power Station recordings, and Alf arranged for him to work with the Unreal Gods again, this time at Crystal Studios in Los Angeles in November and December of 1982.

The session at the Power Station had been a huge success. Billy, and everyone in the band, had been amazed at the quality of those recordings, which made "Boom Chuck Rock Now!" seem primitive in comparison. So, coming off that success, you'd expect Billy to trust Joe Delia to run the show.

"We burned people up really quick," Jon DuFresne says. "As good as Joey was for us at the Power Station, by this time Billy was already getting to him. Joey couldn't be an authority any more. We went back to doing things Billy's way. Joey just couldn't get control of the situation, we didn't have as much rehearsal time as we needed. It was very unorganized. The preparation just wasn't there. Basically, it just wasn't a focused session. We were in a gig mode, not a recording mode."

Crystal Studios was a hotspot in the '70s, the recording home for Stevie Wonder, War and other R&B acts. The studio is located at 1014 North Vine Street in Hollywood, which sounds like a much more glamorous location than it actually is. The studio faces an alley off of Vine, just across from an auto repair shop littered with broken down cars and flat tires. It wasn't much, compared to the Power Station, and neither were the band's recordings there.

"The LA stuff didn't come out very good," DuFresne says. "In fact, it really sucked."

Well, it wasn't that bad, according to Joe Delia. The songs they recorded were all favorites from the Unreal Gods' live sets — "Used to Hang Around," "Upstroke Down," "Symmetry," and "Chances Are." Andrew Berliner was the engineer for the Crystal Studios session. The tapes were sent to Larry Alexander, to be mixed at the Power Station.

"Billy was a talented guy, who seemed to think he knew the right way to do everything," Joe Delia says. "He was very stubborn, but I got along with him well. What I tried to do was put some form in the songs. Billy could make up a lot of songs, good songs. I'd see him one day and he'd say, 'Oh, I just wrote 10 songs yesterday.' Nobody can write 10 complete songs in one night, nobody. You might come up with 10 germs of ideas, or 10 half-songs, or 10 pretty good grooves. But I think

Billy and Fritz Johnson, a Portland businessman, "were like brothers," according to Karen.
(Courtesy of Karen Sage)

some of his songs tended not to be done. That was my take. He definitely wrote catchy songs, and had great ideas, but I think he was too quick to call a song a song."

Still, Billy and the boys had a couple of fun weeks in LA. They stayed in a plain-looking Best Western Hotel on Franklin Avenue in Hollywood, walking distance to Crystal Studios. When they weren't in the studio, Billy and Jon would cruise the Hollywood Walk of Fame, looking for stars of their heroes. Gene Vincent. Chuck Berry. And they'd shop for rock 'n' roll clothes, or check out other bands at clubs up and down Sunset Boulevard. This was a long way from Portland.

"I remember thinking, 'Wow, LA,' " DuFresne says. "It was just wild."

Joe Delia noticed.

"It was a wild time for everybody, but certainly a lot of fun," he says. "But Billy was really hellbent on self-destruction, or so it seemed. I did a pretty good job with the guys, I thought, but I'm not sure they were all there. They were doing a lot of partying."

The plan now was to package the Power Station and Crystal Studios recordings and shop them to major labels. And if none of them bit soon, Billy was prepared to release the package as early as May of '83 as another independent album, titled "Made in Hong Kong."

A couple of months after the Crystal Studios sessions, Billy announced that it was time to make a video, and that the band would be going to LA to work with another Delia brother, Frank. Frank Delia had produced videos for the Ramones, and was just wrapping up "Mexican Radio," which became a quirky MTV hit for the techno band Wall of Voodoo.

A new friend of Billy's, Fritz Johnson, was going to help pay for the video shoot. Johnson is from an old-money Oregon family. His circle of friends included other late 20s and early 30s Portlanders like Annie Farmer. "We'd all kind of gravitated toward each other," Annie says. "We were all from families with money, but we were all like the black sheep of our families. We were all creative, all interested in music."

One of Fritz Johnson's many investments was a company that made pool cues. Fritz was quite a shooter himself, having played in 9 Ball tournaments at Casears Palace in Las Vegas, and around the country. The night Fritz was introduced to Billy by friends Chris Rathe and Mo Stevenson, they went to a bowling alley and played pool. Fritz enjoyed being Billy's friend, and hanging out at the clubs, being backstage with the band. He was a true friend to Billy, more like a brother, actually. And he pumped a lot of money into the Unreal Gods.

Fritz donated $20,000 for the video shoot in LA. And John Flaxel was still a regular contributor to the Make Billy Rancher a Star Foundation, although certainly he was also interested in helping Billy Flaxel.

Cheryl Hodgson was a lawyer in Portland who did legal work for John Flaxel. Hodgson became a friend of Billy's, but her first meeting was not very pleasant. John Flaxel came to Hodgson and said he wanted to negotiate a contract between himself and The Unreal Gods. This was after the "Boom Chuck Rock Now!" album was out, and he said that after the contributions he had made that — if the record ever made any money — he should be entitled to a share.

"Dr. Flaxel is a tremendous man who had given Billy a lot of financial and moral support," Hodgson says. "He would have continued to support the band without a contract, but as things looked like they were starting to happen, he needed some protection for himself. At that point in his life, Billy was a typical young musician, and he really wanted to make it. I wouldn't say he was heartless, but he was taking counsel from some wrong people. Sometimes people want it to be real so bad that the people that really have their best interests at heart are the ones most easily disposed of. We negotiated this contract three times, and Billy kept changing lawyers in California, and each one kept telling him he was getting screwed, when that was as far from the truth as anything could be. All Dr. Flaxel was asking was to get paid back out of the profit, if there ever was any. This was a very high-risk situation for him, financially.

"At the time, I didn't think Billy was a very nice guy, because Dr. Flaxel had done such a tremendous amount for that band, he had made such a tremendous contribution to their lives and to their careers. I mean, this was family."

Eventually a deal was worked out between John Flaxel and the band. So, bankrolled again by Flaxel and Fritz Johnson, the Unreal Gods were off to LA, this time to shoot a video for "The Police Tol' Me." Again, Billy was rushing things. The safest way to make sure a video is going to be played is to wait until you've been signed by a major label, then let them pay for the video and make sure it falls into MTV's hands. But Billy just figured they'd make the video, then everything would work out.

The video was recorded on the second floor of an old, brick office building on the corner of Hollywood Boulevard and Cherokee Street. "They shoot a lot of porno movies here," Frank Delia said as he led the band through the courtyard on the inside of the U-shaped building and up the stairs to the second floor.

Billy wrote the story line for the filming of the video, in which his girlfriend gets busted for selling cocaine, and tries to frame Billy. The video action starts with Billy's girlfriend (an actress, not Karen) running to her car, then speeding away, with the police in pursuit. Then the video cuts to the band, with Billy in front, playing in the second-floor studio, which looks like an abandoned warehouse. Billy's blond hair is long, and it drops in front of his eyes and bounces from side to side in the back as he sings and strums his rhythm guitar parts. Billy's girlfriend is caught by the police, and after a guitar solo by DuFresne, Billy is seen being interrogated by the police. Then it's more shots of the band, Billy out in the snow, with icicles hanging from his hair, Billy lying on a bed in his underwear. The song ends with a shot of Billy's face, against a black background. His hair is slicked back, and a tear rolls out of his eye as the song fades out.

It's interesting visually, a professional-looking video and a good song, and it would have fit nicely into MTV's rotation at the time.

It was at the filming of the video that the Unreal Gods met William Gladstone, the man Alf suggested should be the band's manager. Sounded OK to Billy, who filled Gladstone in on the idea of taking the songs recorded in New York and LA and using them to secure a record deal.

"Don't worry," Gladstone assured Billy. "I'll get you a deal."

No one really liked William Gladstone, even at the first meeting, but Billy and other band members thought maybe he was the type of tough manager they needed.

After the video shoot was done, William Gladstone stayed in LA and sent his brother David to Portland to watch after the band.

The band returned to Portland with a video to go along with the recordings. Whether they needed one or not. The problem was, the video didn't have much of a chance of being played by MTV without a push from a record label, which Billy didn't have yet. For the first time in his career, Billy found out that talent alone wasn't always enough. It was a good video, a good song, but now it was going to have to sit on a shelf until the Unreal Gods signed a record deal. Maybe the experience wasn't a total loss, but the fact was, Billy should have waited until he was signed, then shot a video.

Maybe MTV didn't want the video, but that didn't stop Billy from showing it to Portland. April 15th was dubbed "Video Premiere Night" at the Starry Night Theater, Larry Hurwitz's 1,000-seat club. A band called Go-90 opened the all-ages show. When they were done, a giant screen was lowered over the stage. After a long wait, MTV videos were played for a half-hour or so. At 11:30 p.m., Billy and the Unreal Gods played a 40-minute set. Then the screen came down, and more MTV videos were played. At 12:25 a.m., "The Police Tol' Me" made what MTV likes to call a "world premiere." The response was enthusiastic. Fans were reminded to pick up Billy Rancher autographed posters and T-shirts on their way out.

Actually, this wasn't the Unreal Gods' first video. They'd put one together several months earlier for the song "Uptown," filmed at the grand Pittock Mansion behind the Portland Zoo. Getting permission to film at the mansion wasn't easy, and was given only after Billy promised

Billy and the boys filmed a video for "Uptown" at stately Pittock Mansion.
(Bart Danielson)

to shoot at sunrise, then get off the premises.

"You wouldn't believe what we had to go through to get that open," Billy Flaxel says.

The band played a show the night before, stopped off for Bloody Marys and breakfast, then headed up the hill to the mansion. The video features the band playing on the front porch, with a spectacular view of Portland. The band is more prominent in this video than in "The Police Tol' Me." There are lingering, loving clips of the band playing, some of the shots in slow motion, and a segment in which the band members are lined up, clapping their hands and snapping their fingers to the song. The footage at the mansion is mixed with shots of Billy and Karen walking through downtown Portland, of Karen frolicking in a fountain, being helped out by Billy.

It's another good song. Another good video. Another piece of work you never saw on MTV. Billy was in a hurry. He knew he wanted to make records. He knew he wanted to make videos. He knew he was writing great songs, and he figured that would be enough. In Portland, it always had been.

When Billy and the band weren't recording, or making videos, or waiting for their managers and lawyers to nail that deal with a record company, they continued to play around Portland. The fall of '82 turned into the winter, then the summer of '83, and they kept playing. They were playing the same places, but it didn't seem the same.

"At first, we were young kids, just naive idiots," Billy Flaxel says. "Then the music became a business. Billy Rancher and the Unreal Gods to me was liking drinking a couple of beers and puking when you were a kid. Once we got corporated, it was like drinking a fifth of whiskey and waking up with a hangover. It was a pain in the ass."

20 The Fast Life

"People usually don't quote me on this. They say, 'Oh, Saint Billy, everybody loved him.' Well, there was no Saint Billy, never was, never will be. He was the greatest party animal since Jim Morrison. I remember running around at 8 o'clock in the morning with him, throwing rocks at drug dealers' windows to score more cocaine. And there was a time when alcohol was a real big problem for him." — Alf Ryder.

It should be noted that Alf isn't exactly the "Just Say No" poster boy.

"I was always 100 percent for it," he says of Billy's habits. "I think drugs are great. I still do."

Billy didn't need to drink or take drugs to be the life of the party. But he did anyway. The truth is, it was probably hard to be Billy Rancher and *not* take drugs.

"He was getting blow from everybody," Jon DuFresne says. "My first introduction to cocaine was people coming back and just pouring big mountains of it backstage. It was the '80s, and coke was going crazy through the roof. We were the cool band, so every coke dealer and every rich person who had enough money to buy drugs was always there around us, and Billy obviously liked it a lot. We all had our habits, we all indulged in whatever we indulged in. Billy was really into it."

It's only rock 'n' roll.

"He didn't do anything when we were at Mount Hood," says Glen Baggerly, his old college baseball teammate. "Maybe he'd drink a beer or two once in a while. I think the scene really got to him. Every dealer was his friend. 'Hey Billy, here's a line.' 'Here's a line.' "

Karen remembers there were a lot of people at the shows, with drugs, who wanted to be Billy's friend.

"It was the same thing, all the time," she says. "These people would say, 'Hey, come with me to my car for a minute.' 'Step into my car.' 'Join me in the back seat of my car.' It was just part of the deal, and everybody was caught up in it. Everyone I knew, including my friends, was doing it."

Keith Cox, being a roadie, usually got to the parties after the girls and most of the drugs had already been taken. But he saw what was going on. Like others in the Unreal Gods' family, he acknowledges Billy did a lot of partying, but doesn't think it affected his performance on stage. As for any deep psychological meaning behind Billy's drug use, forget it.

"Billy attracted a wide, diverse crowd, from doctors to drug dealers," Cox says. "They were always trying to ride his coattails. Being able to sit back and watch was interesting. You could see the different people, see the different means they'd try to use to hang around. There was every kind of drug available. But with Billy, it was always coke and pot, nothing harder. This was before anybody thought of saying no to drugs. No one was doing it to get away from anything. It was just something to do, and everybody did it."

Jim Basnight was the leader of a Seattle punk band, the Moberleys. He always enjoyed seeing Billy come to Seattle.

"I always used to go to their parties, because I figured if Billy was there, there'd be lots of cute girls. Good weed, too," Basnight says. "He was somewhat into smoking pot, but not into hard drugs. It's not like he was buying heroin or something, he was just kind of a pothead. And I never saw him on stage where he was fucked up."

Billy usually did his partying after shows. It always took him several hours to wind down afterwards, anyway. And he didn't want anyone doing anything that would hurt the show. Billy was always in control when he was on stage. He did, however, miss out on a chance to play on a night when all he had planned to do was help Dave Stricker celebrate his birthday.

Billy was pretty looped when when he got the word that bass player Lee Rocker and drummer Slim Jim Phantom, two-thirds of the Stray Cats, were at La Bamba and ready to jam. They were in town for a show — that the Unreal Gods would be opening — a few days later at the Euphoria Tavern. Billy had seen the Stray Cats in England when he and Karen had been to Europe, and he was a big fan. Billy and Karen hurried to La Bamba. The Unreal Gods took it upon themselves to show the Stray Cats a rock 'n' roll good time, complete with drugs and drink. Finally, Jon DuFresne, the two Stray Cats and their road manager, on harmonica, took the stage in the La Bamba basement. Billy would have too, if he hadn't been too drunk to plug his guitar into an amp. He didn't miss much, according to DuFresne.

Billy insisted that Astrid get married in grand style at home instead of simply going down to the courthouse. She did, to Jack Hanke, on July 2nd, 1983.
(Courtesy of Karen Sage)

"It was a real uptight situation," he says. "There were just too many people there trying to meet them, or shove something up their nose."

When they played together later that week, Billy apologized for his behavior. Or what he could remember of it.

All just part of the rock 'n' roll lifestyle, the way Billy Flaxel saw it.

"Sure, we did a lot of partying," he says. "We were very into the fast life. We did a lot of coke, a lot of booze. But all kind of harmless, when you look back at it. For me, personally, I drank a lot, met a lot of women, smoked a lot of dope. We had a good time. The cocaine dipped its head in there. But there weren't any what I'd call drug problems. It's just one of the things that went along with the good times. Hell, we wouldn't play a place unless we got two free cases of beer."

Moderation was not really a concept Billy understood. He'd party for months like a wildman, then decide not just to cut back, but to totally abstain from alcohol and drugs. Then he'd be at a really good party and, well, it would be back the other way.

"He'd slip back and forth between a totally athletic-like regimen and a totally off-the-edge, wild-ass, catch-me-at-7:30-in-the-morning routine," Buck Munger remembers.

Karen would have preferred a little more of the athletic regimen.

"It was all or nothing," she says. "He'd go on the wagon for three months at a time. It was amazing to me. All of the sudden, he'd just say, 'I'm going to stop tomorrow.' Then he'd go three months, or six months with nothing, not a beer. He wouldn't even drink champagne at his mother's wedding."

Astrid married Jack Hanke on July 2nd, 1983.

"We were just going to go to the judge and get married," Astrid says. "Billy said, 'No way, you can't do that, Mom. You're going to have a big wedding. You'll have it here.'"

So Astrid married Jack by the pool in the back yard of Astrid's house, the same home she'd lived in since the Ranchers moved from Oakland, Calif., when Billy was 12 years old. And Billy didn't drink a sip, not even champagne to toast.

Of course, it wasn't long before he'd jumped back off the wagon.

Whether Billy was partying usually depended on who he was spending the most time with. And more and more, people who wanted to party were coming into his life.

"Billy and the Unreal Gods liked their good guy image," Buck Munger says. "They were working out of the punk era, and they were tired of the puking, and the green hair. Billy Rancher was living the life of the clean cut guy. I know he went to parties, I know he snorted cocaine. But as far as those guys not being able to get through a night without it, that's bullshit. There were lots, LOTS, of scumbag people who came backstage and put this shit in front of them. But as far as that being part of them, part of their daily routine, it just wasn't."

Billy had become the hero of the idle rich in Portland.

"The thing was, Billy was the pretty white boy and we were a backwards, honky music place," Munger says. "When Billy happened, he was so white, so wholesome, so beautiful ... the rich guys loved him. He cut across boundaries. There was so much to appreciate with Billy. There was the music, but even if you didn't like that, there was the production of the show, and Billy was so likable, so handsome, everybody just loved this kid."

Fritz Johnson ran with a group of buddies that included his brother, Annie Farmer and Chris Rathe and his girlfriend, Mo Stevenson. Mo, like the rest of the group, was well off financially, the daughter of wealthy parents. She lived in a big house near the town of Hood River, an hour east of Portland on the Columbia River.

"When I first heard Billy, I was so intrigued by his music, it was so happy, so uplifting," she says. "I never minded the drive into Portland. It was so much fun. It was like the band was your friends, whether you knew them well or not."

There were days Mo loaded up her car and took nieces and nephews, some as young as 9 years old, to Portland to hear Billy at an all-ages show. Then she'd take the kids home, and head back for the later over-21 show and dance the night away.

"They'd play at different places, but you'd see the same faces. It became like a big family," she says. "It was the kind of music, the kind of scene where you could just run out on the dance floor and dance. You didn't have to walk up to somebody and say, 'Hi, my name's Mo. Wanna dance?' There was so much energy at those shows."

Mo started doing most of her dancing with Fritz, who eventually took

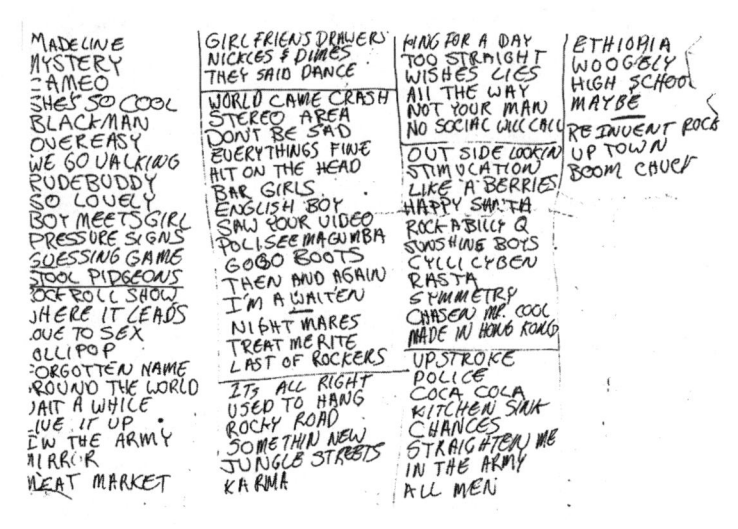

Billy decided on this set list in honor of Portland's 75th Rose Festival in June of '83, playing 75-plus songs over two nights at Lung Fung.
(Courtesy of Keith Cox)

Chris Rathe's place as Mo's boyfriend. Fritz became one of Billy's biggest supporters. "I think he just gave Billy money whenever he needed it," Mick Boyt says. Fritz and some of his pals didn't have much use for Billy's old Malchicks buddies. In Fritz's opinion, Billy hanging out with Lenny and Pete Jorgusen, and Steve Hettum and Joe Dreiling and Wade Varner would be like a country club member taking his shirt off, wrapping his necktie around his forehead and shotgunning beers with the caddies. Of course, Billy didn't grow up in any country club. You can take the boy out of northeast Portland …

"It wasn't cool for Billy to be with his old buddies any more," Hettum says. "One time Fritz invited Billy to some pool hall in northwest Portland, some fancy place with all these antique cars. We all walk in, and Fritz tells Billy, 'We just wanted you and Karen.' So Billy says, 'OK, let's go back to the house and get a six pack.' Billy hung out with Fritz and those other rich guys, but he hated stuffiness, he hated hypocrisy. And when they treated his friends like that, he told them about it."

Or, as Tony DeMicoli says, "If you laid out a line of bullshit, Billy would call you on it."

Billy managed to find time for a couple of reunion shows with the Malchicks. The first was on April 17th, 1983, when the Malchicks played La Bamba on Lenny's 22nd birthday.

"That was a big old party," is the way Karen remembers it.

Lenny remembers thinking Billy considered it a big old pain in the ass.

"I think Billy thought it was kind of an annoyance," he says. "Our relationship was still pretty strained at that time. I think he thought Pete and I thought his music was a joke, that it was thin. I didn't, although he never did ask me what I really thought. He'd never ask us what we were doing. He was just really into his Unreal Gods thing."

"It was kind of like he had something better to do," Pete said of the Malchicks reunion shows. "He'd walk in like he was the star, show up with his entourage."

That's not the way Karen remembers it. "Billy was always excited to play those shows. He always wanted to do things for Lenny and the Malchicks. He thought it was fun."

Of course, Billy *was* the star. Lenny and Pete's band, the Pipsqueaks, hadn't found much of an audience for their white boy reggae in Portland and they were leaving two days after the Malchicks reunion show for

Hawaii. Billy was just waiting for the record deal he knew was coming soon. And a reunion with the Malchicks seemed like a good way to spend an April night while he waited.

Where the Unreal Gods were tight musically, the Malchicks were, well, loose, even in their best days. Now more than two years had passed since they'd played together. They had just one rehearsal before the show. And Lenny was drunk.

Billy, wearing mascara, green and black striped pants, a pink pajama top and a light blue, knitted cap with a ball on top, led the band through a couple of sloppy sets mixing Malchicks originals with Rolling Stones, Chuck Berry and Ron Wood covers.

"This one's called Star Fucker," Billy said, intoducing a Rolling Stones song that was actually titled "Star Star." Of course, listening to the lyrics, it would have been called "Star Fucker," if you could have gotten away with that back in the early '70s. "It's by the ... uh, Malchicks."

Nearly every song was accompanied by a long delay as Billy waited for Lenny to tune his guitar.

"This is why the Malchicks never went anywhere," Billy said during one break. "We didn't have enough money for a guitar tuner."

Lenny continued to turn pegs, trying to get in tune.

"Lenny, you're still way the fuck out," Billy said.

Billy drank beer on stage while Lenny struggled with his guitar. He showered the crowd with pitchers of beer. He poured beer on Lenny. He tossed rose petals to the crowd. And he waited for Lenny to get in tune.

Finally, they were ready, and Billy, Lenny, Pete, Dave Stricker, Rod Bautista and keyboard player David Diaz did a twangy country version of "Beast of Burden." Then it was time for an old Malchicks-turned-Unreal Gods song, "Too Straight for the New Wave." It was one of the most coherent tunes of the evening, featuring Alf on keyboards, but still included an improvised verse:

My brother's a musician,
the piper in the band
He's such a fine composer,
the best in all the land
he's a prodigal maniac,
imagines everything

His music's a Fantasia,

a Rhapsody in Blue
He's got more improvisation
than most niggers do

If that didn't offend anyone, maybe a rousing version of "Cocksucker Blues," would do the trick. (In 1970, the Rolling Stones thought they had fulfilled their contract with Decca Records, and were looking for a new label. But Decca told the Stones they owed them one more song. No problem. Mick and Keith sat down and penned a happy little tune called "Cocksucker Blues." It was never recorded.)

Well, I'm a lonesome schoolboy,
I've been hangin' around too long
Yes, I'm a lonesome schoolboy,
And I just came into town
And I heard so much about La Bamba,
I just had to check it out

I asked the young policeman,
Can he lock me up for the night?
Some of them pigs,
some of them pigs, they're all right
And he fucked me with his truncheon
and his helmet was way too tight

About now, the crowd that had been doing its best to dance along as the Malchicks lurched through one song after another, was mostly standing in dazed silence, gaping at Billy.

Where can I get my cock sucked?
Where can I get my ass fucked?
Well, I may have no money,
But I know where to put it every time

OK, everybody now!
And on it went. Joe Dreiling and Jon DuFresne sat in on guitars during a messy blues jam. Billy even invited Tony DeMicoli on stage to sing a chorus of "Star Star."

Billy thanked the opening act, the Harsh Lads, a band fronted by his young friend Houston Bolles, a high school senior who'd met Lenny a year earlier and worked his way into carrying the Pipsqueaks' gear around, then put together his own band. Houston was a regular at Unreal Gods all-ages shows at Lung Fung. A few times Billy spotted him in the crowd and made the Unreal Gods play an old Dean Martin song, "Houston."

The Malchicks were their usual selves at the four-hour reunion show. Dave Stricker stood in one place, as though he were bolted to the La Bamba stage, playing his bass. Pete Jorgusen sat behind his drums wearing a yellow T-shirt that had Stockholm, Sweden written in bold letters on the front. He was wearing a green Army cap that made him look like Max Klinger (the later years, without the dresses). The Human Stage Prop, guitarist Rod Bautista, wore a sleeveless shirt, and a flower in his hair, and he looked marvelous, as usual. David Diaz, who sat in occasionally back in the old days with the Malchicks, did his best on keyboards to hold the songs together.

And then there was Lenny. He wore red jeans that had ripped out in the crotch during the second set and a red T-shirt. It looked as though he'd combed his hair with a brick.

There were more breaks while Lenny attempted to tune his guitar ("Lenny's so fucking far out of tune now he can't even play," Billy reported at one point to the anxious crowd). Finally, Mick Boyt had to rush in from the side of the stage with another guitar before Lenny could play "Start Me Up," another Rolling Stones song.

Before "You Can't Always Get What You Want," Lenny stepped to the microphone and slurred, "This is the kind of song where you just need to sit back ... and think about all the bad notes I hit."

Lenny still managed a few searing solos, and even sang a couple of songs. Toward the end of the set, the Malchicks grabbed Lenny, wrestled him to the stage floor and gave him 22 birthday spankings.

Then Billy wished Lenny and the Pipsqueaks good luck in Hawaii.

"We had a deal with some shady promoter over on the big island," Lenny says. "I thought, 'Yeah, Hawaii, that sounds pretty tropical. We'll play reggae and drink beer.'"

Sammy Reeves was the promoter who talked Lenny into moving to Hawaii. The Pisqueaks lived in an old, rat-infested theater, the Aki Bono, built in 1909. The deal was, they got to live there for free, if they restored the theater. The Aki Bono was located in Pahoa, a city 20 miles from Hilo on the big island of Hawaii. It's an area that's as Third

World as you can get and still be in the United States. Lenny lived in the balcony of the theater, sleeping next to the movie projector. For one year, the Pipsqueaks cleaned up the Aki Bono, getting it ready for hula lessons and movies. They played their music for the amused locals, ate mangos and avocados off of trees, did odd jobs for Sammy Reeves, and hung out with his teenage son, an aspiring actor and musician named Keanu. Yes, that Keanu Reeves.

The Unreal Gods had bigger plans.

During the spring and summer of '83, they made several trips to Seattle for shows at Astor Park, the Backstage and the Hall of Fame. Billy Rancher and the Unreal Gods were still the biggest draw in Seattle. They also played Tacoma, Washington; Vancouver, British Columbia; and all the usual Portland haunts — La Bamba, Lung Fung, Starry Night, the Copper Penny, Last Hurrah, Pine Street Theater, the Orange Peel, Beckman's Place.

Steve Hettum was still helping the Unreal Gods book Lung Fung, although he had to get a real job, driving a delivery truck. He set Billy up for two nights in June at Lung Fung. Billy decided that in honor of Portland's 75th annual Rose Festival, the band would play 75 songs during the two nights. Hettum put up 1,000 posters between stops on his delivery route. The first night started with "Madeline," and the second show ended with "Boom Chuck Rock." Each song was an Unreal Gods original, written by Billy. They were great shows, and a testament to Billy's songwriting ability.

The Goddesses A-Go-Go were gone-gone. Candyce Dru had been with the Unreal Gods since the first show, teaming with Mary Smith, then Celeste Johnson, then Alaina Pereira. Alaina quit after she got sick in New York the previous fall and had to come home early. She was replaced by Patti Hatfield. At their last performance with the Unreal Gods, Candyce and Patti performed in sheer chiffon tops that didn't leave much to the imagination. Their nipples were covered only by tiny patches they call pasties in the exotic dancing business. "It was very suggestive, very seductive. Pretty bold," Candyce says. "It was legal, though."

And the band played on, around Portland, and all over the Northwest. William Gladstone, meanwhile, was busy shopping the recordings and videos. He managed to get a glimpse of the video for "The Police Tol' Me" played in the movie "Firstborn," starring Teri Garr and Peter

Weller. And the Power Station and Crystal Studios tapes were in the hands of executives at Polydor, A&M, EMI, Capitol and Geffen, among others. William Gladstone was using the shotgun approach.

"William Gladstone would have signed us with anybody, just to say he did it," Jon DuFresne says. "He didn't have enough sense, enough knowledge about the business, to know it was important what label we signed with, what producer we'd have, that it was important to be hooked up with the right people."

Clive Davis seemed like the right people to Gladstone. Clive ran Arista Records, and nobody had a bigger reputation in the business. Clive Davis dragged Columbia Records into the rock 'n' roll era, signing Janis Joplin, Santana, Billy Joel and Bruce Springsteen to a previously dreary label whose stars had been Andy Williams, Barbra Streisand and Doris Day. In 1977, he took over Bell Records, the lackluster record division of Columbia Pictures, renamed it Arista and turned it into one of the biggest money-making companies in the business. Clive Davis was a bigshot, a 51-year-old, flashy dressing, egomaniacal New Yorker.

Actually, Arista had already had one chance at the band. Joe Delia sent the Power Station tape to Neil Portnow, Clive Davis' right-hand man at Arista.

"He passed on the band, which I thought was very curious," Delia says. "He said he wasn't interested, just out and out passed on the deal."

Well, they were interested now. Arrangements were made for Clive Davis to see Billy and the Unreal Gods August 7th at the Starry Night Theater in Portland.

Billy thought that sounded like a good reason to have a party.

21 Does God Have to Call Shotgun?

"Uh, can I get your bags Clive?"

What is the proper form here, Jon DuFresne wondered. *I mean, this is Clive Davis, the most important record company executive in the world*. And on the afternoon of August 7th, 1983, he was standing in the parking lot of the Portland, Oregon airport, waiting to get into Billy Rancher's Saab.

OK, Clive gets to ride in the front, Jon had figured that much out for himself. He'd slip into the back with Neil Portnow.

"Glad to meet you Clive," Billy said, taking Clive's hand with his own big mitt of a right hand and shaking it enthusiastically. "This is John Davis."

John Davis! Jon couldn't believe what he was hearing. He glared at Billy. *You idiot, what are you doing?* He understood that Billy might be a little nervous, but after spending almost every day the past two years together, he didn't expect Billy to confuse him with John Davis.

"I mean Jon DuFresne," Billy said.

Billy, Clive, Jon and Neil spent their cramped 15-minute drive talking music, until they arrived at Astrid's house, where they met the rest of the Unreal Gods. Astrid and Jack were vacationing in Sweden. Karen, against Billy's wishes, was in Mexico where one of her cousins was getting married. Clive, Neil and the Unreal Gods pulled up chairs around the pool in the back yard.

"We were all just staring at him like he was an alien or something," DuFresne says. "But he was real nice, very dignified, very low-key."

Dignified and low-key were not traits the Unreal Gods had mastered yet. Billy Flaxel got up to get another beer, walked behind Clive and pointed at his bald head. One by one, the Unreal Gods made excuses to get up and walk behind Clive, each stopping to try to figure out what he had done to his bald spot.

"He was using that stuff that men paint on their scalp to make their hair look thicker," DuFresne says. "I remember we were all going, 'Look at his head, man, look at the back of his head,' and just cracking up. We kind of treated everything as a joke, and just because he was Clive Davis didn't make this an exception."

Four months earlier, Clive had signed a 19-year-old singer named Whitney Houston. Now he wanted to add a rock 'n' roll band to the Arista lineup, and he liked what he'd heard of Billy Rancher and the Unreal Gods. He wanted to see them, which he would do later that evening at the Starry Night.

Just before the show, Billy peeked from backstage to see Clive and Neil's silhouetted heads in the roped-off Starry Night balcony. Billy wanted to make sure everything was perfect that night. Billy Triplett was handling the sound, and Keith Cox was ready with a bigger-than-usual light show. The large Starry Night stage gave Billy plenty of room to work. The only thing he didn't think of was changing the order of the set.

The other band members were trying to convince Billy to put all their best songs first, to make sure they blew away Clive early.

"Our fans wouldn't understand if we started with 'Boom Chuck Rock,' when we usually finish with it," Billy said.

"Who gives a fuck?" DuFresne said. "We could go out there and take a shit on the stage and these people are still going to be our fans tomorrow. But none of them runs Arista Records."

Jon had been in enough arguments with Billy to know when he actually had a chance, and when Billy wasn't going to budge. This was one of the times Billy wasn't going to budge.

The band did a nearly three-hour set, finishing with "Boom Chuck Rock." Clive left halfway through the show, and never heard many of the Unreal Gods' best songs.

22 Let's Make a Deal Already

The show for Clive was a success, as best anyone could remember the next morning. Billy, the Unreal Gods and assorted girlfriends, managers, roadies, Malchicks and guys who just came for the beer woke up Monday, August 8th in or around Astrid's house. Astrid and Jack were gone, and Karen was in Mexico. Billy put two and two together and figured there was no reason for anyone to go anywhere, so long as there was water in the swimming pool and beer in the fridge.

The party lasted for two weeks. Jon DuFresne rubbed the sleep out of his eyes one morning (or afternoon maybe, who could tell any more?) and came to the conclusion that life was about to pass him by.

"Enough, enough, enough already," he mumbled to no one in particular. "Let's go back to work. Hey by the way, we're signed right?"

Not exactly.

Milt Olin, the band's Los Angeles lawyer, was trying to work out the details with Arista. Clive Davis' schedule, according to Olin, was to sign Billy by the end of August, find a producer in September, record in LA in October, and release Billy Rancher and the Unreal Gods' first album for Arista in February. Oh, and one more thing: Clive was signing just Billy, not the band. Standard record industry practice, everyone was assured.

Alf Ryder feared the worst, though. In fact, if it hadn't been for a contract the band had signed, forming a corporation, they'd have been left behind, he says. "He was ready to dump the band, but I'd insisted on that contract. If we hadn't had that, we'd have all been up here, and Billy would have been in LA, going, 'Well, I think I'll have Jon come down and play guitar.' The deal was with Billy, but I made it clear to him that if he didn't have the band he was going to be dead in the water."

None of the other Unreal Gods shared Alf's concerns. Dave Stricker, Jon DuFresne and Billy Flaxel were all confident that they were going to LA to make an album, no matter who Arista signed. "Arista liked the songs that we did, as a band," Flaxel says. "Billy wouldn't have done a deal with Arista unless it involved us. Billy always stood very strongly behind the Unreal Gods. There was absolutely no thought at all that he would drop the band."

There was a precedent for Portland bandleaders making personnel changes. Johnny Koonce (Johnny and the Distractions), Marv and Rindy Ross (Quarterflash) and Jeff Lorber (Jeff Lorber Fusion) all shook up their lineups after signing major deals. Shortly after Clive's trip to Portland, Billy made it clear to interviewers Gary Aker of Scene Magazine and Michael Burgess of Multnomah Magazine that he wouldn't be pulling the same trick. "The record company likes our sound, and I made the stipulation when we started talking that the band stays the same," Billy told Burgess.

August came and went, and still Billy was not signed. Patience was never one of Billy's strengths, and he was going crazy waiting for Olin to close the deal. In the meantime, Billy spent a lot of time in record stores with Karen, looking at albums, trying to decide who would be a good producer for the Unreal Gods' sound.

It was more of the same in September and October. Lawyers, managers and record company executives were haggling over the details, with Billy's career on hold until they got it straightened out, and there was nothing he could do about it.

In the meantime, the band played a few shows, but was also spending a lot of time trying to figure out what songs they were going to put on the album.

Clive's favorite Unreal Gods songs were "Police Tol' Me," "Straighten Me Out," "Made in Hong Kong," "Chances Are" and "Rocky Road."

Arista Records president Clive Davis came to Portland to see Billy, then signed him, convinced he'd found an MTV star.
(Bart Danielson)

Billy and the band were working on a new bridge for "Rocky Road." Clive was encouraging Billy to write more "serious rock songs," trying to steer Billy toward the early '80s MTV sound. Songs like "Boom Chuck Rock" and "Symmetry" weren't what Clive was looking for, and there was no way in hell "Go Go Boots" and "Girlfriend's Drawers" were going to be on an Arista record. The only concession to silliness Clive was willing to make was that he liked "Upstroke Down," even if he misinterpreted its meaning. "Clive dug that song because he thought it was some kind of homosexual reference," Billy Flaxel says. "It wasn't at all, it was just about getting your shit together, but we just laughed and said, 'OK, Clive, cool. Whatever you say.' "

Billy's favorite songs always were the lighthearted, silly pop songs. Trying to write songs that sounded like Bryan Adams, or Asia, or Duran Duran bored him, but he was willing to give it a try if that's what Clive thought was best. What it came down to, Clive told Billy, is that he had to come up with one sound, and stick with it. "You can't confuse your audience," he told Billy. Funny, Billy thought. No one at La Bamba ever seemed confused.

Of course, having an American rock 'n' roll band was a new experience for everyone at Arista. The label's biggest American acts were Barry Manilow and Whitney Houston. Its only rock bands were English — Graham Parker and the Rumour, Flock of Seagulls, the Kinks. But Clive knew Billy wrote good songs, even if you had to sift through them to find the ones he thought would work. And he knew he was going to look good on MTV.

Billy was still sitting on "The Police Tol' Me" video, which cost more than $20,000 to produce. Until Arista got involved, the plan had been to release the video, and an album that combined the songs recorded at the Power Station with the ones done at Crystal Studios in LA. Now all that was being delayed while Billy waited for the lawyers to do their jobs, so he could do his.

Finally, in November, Billy signed with Arista. Billy marked the occasion by throwing a party in a suite at the Benson Hotel in Portland. Billy invited all the media. There were TV cameras. Everybody got dressed up, drinks were served. Billy and the Unreal Gods were all interviewed. The event was a top story on the Portland TV news broadcasts that night.

Billy Rancher and the Unreal Gods were about to be stars.

23 Welcome to Arista, Now Change Everything

During the first half of 1984, Billy learned a little bit about how the music business works, which is to say, at a much slower pace than the one he was used to. For the past five years, from the first Malchicks show, Billy had been making things happen. Fast. Need some local press? No problem. Where's Buck Munger's office, anyway? Wanna start a new band? See ya later, Lenny. A few auditions, a couple rehearsals, next thing you know, John Wendeborn's telling the world about the Unreal Gods. Just can't wait to put out that first album? Hey, Jack Barr's got a new studio, and Dr. Flaxel's good for whatever it costs. One, two, three, it's called "Boom Chuck Rock Now!"

Billy made himself the star of late-night TV commericals promoting his band. He turned a Chinese restaurant's lounge into one of the Northwest's hottest rock 'n' roll clubs. He wanted to go to New York, so he went. He recorded at the Power Station. He made a couple of videos. He talked Clive Davis, the most influential record company executive in the world, into coming to Portland to see him play. He wasn't afraid of anything. Billy's attitude was always, "Let's try it."

But now, for the first time in his career, things were out of Billy's control. Signing with Arista meant waiting for Clive Davis to decide who his producer would be, where he would record, when he would record, what songs he would sing. Each time Billy heard from a lawyer or a manager that it was almost time to record, he'd schedule a grand farewell party for the Unreal Gods. It turned into more of a farewell tour.

In February, Billy and the band played farewell gigs at Pine Street and the Last Hurrah. Billy ended a wild show at the Last Hurrah at 2:15 a.m. with a rollicking version of "Money." But the farewell shows didn't really mean farewell. Billy was stuck in Portland, while Arista tried to figure out what kind of music they wanted the Unreal Gods to play.

Finally, a producer was chosen. During their naive strolls through record stores, Billy and Karen probably never stopped to look at "Business as Usual," a 1982 album by Men at Work, an Australian band that hit it big with quirky pop songs like "Who Can It Be Now?" and "Down Under." If they had, they'd have seen the producer's name — Peter McIan. In 1980, McIan, a keyboard player and singer, released an album of his own, a lifeless, synthesizer-heavy, by-the-numbers formulaic collection of love songs recorded by a group of LA studio musicians. Anybody remember Toto? Actually, most of the songs on "Playing Near the Edge" sound like soundtrack rejects, the ones Frank Stallone didn't sing for his brother's movies. McIan produced his own record, and he produced Men at Work. He must have done something right, because "Business as Usual" sold millions of copies.

Billy and the Unreal Gods played a series of farewell shows in Portland before finally leaving for LA in the fall of '84 to record an album.
(Bart Danielson)

But Men at Work was a different type of band than Billy Rancher and the Unreal Gods. For starters, Men at Work was a terrible live act, and was content to spend most of its time in the studio. The lack of a decent live show no doubt eventually hastened Men at Work's quick descent into rock 'n' roll oblivion. The Unreal Gods, on the other hand, were at their best live, thriving on the energy between band and audience. Still, no one could argue with McIan's success, and besides, Clive said Peter McIan was the producer, so Peter McIan was the producer.

On April 13th and 14th, McIan was in Portland to watch the band during yet another farewell weekend, a couple of shows at Lung Fung. Lenny's band, the Pipsqueaks, back from Hawaii, opened the shows. Then Billy and the Unreal Gods played their usual sets. They were good shows, well received, as always, by their enthusiastic fans. But the band clearly was nervous with McIan watching. What did he want? Why was he here? Was he going to replace some of the band? McIan suggested a few changes, then Billy set about putting together a demo tape of new songs, and new versions of old songs, like "Rocky Road" with a new bridge.

"I really didn't like that tape," Dave Stricker says. "Peter had come to Portland a few times and was working with us, but they wanted a little bit of a formula, where certain things have to be in each song. 'Rocky Road' is just the same thing over and over, but there are dynamics to that song that make it work, but Peter thought it needed these other parts. We took parts of other songs, and were screwing around with the arrangements. These were good songs, and we were changing them. I don't think anything good really came from that."

Other than the premature farewell shows, the Unreal Gods weren't playing much in '84. Billy was writing new songs, and the rest of the time would be spent rehearsing at a warehouse he had rented on 28th and Belmont. It was a confusing time for the band, which had kept itself busy for three years with non-stop shows. Shows paid the bills, and without them, the Unreal Gods were broke, bored and wondering when they were ever going to get to LA to start recording.

The delay was caused by Arista, and Peter McIan, who wanted to be sure of what they were getting when they got into the studio. What they were getting was a truly original band that was incredibly exciting in a live environment, performing songs written by Billy that didn't fit neatly into one style. Arista was trying to figure out how to market the band. Should the focus be almost exclusively on Billy, turning him into a Billy Idol or Bryan Adams clone? Was it a pop band, like Duran Duran or Human League? Could they make more of a heavy sound, like Van

Halen? What was emerging on the tape Billy and the band were putting together sounded an awful lot like The Fixx, a popular MTV band of the time that was headed for the same fate as Men at Work. The truth is, Arista shouldn't have tried to make Billy Rancher and the Unreal Gods look, or sound, like anyone else. But that's what record companies do, no matter how much success Billy had in Portland, or how much anybody loved him at La Bamba and Lung Fung. And if this was confusing for Arista, or Peter McIan, it was worse for the band.

As if they didn't have enough to worry about, Arista told Billy they weren't sure they liked the name Unreal Gods. Billy got a good laugh out of that one. He had no intention of changing the name of the band, but thought it might be fun to float a few rumors out there, anyway. The Unreal Gods, at one time or another, were going to change their name to the A-Men, the Magicians, or the Hands, according to the local music press. But Billy had a bigger problem. What kind of music was Arista looking for?

Some bands, or musicians, are blessed (or cursed, depending on your point of view) with one style. Maybe all the songs sound the same, but at least a record company knows what to do with them.

What was so great about Billy Rancher and the Unreal Gods was that they could play any style.

Jim Basnight, who fronted Seattle's Moberleys, was a Billy Rancher fan who saw many of his shows in Seattle.

"At the time, a lot of the Seattle bands were a little too straightforward and mainstream to really capture the imagination of the people," Basnight says. "Everybody was getting by doing stuff that was familiar. But Billy had a real unique style, even his stage rap. He'd say really controversial things, get into a stream of consciousness thing on stage. And he brought a lot of unpredictable musical styles. Others were worried about finding their one place in the market, but not Billy. He would jump all over the place. One song, it was like the Stones, then it was reggae, then something spacy. That's what was so cool about it. And he just kept getting better, every time I saw him. He continued to grow, to expand."

Now Arista was asking Billy to pick a style and stay with it.

"Billy really wanted to do all the reggae stuff, the ska sound, the cornball stuff," Jon DuFresne says. "That's what he really liked. And the record company's going, 'Hold it, what's this, My Girlfriend's Drawers? Get rid of that song. You guys have to grow up now and be a real band. Sure, you had your little local thing, but you've got to approach this like you're going to conquer the world, you've got to meet the marketplace.' Billy was very resistant to that. He'd say things like, 'I'm going to teach Clive Davis what a hit is.' He was very cocky. It was one thing to be cocky to the local press in the early days, but we were dealing now with professionals in the music industry, and that kind of attitude just didn't wash. But that's why it took so long to get into the studio, because Billy was writing all of these obscure songs. The band was feeling like, 'What the fuck's going on? Why aren't we playing?' We all had no money, and we were getting depressed."

So instead of making money by playing live shows, the band spent most of its time rehearsing in the warehouse. For the rest of the Unreal Gods, practicing all the time was starting to feel like a chore. Another day, another rehearsal. And Billy was becoming more of a boss, which, after three years together, was wearing thin with the rest of the band.

Rehearsals started to disintigrate. Billy was drinking a lot of beer during the rehearsals. Some nights, Jon DuFresne or Alf Ryder would get pissed off at Billy and leave. Other nights, Billy Flaxel and Dave Stricker would just sneak out as the session began to fall apart.

There were nights that ended with just Billy and Jon in the big warehouse, Billy trying to teach Jon a new song, but unable to play it himself because he was so drunk. "It was sad," Jon says, "but you couldn't really talk to him. Billy was a very powerful talker. He had a way of shooting you down immediately. I remember a lot of times, trying to talk to him about things, telling him to relax and not be such an idiot. He'd always tell me, 'Oh, don't get your tits in a bind,' or 'Don't worry about it, everything's going to work out.' "

Then there was the matter of the new songs.

"Billy was trying to write these more mature songs, but he wanted to approach it like the earlier songs, which we could learn in a minute and they'd be done," DuFresne says. "But these songs required more finesse, and he didn't really have the patience to work on them. That was very frustrating. Billy could be the coolest person in a way, but he could also make life a living hell. You could do things the easy way, and make them happen, or you could do it the hard way, and Billy always did things the hard way. I think Billy had really become corrupted by the whole stardom thing. I think he really let things go to his head."

Others had noticed. Back in the early days, Billy was the kind of guy who would help David Jester haul his video equipment. At one of the infrequent Portland shows after Billy had signed with Arista, Jester asked Billy if he could grab some equipment. After all, he was recording the show for free, as usual. "Hey, I'm the star," Billy told him. "Carry your own fucking gear, I don't do that anymore."

"He'd beaten cancer, he was going to be a star, and he just kind of ignored all the local people," Jester says. "His head was up his butt. It was amazing to me, to watch this sweet person turning into a superstar asshole."

Stricker, Billy's true, blue friend from the Malchicks days, was more forgiving.

"It was just a real intense period, because we wanted to cross the finish line, to record that album," he says. "For me, I kind of appreciate having someone who's driving the thing. Sure, he was being a little more difficult, but he was just being the boss."

Maybe fame had gone to Billy's head, but he was feeling a lot of pressure at this time. Pressure from Arista, and McIan to come up with a marketable sound. And pressure to keep the band together. Rehearsals, when he could talk everyone into showing up, weren't much fun. Any money they'd made had been spent on new equipment for everyone — Fender Stratocaster guitars for Billy, an amp system for DuFresne, a bass guitar for Stricker, a Koa drum set for Billy Flaxel and some synthesizer toys for Alf Ryder. Alf was playing solo shows at The Metro in Portland. Billy played a show without the Unreal Gods in Eugene, opening for T-Bone Burnett. Jon DuFresne and a standup bassist had been gigging at Tony DeMicoli's new club, Key Largo, as Young Johnny Guitar, playing Gene Vincent and Elvis songs. A drummer had been added, and there were dates scheduled at the Elks Club. *Jesus, we've got to get to LA. If we can just get to LA, everything will be OK.*

On May 12th, it was time for another farewell show, and this time they meant it. The Unreal Gods played at the Starry Night for their last show in Portland before leaving for LA. It was another typically energetic show. Billy's loyal fans wouldn't leave without an encore. They clapped, and screamed, and hollered until Billy ran back onto the large Starry Night stage. With sweat dripping from his blond hair, and through the pajama top he was wearing, Billy promised another song. "But first

I've got a question for you," he shouted to the dancers in front of the stage, and to the rest of the overflow crowd in the balcony. Billy asked the crowd what kinds of songs they thought should be on the album. Why not? Everybody else seemed to have an opinion. First, he asked what they thought of the hard rock sound on some of the new songs, like "Social Will Call," and "Shortage of Variety." Or the tremolo guitar of "Uptown," and "All the Way." And then there was the old boom chuck rhythm of "Boom Chuck Rock," and "Upstroke Down." Billy's fans, unfortunately, weren't any more help than Peter McIan or Clive Davis, but for a different reason. They loved all of Billy's songs, and cheered each of the choices. Billy might have shown his preference when he kicked the band into an absolutely joyous romp through "Symmetry." It felt just like the summer of 1981 again.

In June, Billy Rancher and the Unreal Gods finally left for LA to make a record. All of them, including Billy, were a little shaken by the musical confusion, and the meddling Arista had done. All they were really sure of was that they were about to make it.

Buck Munger remembers the day Billy left Portland, and he couldn't have been prouder if Billy had been his own son. "We were sending him off to the big time."

24 Lost in LA

Billy had been to Los Angeles before he arrived in July of 1984 to record an album for Arista. He was born there, in fact, 27 years earlier. And he'd taken the Unreal Gods to LA early in '83 to record with Joe Delia at Crystal Studios. They'd been back to make a video for "The Police Tol' Me" shortly after that, and there were a couple trips to meet with all the lawyers and managers and accountants during the past year. Of course, this was the first time Billy had been in LA as a Major Recording Star. And it all looked better to him now. From his fancy condo, Billy hardly noticed any smog or congestion. LA was about to become his playground.

The Oakwood Apartments in Van Nuys were a long way from Malchick Manor, or the first Unreal Gods house, or any other dilapidated warehouse or crummy apartment Billy had called home lately. There were fences, and security guards, a sauna and a swimming pool. And, Billy couldn't help but notice, a lot of lovely, tanned bodies in bikinis hanging out at the pool.

Karen didn't go to LA, staying instead with her parents in Lake Oswego. Billy and Karen's perfect relationship wasn't looking quite so perfect lately, thanks to a couple of Karen's habits that were really starting to get on Billy's nerves. For one thing, she had the nerve not to always do exactly what Billy wanted her to do, whenever he wanted her to do it. She had been in Mexico for her cousin's wedding when Clive Davis came to Portland, and now she wasn't going to be staying in LA when they started to record. And Karen wasn't as forgiving of Billy's affairs as he assumed she would be, or that she should be. Billy, to be fair, had sex with very few of the women who had thrown themselves in his path during the past four years. The way Billy saw it, he'd turned away opportunities on a daily basis that most guys could only dream of, and so what if he had given in to temptation a few times. He loved Karen. He only slept with those other girls. Karen, however, saw faithfulness as a two-way street. Besides, it wasn't like Billy was the only good-looking one with other opportunities in the relationship. Maybe Karen wasn't a rock star, but she was pretty, and smart. She also had a notion that being in love meant giving yourself completely to one person, and just to that person. It was an idea Billy was having more and more trouble with.

Billy was always a willing photo subject.
(Mark Rabiner)

After a few days of shopping for rock 'n' roll clothes, relaxing by the pool and wrestling matches in the rooms that were so rowdy security guards were called in, the band headed into the studio to start making a record. Westlake Audio, at 8447 Beverly Boulevard in West Hollywood, didn't look like much from the outside, a one-story stucco building with plain-looking wood slats on the front. But it was one of the hottest studios in the business. Michael Jackson recorded "Thriller" there. This was the big time. And right away, everyone noticed something was different. Billy wasn't in charge anymore.

When the Unreal Gods recorded "Boom Chuck Rock Now!", when

they played live, when there were band meetings and business dealings, when they went to New York and when they made videos, booked clubs or decided where to eat dinner, Billy had been running the show, from day one. Now producer Peter McIan was the boss, and Billy was finding that hard to get used to. Billy wasn't going to be able to get his favorite songs, the reggae and ska-influenced stuff, on the album. Arista was pushing the hard rock, the early '80s MTV sound. Billy's songs "Made in Hong Kong," "Three Kilometers Down," "Police Tol' Me" and "Thinkin' Zebra" were to be recorded, plus the awful new version of "Rocky Road" and even a Bryan Adams-like song that Clive Davis had suggested. The band's sound was changing, and what life, and fun, was left in the songs was being sucked out by McIan's heavy-handed production.

"I wanted to like Peter McIan, so at the time I liked him," Jon DuFresne says. "But in retrospect, it was just such a slow pace. He was so anal about everything. He really turned us into something we weren't. It's the proverbial story: They sign you for what you are, then immediately change you into something you're not. We didn't really know how to play the game, so we just went along with it."

Actually, Billy did his best not to go along with anything. He had his artistic vision, and it sure wasn't the same one Peter McIan had. The problem was, Billy didn't win any arguments with McIan or Clive Davis, which meant he usually ended up doing things their way in the end, and having a bad attitude while he did it.

The band was just trying to get to the end of the tunnel before the train flattened them.

"I remember we were all thinking, 'God, let's get this done and have some success so we can get on with our lives,' " DuFresne says. "We were starting to think that Billy would get rid of us sooner or later, anyway, so let's just try to get through this record, try to cash in. It was pretty crazy. Clive brought us these really schlocky songs, but I just said, 'I don't care, we'll do them, let's just get on with it. We can't be in a holding pattern forever.' We were tired, and the magic was pretty much gone, but we were just trying to hang in there for our big payday."

Billy and Peter's relationship was deteriorating daily, further slowing the process. Some of the Unreal Gods were willing to work with McIan, just to get the record done. "We'll do what we want to do on our next album," was their theory. It's not one that Billy was buying, which caused some problems, especially between Billy and Jon. One day, as they were driving away from the studio after yet another interrupted and unproductive day of recording, Billy and Jon got into an argument. The conflict was Jon's desire to go along with Arista and with Peter McIan, and just get the damn record done and Billy's insistence that his way was the best way, and, in fact, the only way. "You have to give up some control," Jon told Billy. "You see? You see what's happening here? You can't always run everything. Just go along, and we'll call the shots on our next record." Billy was having none of it, in fact was in a particularly obnoxious mood, and the argument ended with Jon smacking Billy on the back of the head. They really needed to get the record done.

Karen decided to visit, which lightened the mood a little.

"It was pretty much boys camp for them down there," Karen says. "They'd wrecked a rental car, furniture had been thrown around the apartment. They were plugging holes in the wall with toothpaste. I told them, 'That's not going to work.' They slowed down a little bit while I was there, though."

Having Karen around put Billy in a better frame of mind. He could talk to her about his problems with Peter McIan. Billy spent every minute he had outside the studio with Karen. He showed her around LA, and a night at the Comedy Store on Sunset Boulevard helped Billy forget any problems he was having. The band took a few days off during Karen's stay. Things were looking up for Billy. But after a week in LA, Karen went home to Portland, and Billy returned to the studio to face the same old problems, and a couple new ones, just to make things interesting.

Problem No. 1 was Peter McIan. Alf Ryder didn't like McIan for many reasons, not the least of which was the fact that McIan, a keyboard player, was constantly criticizing Alf, then playing the parts himself if he didn't like the way Alf played them. Alf also resented the fact that his brothers Joe, Frank and Matti weren't involved any more. The Unreal Gods stayed with Matti during the New York adventure in the fall of '82, and Matti set up a chance to play with Bruce Springsteen, even though Billy blew that. Joe produced the Power Station recordings on that trip, the best work the band had ever done in a studio. And Frank directed the "Police Tol' Me" video, which would be playing on MTV by now except that Arista was holding that up. Alf was developing a hatred for everything Hollywood, and to him Peter McIan represented the worst of the corporate machine that was suffocating Billy Rancher and the Unreal Gods.

"Peter McIan put the band down, he changed the lyrics," Alf says. "They infuriate me, the whole big record company scene. I think they suck, period. They love to get jokers in from out of town who were popular because they were real, then whip them into shape. 'Can you play every note the way I tell you to play it?' That's their test. I'm like, 'Fuck you.' I'd bang my fist on the keyboard halfway through a song just to piss him off. That producer could have made it a success if he wanted to, but he didn't. All he wanted to do was show what a bunch of hicks we were, collect his bucks and move on to the next project. He didn't give a shit about the band, and neither did the company."

Jon DuFresne liked McIan better before the band got to LA.

"He was OK when he came to Portland to watch us," he says. "When we went to LA, it changed. He treated us like we didn't know shit, to the point of not even telling us what was going on."

One comment McIan made to Jon provided some insight into the slow pace of the sessions. "I remember he told me that you've got to make it cost a lot in the studio. 'The more it costs to make, the more the label will spend to promote it,' he told me."

The mistake McIan and Arista were making was focusing on Billy's voice, instead of the band's total sound. Of course, they didn't know any better. Arista's big stars were Barry Manilow, Melissa Manchester and Whitney Houston. All Clive Davis knew was that Billy Rancher was a good-looking kid from whom he might be able to squeeze out a few MTV hits.

"It's the shotgun theory with these big record companies," Alf says. "You get 20 acts, throw them into the hopper, and see what comes out the other end. The greatest thing about our band was that it was totally natural. We just went out and did it, and they proceeded to tear it all apart. Look at Peter McIan's last project before he worked with us. Men at Work. A shitty performance band. That wasn't us. The only reason it wasn't working is that the producer wouldn't buy Billy's vocals. He was pressuring him on the vocal shit like he was Barbra Streisand or something. I could have produced Billy and made it sound great. They didn't want him to come out. They wanted to chew him up and spit his ass out, and that's what they did."

"Arista was the wrong label, and Peter McIan was the wrong producer," DuFresne says. "The whole thing got off track when William Gladstone was shopping us as Billy, not as a band. Then he gets us signed, and says, 'Hey, I told you I'd get you signed, and you're signed.' He didn't give a shit who it was with."

Billy and the band were confused and more than a little disillusioned. But they were still in the studio, which meant there was still hope they were going to get an album recorded. Whether anyone would recognize it as the Unreal Gods was another matter.

"We had to so some song that Clive Davis forced on us," Alf says. "It was so unlike our band, and they just shoved it down our throats. I'd rather be a fucking nobody the rest of my life than eat that kind of shit."

That's about the way Billy saw it, too. DuFresne, Stricker and Flaxel were more willing to go along with Arista.

"As we got further and further into this, we saw how much of our say was being ripped away from us to work with people of this stature," Flaxel says. "So we're starting to compromise. Billy took it hard, harder than we did. We wanted to do it. We felt that if we just did it, we could roll the dice at a later date. That turned out to be a disaster, which has been a big lesson in my life. Our music was fun, then it became a business. It was becoming someone else's interpretation of our music. Instantly, it turned out not to be fun, it turned out to be an alteration of our music."

Cheryl Hodgson is an entertainment lawyer in Los Angeles. In the '80s, she worked in Portland, and knew all about Billy Rancher and the Unreal Gods, having represented John Flaxel in his deal with Billy. She met with William Gladstone before Billy hired him as the band's manager. She watched as Billy signed with Arista, and wondered why. And she wasn't surprised when she heard what was going on at the recording session in LA.

"Arista was a bad label choice for the band," Hodgson says. "Arista might have been a good record company for Whitney Houston, but they've never been good with rock bands. The label, and the producer, couldn't have been much worse for Billy. But he made the same mistake a lot of people do. They endow people in this business with all these attributes they don't have, and don't deserve. It's the expert myth. You assume other people know more than you. Well, there are more idiots with six-figure incomes in the record business than in any business

I've ever seen. It's rampant in this industry. I'm sure what they thought was, 'Well, it's Clive Davis, he must know what producer we should use.' Clive Davis might be great at Whitney Houston, but he didn't know shit about boom chuck rock, and I'm sure he'd be the first to agree. But because he's who he was, because the record company was what it was, they went along with it. Billy didn't say 'This is who I want, and this is why.' So he got Peter McIan."

And Peter McIan made the mistake of trying to make Billy Rancher something he wasn't. He wasn't Bryan Adams or Jon Bon Jovi, and the Unreal Gods weren't some flash in the pan band like Men at Work or The Fixx. If McIan really thought he had to turn Billy into someone else, he'd have been better off using Buddy Holly as the model: *Fair guitar player and singer. Writes great songs that make people want to sing along and dance.* All Billy would have had to do then was be himself.

Billy probably had enough to worry about just trying to get this record done, but now he had a few more problems. For starters, his relationship with Karen was slipping away. She was dating another guy back home, and there was nothing Billy could do about it until he could return to Portland.

"We were having some problems, and I took a few trips with this other guy while Billy was in LA," Karen says. "We were playing games with each other."

If that wasn't bad enough, Billy could always count on his management situation to make life a little tougher. William Gladstone, who never did much for the band anyway, had been fired, leaving Billy without a manager for the time being. And he could have used one. Billy owed money to John Flaxel and Fritz Johnson. He'd signed a deal with Joe Delia, giving him the right to produce any project undertaken by Billy Rancher and the Unreal Gods. Delia filed a lawsuit to attempt to stop Billy from recording with Arista.

"I remember Peter McIan just freaking out one day," Jon DuFresne says. "He's screaming, 'I can't work with you any more. I just got served these papers.'"

That legal fiasco was worked out, but another was right behind it. William Gladstone, a little steamed, apparently, that his services were no longer desired, sued Billy Rancher and the Unreal Gods for $25 million.

Let's see ... I hate my producer, my girlfriend's seeing someone else, I'm in contracts up to my ass with people whose names I can't even remember, and my former manager just sued me for 25 million dollars. Could anything else go wrong?

Well, there were the constant delays in the recording session. In fact, they'd reached a point by early September that the Unreal Gods were sent home. The bass and drum parts were basically done on a few songs, and any keyboard parts that weren't finished, Peter McIan could play himself. But McIan still wasn't satisfied with Billy's vocals. McIan told the rest of the band that he needed to work with Billy, and there was no sense in them sticking around for now. Go home, he told them, we'll mix the vocals, then you guys will come back down to finish the record. That was the last time Billy Flaxel, Alf Ryder or Dave Stricker saw the inside of Westlake Audio. Billy and Jon stayed on for another week to work on vocal and guitar parts. Billy and Jon were back and forth, between Portland and LA, a few times the rest of the month. They'd work with Peter McIan in the studio for a week, go home and play Unreal Gods shows in Portland for a week, then head back to the studio. Nobody knew exactly what Arista had while this was going on, but everyone could agree on one thing: It wasn't a finished record.

"We didn't play our cards right," DuFresne says. "We had a shot at it. But we were preoccupied with too many other things, like gigs, fighting with our manager, and Billy making sure he was treated a certain way. Billy's arrogance, and ego didn't help."

On one of the trips home to Portland, Billy decided he was going to put things straight with Karen.

"Notice anything different?" he asked, stripping off his shirt.

She pretended not to, but she saw it. Her name, Karen Marie, was tattooed on his right shoulder.

"He was trying to make up," she says. "I just thought, 'Oh, come on.' He was trying to prove he was loyal, which everyone knew wasn't the case anyway. I was not impressed."

With Billy and Karen's relationship in a precarious form of limbo, Billy and Jon headed back to LA to work with Peter McIan, with the hope of finishing the vocal and guitar parts on this trip. They were no longer staying at the luxurious Oakwood Apartments, but at the Hyatt Hotel on Sunset Boulevard, famous for the parties thrown by Led Zeppelin in the '70s and nicknamed The Riot House. Each morning, Billy and Jon trudged off to Westlake Audio. Jon was happy with his guitar work. In fact, he did some of Billy's rhythm parts, too. Billy still was having a hard time making his voice sound exactly like Peter McIan thought it should. And now he was sick, which wasn't helping any. Billy and Jon had gone to Tijuana on one of their weekend breaks from recording, and Billy made the mistake of sampling some of the fine local cuisine.

"Man, I think I've got food poisoning," he told Jon after they got back to LA.

"He didn't feel good after the trip to Mexico," DuFresne says. "I figured the stress was getting to him."

Stress usually doesn't cause a softball-sized lump in your stomach, such as the one Billy discovered one afternoon relaxing by the pool. It had been almost three years since he'd been diagnosed with cancer and had surgery to remove one testicle and 63 lymph nodes. The surgery had been a success, and examinations the following 10 months didn't show any traces of cancer. He hadn't worried about it for more than two years. Billy called Stephen Kimberley, a Portland doctor who had never actually been Billy's physician, but had become a close and trusted friend.

"Get back up here and we'll test you and find out what's wrong," Kimberley told Billy. "Don't worry about it."

Don't worry about it. Easy for him to say.

25 The End of the Unreal Gods

Billy returned to Portland, and was seen on the first day of October by Dr. David Paull, who had performed the surgeries in 1981. Dr. Paull ordered X-Rays and ran some tests, and conferred with Rebecca Orwoll, an oncologist with an office at the hematology clinic next door to Providence Medical Center. The doctors told Billy they'd let him know as soon as they had the results. But Billy had a pretty good idea what was coming. Food poisoning, or stress, didn't give you lumps in your stomach. Cancer did.

The Unreal Gods, devastated and demoralized by their experience in LA, hoped to find themselves again by playing in Portland. Billy and the band played a few shows, and Billy didn't let anyone know about the tests he'd had at Dr. Paull's office. No sense scaring anyone yet.

Billy got the news on a Saturday afternoon in Karen's apartment in Eugene. Karen was just two terms away from graduating from the University of Oregon, and she had started fall term classes in Eugene. Billy and Karen and their friends Fritz Johnson and Mo Stevenson were relaxing in the apartment, just a few hours before an Unreal Gods show, when Dr. Orwoll called.

"The cancer's back, Billy," she said.

Billy sighed, and looked at Karen. "I know."

The last thing Billy wanted to do that night was play, but he did. He didn't want the band to drive all the way to Eugene for nothing. Besides, it might be awhile before he played again.

Billy didn't want to go through cancer treatments alone, and wanted to resolve his problems with Karen. She had been dating someone else while Billy had been in LA ("Billy was pretty jealous," she says), but she still loved Billy. She just wasn't in a real forgiving mood, particularly of Billy's affair with a Portland woman.

"This girl had gone around with everybody, including Billy, and I had always known this had happened," Karen says.

The woman visited Billy frequently at the studio apartment he was living in near Portland's Rose Garden. In fact, she had moved nearby to make her trips to see him more convenient. Sometimes Karen was there when she dropped by, sometimes she wasn't.

"It was driving me crazy," Karen says. "I was kind of seeing someone else, but I was just disgusted by the way the whole thing was turning out. Billy says, 'Why don't you go talk to her?' So I did."

A few days after they found out Billy's cancer was back, Karen went to Key Largo, Tony DeMicoli's downtown club, to have it out with the woman.

"Listen, Billy really loves you," she told Karen. "I want you to take care of him."

In the Sage family, emotional outbursts were rare, if not unheard of. Demure, in fact, is a word that comes to mind when describing Karen. But this was too much, especially with the news of Billy's cancer returning. What right did this woman have saying something like that to her?

"Where have you been the last five years when I've been taking care of him, honey?" Karen screamed.

Billy sat back, watching the incident, amused. His arms were crossed, a big smile on his face.

"I'm sure he was loving it," Karen says.

And Billy and Karen were together. "We kind of dropped everything when Billy got sick again," Karen says. "All the stupid little problems we had kind of dissolved, and reality hit. It's like, 'What really matters here?'"

Once the results were back, Astrid took Billy to see Dr. Orwoll. The doctor told Billy and Astrid that heavy doses of chemotherapy could make the tumor in Billy's stomach shrink. Then surgery would be scheduled, and Dr. Paull would remove what was left of the tumor. She told them that the 12 weeks of chemotherapy treatments would be brutal, and that side effects would include hair loss and nausea. She also explained that it was Billy's only realistic chance of beating cancer.

Astrid dropped Billy at Providence at 7 a.m. for his first treatment, then headed off to work at the Sky Chef restaurant at the Portland airport, where she was a hostess. Billy was taken to a room he shared with another half-dozen cancer patients. Billy, like the others, was placed in a reclining chair. A nurse strapped a thick rubber tubing around his right biceps muscle. Billy was asked to open and close his fist rapidly, producing a vein for the nurse to force in a 2-inch long IV needle. He leaned back in the recliner and watched the drugs rush into his body. Within minutes, he could feel his insides tingling. The needle stayed in his arm for 10 hours. When it was over, he could barely get out of the chair, or stand up, he was so weak, and sick, from the treatment. As Astrid drove him home, Billy asked her to pull over so he could vomit.

Billy's treatment alternated five straight days of the 10-hour sessions, then two weeks off to recover, for 12 weeks. After his first week of treatment, Billy woke up one morning and found clumps of blond hair on his pillow. Astrid and Karen were told Billy would have to be monitored for infections, because the chemotherapy would change his platelet count. Any fever was a real danger sign, Karen was told.

On November 5th, his fever shot up, and Astrid and Karen rushed Billy to Providence Medical Center. He required transfusions to get his fever down, and had to stay in the hospital for six nights.

The Unreal Gods, meanwhile, weren't sure what to do, so they kept playing. The four of them convinced themselves it was a chance to grow as performers, to write and sing their own songs. And besides, they needed to make money somehow. It was a miserable failure.

"It was a stupid idea," Alf Ryder says. "We shouldn't have done it at all. We played for a couple of months, but there was no way that was going to work, and we knew it."

Jon DuFresne: "The shows were horrible. That was the lowest low. We kept saying, 'It's OK, we'll just do this until Billy gets back. He'll be back.' But we didn't really know if he would be. We were just playing for the money, basically. It just didn't work. It was, 'Let's just get through these shows so we can pay the rent for another month.' That was really a tough time."

Midway through his chemo treatments, Billy made his first public appearance, playing at a John Lennon memorial show December 7th in Portland. Billy was one of the last performers, taking the stage at 10:30 p.m. in front of 2,500 fans at the Arlene Schnitzer Concert Hall. He cradled a blue acoustic guitar with arms and hands that were constantly sore. He wore a $55 women's wig in an unsuccessful attempt to hide the fact that he'd lost his hair. He had also lost a lot of weight. Blisters on the inside of his mouth made speaking painful. Of course, for Billy, the only thing more painful would be not speaking. He started by telling the crowd about his trip to Los Angeles.

"... then one day I was out by the pool lying on my back, and I noticed my stomach, instead of being flat, kind of rose like a little hill. I thought it might be some scar tissue. I didn't say anything to anybody, but when I came back to Portland to play a couple of live engagements, I had a checkup. I found I had cancer."

By now, anyone close to Billy, and most of the Portland music community knew. From those in the crowd that night who didn't know came an audible gasp when Billy told them.

Then he strummed the A, D and G chords of the Beatles' "In My Life," dedicating the song to Karen. The next Monday, he was back at Providence for another round of chemotherapy treatments.

Billy was interviewed by Tom Hallman Jr. of The Oregonian newspaper six weeks into the treatments. "It hurts when the needle goes in, because it scrapes the vein," Billy told Hallman. "And all day long I have a needle in my arm. When I try to sleep at night, my body feels like it's being pressed from the inside out. It's tough on the body and I admire and respect the older patients in here because it must be even harder on them."

In the same story, Rebecca Orwoll said she was hopeful of a full recovery for Billy. "Dr. David Paull and I feel we've caught it early, and that's good. We're hoping for the best, and hoping for a cure. There is a high cure rate in cases like this. A lot of people hear the word cancer, and think it's all over. That's not always the case."

If chemotherapy wasn't enough to worry about, Billy still had the $25 million William Gladstone lawsuit hanging over his head.

Billy hired a law firm in Santa Monica, California, coming up with a

$20,000 retainer to represent him and the band against Gladstone. The firm filed an answer, but didn't pursue a defense, then told Billy he'd need to come up with some more money for them to continue their efforts, such as they were. Problem is, there wasn't any more money. Billy wasn't currently making any, and the medical costs were sucking up any money he did have. (Astrid's medical insurance, which she decided to buy as a Christmas gift for Billy a few years earlier because she didn't know what kind of clothes to get for him anymore, was coming in handy. The chemo treatments cost more than $1,500 per visit, and there was another surgery that would have to be performed. The insurance covered 80 percent of the medical costs.)

Fritz Johnson, on Billy's behalf, went to see his good friend, attorney Cheryl Hodgson.

"Billy was sick, there was no money, the band wasn't playing ... it was a tragic situation," Hodgson remembers. "Fritz asked me to take a look at the file."

She talked to Billy, then met with the rest of the Unreal Gods at her Portland home. She remembers a great deal of dissension within the group. Billy was the one who had hired and fired William Gladstone after all, so why were they all being sued? Hodgson patiently explained that the fact of the matter is that anyone can be sued for anything, and that this particular suit was just as groundless against Billy as it was against the rest of the band.

"I didn't feel like there was a lot of loyalty with a couple members of the band," she says. "Quite frankly, it was rather appalling."

Hodgson's husband found Alf Ryder to be so obnoxious he wanted to throw him out of the house. Cheryl talked him out of it, though she was no less disgusted by what she viewed as Alf's selfish attitude.

Eventually, Hodgson found a way to get the suit dismissed, using the California artist manager statute. Loosely translated from legalese into English, the statute prohibits anyone who does business as a talent agent from also engaging in booking agreements. Hodgson found a letter in which Gladstone had agreed to help the band get bookings. Gladstone lived in California, and the suit was filed in federal court in California, therefore the statute applied. Hodgson flew to LA, filed a motion to dismiss for summary judgment and had the case thrown out of court. A judge never had the opportunity to listen to William Gladstone explain why his dismissal as the Unreal Gods' manager was worth 25 million bucks.

Of course, Billy still didn't have a manager, which he could have used to sort out some messy business deals and financial commitments that involved Arista, Dr. Flaxel, Joe Delia and Fritz Johnson, among others. At least he was going to get a chance to play soon.

Billy's last chemo treatment was January 15th, and he was scheduled for surgery on February 7th. In-between, he planned to play a few gigs with the Unreal Gods. He was still weak, and had barely been able to play his guitar at all during the chemo treatments. But the return of Billy Rancher and the Unreal Gods was scheduled for Saturday, January 26th at the Starry Night in Portland.

Not long into the show, Billy started to feel tired, and sent the band into an extended reggae jam, which wasn't as demanding physically as the usual high-energy Unreal Gods songs. A reggae set isn't what Billy Flaxel had in mind that night, though.

"I know now that he did it because he just didn't have the energy to keep it up," Flaxel says. "But at the time, I was fed up. I was really frustrated anyway by what had happened in LA, and the fact that we weren't moving as fast as I wanted us to. The whole thing had been laid out for us, then we kept getting things pulled out from under us. I was pissed, and when Billy started this reggae thing I just didn't dig it. I was a young kid, and I was saying, 'Come on, let's rock.' I'd had enough."

Flaxel tossed his drumsticks down and walked off the stage. The only thing left for Billy Rancher to do was to sit down behind the drum set and start playing. When he did, Flaxel ran back on stage, grabbed a microphone and started singing.

"Through all the time together, other people in the band would bitch about things, but they'd never really stand up to Billy," Jon DuFresne says. "I felt that I did stand up to Billy a lot. Not that it ever did me any good, but at least I wasn't carrying around this big ball of anger. Billy was always directing the band on stage, which can be a little embarrassing. When he started doing that to Billy Flaxel, he just quit, walked off the stage. Talk about airing your dirty laundry in public."

It was an ugly end for Billy Rancher and the Unreal Gods.

26 Helping One of Their Own

Portland's best bands and musicians came together on February 3rd, 1985. Quarterflash. Nu Shooz. The Dan Reed Network. Johnny Koonce. The Crazy Eights, a rocking reggae outfit heavy on the horns, played an awesome set. But the reason the Starry Night was overfilled to nearly twice its capacity of 812, to the point, in fact, that the Portland Fire Bureau cited the club, was to honor a hometown hero.

Midway through the evening, Starry Night owner Larry Hurwitz walked to the center of the big stage. "Put your hands together for the star tonight ... Billy Rancher."

Billy strode confidently to the microphone, blowing kisses and waving to the crowd. The effects of the chemotherapy treatments, which he had completed two and a half weeks earlier, were obvious. He was wearing a wig to hide the fact that his stringy blond hair had all fallen out. He didn't have any hair where his eyebrows used to be. He was scheduled for surgery four days later to remove the cancerous tumor the doctors had found four months earlier. Still, he managed to look happy, and very much alive. This was show business, after all, and Billy always knew what to do on stage.

Wearing a bright yellow shirt and a multicolored, checkered suit, Billy waited for the warm applause to subside. It didn't, so he started talking anyway, which managed to quiet the crowd. He thanked his brother Lenny, who had come up with the idea for the benefit to help cover some of Billy's medical expenses. Lenny pitched the plan, and Larry Hurwitz made it happen, getting all of Portland's best musicians to play for free. Lenny's band, the Pipsqueaks, performed.

"This is really going to help someone very important to me, my mother," Billy said. He pointed in the crowd to Astrid, who came to the show with Billy in a limo. Billy talked about the bills that had been incurred during his illness. His tone was matter-of-fact, with no trace of self pity.

He thanked the Portland music community, which clearly had done itself proud in this effort to help one of its own. Several of the bands that played that night were major label stars, with Top 40 hits to their credit, and national tours to make. But they were there on this night for Billy.

"Tonight, I feel like it's one big band," Billy told the crowd. "It's a band of people who came here to watch, it's a band of 10 groups who played. It's just one big band. That's a special feeling."

Many of Billy's friends, fans, and fellow musicians cried as they listened.

"I'd also like to thank the Unreal Gods, my four band members who have been very supportive," Billy said. Either Billy was being extremely gracious, or, more likely, four years together outweighed the events of the past few months, during which time supportive is not exactly the word you would have used to describe the behavior of a few of the band members.

The benefit was a genuine expression of compassion by Portland's music scene, generating a high energy level on and off stage. The show was seen by everyone who was anyone, including the Rose City's favorite aging hipster and Unreal Gods fan, mayor Bud Clark. It was also a hot, overcrowded nightmare, according to police and fire department officials. By 9 o'clock, people were being turned away at the door, even those with tickets. Policemen were called to clear crowded stairways and aisles. The crowd was estimated at close to 1,500. Part of the problem was that each of the 10 bands had large guest lists, in addition to the tickets that had been pre-sold.

The Starry Night was cited the day after the show for overcrowding.

Then Hurwitz took a pounding in the Portland press for expenses that cut into the net proceeds. Still, the show raised $4,827 for a grateful Rancher family.

Billy was still talking about the show when he checked into Providence Medical Center on February 6th for surgery scheduled the next day.

The day of the surgery was a long one in the waiting room for Billy's family, and Karen. At one point, Astrid heard an urgent call over the loudspeaker for Dr. Richard Rogers. She didn't find out until later that he had been called to save Billy's life.

Richard Rogers was a well-known Portland heart specialist who happened to be at Providence that day for another surgery. When Dr. Paull discovered the tumor had wrapped around Billy's aorta, Dr. Rogers was called in to perform the delicate rescue. The surgery lasted eight hours, finally ending successfully with the removal of the tumor.

Billy recovered quickly, and checked out of the hospital on Valentine's Day, a week after the surgery. The doctors told him all the cancer was gone. He was looking forward to regaining his strength. And getting back on stage.

27 Flesh and Blood

Lenny didn't have to think twice. Billy was putting together a new band, and he wanted his brother. It felt good to be asked.

"Yeah, I'd love to," Lenny said.

The Pipsqueaks had just broken up anyway, so Lenny had no problem putting his career on hold to help Billy.

There was one condition, though, as Lenny learned on a fishing trip with Billy. Fishing, by the way, wasn't just fishing to Billy. It's what he did when he needed to think, or when he needed to be alone. Or, in this case, when he needed to have a talk with Lenny.

"Why don't you quit drinking?" he asked Lenny. "You're a shell of a man. You're never going to do anything you want to do. Drinking is always going to be your number one priority. I need you to be serious about this band."

Lenny knew Billy was right. He also knew he wasn't ready to quit drinking. Billy seemed to realize he wasn't going to convince Lenny to give it up then and there, but he told him he was going to keep after him until he did quit. It was for his own good, he told Lenny, and the good of the band.

Once Lenny was on board, the name came easily to Billy. Flesh and Blood. No, wait. Billy Rancher's Flesh and Blood.

No one really remembers the Unreal Gods officially breaking up. But when Billy Flaxel walked off the Starry Night stage on January 26th, the Unreal Gods were history. That was the last time they played together. Less than two weeks later, Billy Rancher was in the hospital having a tumor removed and Flaxel had stepped out from behind the drum set, dressed up like Alice Cooper and formed Marilyn Monro, a heavy metal band that included the rest of the Unreal Gods. If that's what they wanted to do, that was fine with Billy, but they were all welcome to join him in Flesh and Blood.

"Billy wanted me to be in the band, but Flaxel was doing Marilyn Monro. They were two of my best friends. That was a tough one," says Dave Stricker. "It wasn't like I didn't want to play with Billy Rancher, but I kind of wanted to do something that didn't matter. I didn't have much confidence in Marilyn Monro."

DuFresne considered Billy's offer, but was scared off by Billy and Lenny's volatile relationship.

"He really wanted me to be in Flesh and Blood, but those guys had a pretty rough time of it," he says. "I knew it was going to be a good

Lenny Rancher, right, put his career on hold to join Billy in his band Flesh and Blood.
(Bart Danielson)

band, but their personal relationship was so crazy. Besides, I felt like I had to move on. I didn't just want to be a local hero, reliving the Unreal Gods over and over. I just thought, the whole Billy Rancher thing, enough of that already, I need something new. I'd put everything I had into that band."

Marilyn Monro, as Stricker predicted, didn't last long, and the former Unreal Gods all went separate ways. DuFresne again turned down Billy's offer to play with Flesh and Blood and joined a U2 soundalike called The Nation. That spring, he ran into Peter McIan in Vancouver, British Columbia. McIan gave him a tape of a few Unreal Gods songs he'd patched together from the recordings in LA. Jon barely recognized the music as the Unreal Gods.

"There were a lot of weird new keyboard parts," he says. "I was listening to it going, 'I know Alf didn't play that.' "

Flaxel moved to LA after Marilyn Monro broke up. Stricker stayed in Portland. So did Alf, who thought it was about time he led a band of his own.

"Billy asked me to be in Flesh and Blood," he says. "I said, 'No thanks, I'm going to do my own project.' He said, 'Good luck, you're going to need it.' "

Billy described the sound he was looking for in his new band as "white boy reggae." He needed a couple of horn players, and he recruited Tom Cheek, a saxophone player, and his brother Jim, on trumpet. Billy reunited with another ex-Malchick, drummer Pete Jorgusen. Chuck Retondo, on bass, and singer Mary "Lace" Reynolds completed the lineup.

Billy made it clear to everyone in the band that this had to be their No. 1 priority, this was no side project. The band practiced nearly every day. Now, there was only one thing left to do before the band took the stage — a team fishing trip. The gang headed a couple hours south to Clear Lake off the McKenzie River, rented a couple of boats, and tossed their lines in the water.

"It was one of those Billy propaganda trips," Lenny remembers. "You know, 'We're going to go fishing, and learn how to be better musicians.' We heard his wrath on everything on that trip."

Including another lecture, for Lenny's benefit, on the evils of drinking.

Nobody actually caught any fish, or any that weren't already dead, at least.

Billy spotted a trout floating by the boat, belly up. He distracted everyone, attached the lifeless lunker to his hook, and hauled it in. Wiggling the fish around to prove it was alive, Billy announced that he was going to toss it back in, setting it free to swim again, which would have been quite a trick.

After a month of rehearsals, Billy Rancher's Flesh and Blood made its debut April 19th at the Starry Night.

Just Seventeen, a 17-piece big band, opened the show. At 11 p.m., Billy's backlit shadow could be seen dancing behind a white backdrop, then he appeared on stage, wearing a white suit and top hat. The first song was an old reggae tune, "When You're Hot." The large crowd quickly filled the dance floor.

Flesh and Blood played around Portland that spring at the Last Hurrah, 6th Avenue, Pine Street Theater, Key Largo and Starry Night. The band traveled to Seattle to play Astor Park, a popular stop during the Unreal Gods' glory days, and to Eugene and Corvallis to play frat parties. Billy also managed to get the band a gig on a Portland afternoon TV show.

The combination of the reggae sound Billy was going for, his natural ability to craft catchy pop songs, and Lenny's blues influence gave Flesh and Blood a laid-back island music vibe. The band was tight, and very popular around Portland, although it wasn't creating the same type of excitement the Unreal Gods did in their heyday.

Billy had his chance to be a rock 'n' roll hero with the Unreal Gods, which he clearly was in Portland, but cancer and problems with Arista conspired to keep him from being a million-record-selling, cover-of-Rolling-Stone, I'm-on-MTV-so-much-it-makes-you-want-to-shoot-me superstar. Which was OK with Billy. He said he liked writing reggae music because it was good for his soul. He was more spiritual, and thoughtful, in his songwriting than he had been in the Unreal Gods days, which you might expect from someone who had endured chemotherapy treatments and three cancer surgeries before his 28th birthday.

Tony DeMicoli had been watching Billy evolve as a person, and as a musician, since the day in 1979 Billy strutted into the Long Goodbye with the rest of the Malchicks and told him he was ready to raise the roof off his little club. Billy had certainly come a long way since those days of covering Rolling Stones and Chuck Berry songs, and had continued to grow after the demise of the Unreal Gods.

"Flesh and Blood was more intense, leaning toward emotion,"

Billy wore a wig during some of the Flesh and Blood shows, to hide the effects of chemotherapy treatments.
(Bart Danielson)

DeMicoli says. "The Unreal Gods was 100 percent entertainment."

The next logical step for Flesh and Blood, the way Billy saw it, was to record an album. But Billy remained under contract to Arista, which wasn't interested in recording Flesh and Blood. In a phone call on June 3rd, Billy told Roy Lott, the vice president of business affairs at Arista, that he wanted to make an album with his new band. Two weeks later, he received a letter from Lott:

> *Dear Billy:*
>
> *This will confirm our conversation on June 3, 1985. Arista Records will waive its rights of exclusivity with respect to your services so that you may record up to five songs for inclusion on an EP that will be released only in the Northwest United States. (We will obviously not have any responsibility for payments nor have any other obligations in connection with this EP or with your performances on the EP). In connection with this EP, you will not re-record any of the songs that you have recorded for Arista except for "Thinkin' Zebra."*
>
> *Finally, as discussed, except as expressly provided above, Arista's rights to your exclusive recording services will remain in full force and effect.*

> As discussed, please send us a copy of the EP as soon as possible. Thanks.
>
> Best regards.
> Sincerely,
> Roy E. Lott
> Vice President
> Business Affairs

Astrid and Billy had always been close, and his second round with cancer brought them even closer. Astrid went to as many of Billy's shows as she could, she took him to and from his chemotherapy treatments, and her's was always the first face Billy saw when he woke up in a hospital bed. If it hadn't been for her foresight in buying health insurance, the family would have been wiped out financially. She'd always supported Billy, and his music, every way she knew how, short of hopping on stage and playing some kickass piano.

So Astrid knew exactly what to do when a friend of Billy's, Portland accountant J. Bryan O'Doherty, suggested that Billy needed someone to handle the business side of his new venture. She took an accounting class at night at nearby Mount Hood Community College, told Billy she'd be handling the books and helped him form a corporation named Karactor Records. Astrid and Karen were the major shareholders. "You just worry about the music," Astrid told her son.

Sounded good to Billy. He wanted to get into the studio to make some music, even if he could do only five songs.

And he had something to say now. With the Unreal Gods, Billy wrote these lines:

> From "Girlfriend's Drawers" :
> *I found the key to life*
> *inside my girlfriend's drawers*

> From "Rude Buddy Holly" :
> *Buddy, it was so rude for you to leave*
> *Mr. Holly, would you please move your Cadillac?*

> And from "Go Go Boots" :
> *Go go boots are comin' back,*
> *don't throw yours away*

With Flesh and Blood, he'd moved on to more serious topics: Karen, God and cancer, in that order, more or less. And as far as Billy was concerned, the three were related.

On "Please Don't" Billy expresses his love for Karen, and asks her not to forget him.

No one that I know, not even me,
can live on promises too hard to keep
So please don't, please don't ever hurt me
Please don't, please don't ever desert me
Please don't, please don't forget me girl
I'm so in love with you

From "Oh God":

Don't be a playboy every night
Love your companion
you've got to treat them right
If you want a family
you better find your wife
Oh God's been 'round for years
Yes God's shed many tears

In the songs "Boyish Tears" and "Feels So Nice (Love)," Billy acknowledges his life is different because of cancer, but that he's closer than ever to Karen because of it. From "Feels So Nice:"

Put your dancin' shoes on,
make me feel like Fred Astaire
Where have all my moves gone?
I'm so glad you don't care
It feels so nice
It feels so nice
I thank you,
for showing me all about love

These are love songs, but love songs written by someone who understands now that he won't be around forever, and is determined to make the most of whatever time he has. His commitment to Karen was certainly stronger than it had ever been.

Karen finished school at Portland State in March, moving home for her last term so she could be closer to Billy while he was undergoing chemo and surgery. Once she was finished with school and Billy had regained his strength after the surgery, they took a vacation to Victoria, British Columbia.

Karen remembers that Billy was excited about putting together Flesh and Blood, and in better spirits than she'd seen him since before he'd gone to LA the previous summer.

His hair had started to grow back, thicker and curlier than it had been, but he still took his wig with him wherever he went. He liked to wear it when he left the hotel in Victoria, then take it off when he came back in, just for the fun of confusing hotel employees. While they drove around Victoria, Karen would put the wig on and make funny faces at startled drivers. They were having a good time again.

When Billy and Karen returned to Portland, they rented an apartment together. Billy had spent many nights with Karen in Eugene or at her parents' house in Lake Oswego, and she had stayed with him in his apartments or at Astrid's house, but this was the first time they'd actually lived together.

The new songs Billy was singing were more meaningful than the Unreal Gods' pop songs, and Billy seemed, to others, to have changed, but Karen says it was simply a side of Billy that had always been there.

"He was headstrong and stubborn, but also a very giving person," she says. "He gave people too much, sometimes. He always had that in him, he was very warm to people. Even in the heyday of the partying, and the Unreal Gods, they'd do shows for solar energy, and Native Americans. He cared about other people."

Even convicts. Billy scheduled a show at the Oregon State Penitentiary in Salem for 1 p.m. on June 16th. That was fine, except that at 10 a.m. on June 16th, he had the worst hangover of his life. He'd been out all night with Pete Jorgusen.

"We were on the biggest coke binge. Coke and drinking, all night," Jorgusen says. "We were so sick that day. I said, 'Billy, we've got to get ready for the show at the penitentiary, it starts in three hours. Billy says, 'Fuck it, I'm not going to do it.' He calls and finds out the equipment's already there, Mick Boyt and Billy Triplett are setting everything up. And he just says, 'Tell them we're not coming.' "

Mick was in the prison yard, unloading the equipment, wondering why

Billy and Pete weren't there yet, when he was told he had a phone call.

He was taken to see the prison superintendent. "I've got information that Mr. Rancher won't be showing up today," he told Mick. "I don't know how you're going to handle this, but I'd be careful." He opened a gate and sent Mick back to face the crowd of inmates that had gathered to see the show.

Mick told Billy Triplett the bad news. Norm Hunter, an inmate who set up the gig, overheard.

"Oh Jesus, they're going to fucking kill me," he told Mick.

"Better you than me, man."

Mick told the inmates that Billy was sick, which, technically, was true. The reaction?

"Nothing got destroyed as I remember," Mick says.

News of the cancellation didn't thrill Lenny, who was still drinking, but doing his best to keep it in moderation, at Billy's urging. Lenny had a new wife, Ilme, and he definitely had slowed down, compared to the old Malchicks days.

Houston Bolles, leader of a band called the Harsh Lads, remembers Billy's constant pleas to Lenny to quit.

"It wasn't mean-spirited," he says. "What he would say is, 'Lenny's a better guitar player, a better singer, a better songwriter than me, but I'm the one having the success. Why isn't Lenny doing as good as I am?' "

Lenny had actually had about as much of this as he could stand, especially when he kept hearing stories about Billy's partying.

"Had Billy quit? Supposedly he had," Lenny says. "But I'd hear from Karen and other people that Billy had been out the night before snorting cocaine and drinking like a fish, and here I was, trying not to party so much because Billy didn't want me to. It didn't bother me that he wanted me to be straight and sober. But here was a guy who had just had surgery, who had been sick. Each time, I would get madder. I told him I heard what he did, and he would deny it. That totally pissed me off. An occasional beer wouldn't have bothered me, but the cocaine ... coming down from cocaine if you're healthy is terrible, and in Billy's case, it was definitely something he shouldn't have been doing."

Billy rescheduled the prison gig for July 4th. Each member of the band was frisked on the way in. It was hotter than hell, and the prison stage offered no shade, no relief from the relentless sun.

"I apologize for not making it a couple weeks ago," Billy told the inmates who had gathered on the grass in front of the stage. "I had some problems, and I let them get to me. I went out and got a little drunk and couldn't make it."

Billy and the band played an eclectic 45-minute set that included covers of songs by Marvin Gaye, the Beatles and the Supremes, a few original reggae songs, a country version of "Girlfriend's Drawers," and a blues jam featuring Lenny and a shirtless, suntanned inmate named Skeets who had apparently had plenty of time to practice his licks in the Big House. Toward the end of the set, as inmates shouted, "AC-DC!" and "rock 'n' roll!" Lenny played the opening riff of "Jumpin' Jack Flash."

"Don't stop, Lenny," one inmate screamed.

"Was that Jumpin' Jack Flash I heard?" Billy asked. He led the band through a rousing version of the Stones' classic, to the delight of the inmates.

"Thinkin' Zebra" is a song Billy had written for the Unreal Gods, in fact, was one of the songs they planned to record for Arista. It was one of Billy's favorites, and he intended to make it the title track of the Flesh and Blood EP. "Thinkin' Zebra" and "Jailhouse Rock" closed the prison show.

"You guys have a prison band here?" Billy asked. "That's good, because music is one of the most important things for the soul, it keeps you going on a day-to-day basis. I know I need it. I've been going through some pain. I've been back and forth to the doctors for four years with a cancer situation.

"Two weeks ago, they told me I had another tumor, which is why I got drunk and couldn't make it here the first time. I'm changing my lifestyle, what I eat, what I believe in, my physical exercise, because I have to.

"I have empathy for you guys. I believe in you, I believe in everyone. Hang in there."

With the Unreal Gods, Billy wrote about go go boots and his girlfriend's drawers. With Flesh and Blood, the lyrics were more introspective, covering topics such as cancer, religion and love.
(Courtesy of Karen Sage)

28 Looking For a Miracle

When Billy had been released from Providence Medical Center on February 14th, he was given a clean bill of health. The tumor had been removed, there was no more sign of cancer. Billy decided it was time to celebrate.

He played hard, and lived hard. He'd sacrificed to chemotherapy, and figured life owed him. He realized now, with the cancer back again, that had been the wrong way of thinking.

Billy decided he'd heal himself this time. He'd watch what he ate, he'd exercise. And no more partying. He heard about a magnetic coil that doctors in Sweden used, and convinced Astrid to order a couple. The one treatment he wasn't interested in was more chemotherapy.

Billy's diet consisted of onions, garlic, herbs, kelp, raw fish, vegetables and blueberries he picked at Mo Stevenson's house in Hood River. He and Karen spent a lot of time in Jim West's fishing cabin on the Sandy River, walking, eating vegetables

Billy and his sister Ellen, in Astrid's house in 1985. "I didn't know how to tell him I thought he was going to die," Ellen says.
(Courtesy of Karen Sage)

and drinking wheat grass juice.

Everybody seemed to have an answer for Billy, and he was willing to listen to most of them.

"We were constantly screening people away from him who had these weird cures," Mick Boyt says. "There was a time he'd eat, like, 100 vitamins a day."

He also walked a lot.

"He'd heard it was good to walk," Astrid says. "He'd walk up the hill behind our house. He'd walk all over. He tried everything. You couldn't say he didn't try. He had such a will to live. He never discussed dying, even though in his songs you could recognize that he might be getting closer to his maker."

Billy kept himself busy recording the "Thinkin Zebra" EP with Flesh and Blood, working with Billy Triplett and Steve Branson at Dogfish Studios.

Billy asked Dr. Stephen Kimberley, who had become a close friend, what he thought of his plan to heal himself.

"He'd gone through a bad period when he was feeling sorry for himself, drinking a lot," Kimberley says. "Tony (DeMicoli) wouldn't serve him. Then he decided to do the juices, the coil. I said, 'Hey, go for it.' "

But Billy was losing weight, and it became obvious the holistic methods he was trying were not working. The tumor was growing inside him. Kimberley, and Billy's friends and family, urged him to give chemotherapy another try. Billy insisted it wasn't necessary.

Billy and Karen were living together in their little apartment. "He never talked about dying," she says. "He decided he was going to do it his own way, with the coils and the macrobiotic diet. He went overboard with that stuff, and it wasn't working."

Billy's sister Ellen, who was still living in Seattle with her husband Steve Pearson, found it difficult to visit Billy.

"He was getting really thin, but he told me he was going to be OK, that he didn't need chemo, that he'd get better through this holistic stuff," she says. "I would get very depressed. I just said, 'All right Billy, if you're sure you're going to be fine. I'm not sure when I'll be able to get back into town, I'll see you later.'

"How do you tell somebody they're making a big mistake? What can you do? I didn't know how to tell him I thought he was going to die."

29 A Close Call

Stephen Kimberley couldn't take it any more.

"Billy, you're going to die if you don't get something done," he said. "We don't want to watch that happen."

So on September 18th, Billy admitted that exercise, and diet, and whatever else he was trying wasn't working, and was admitted to Good Samaritan Hospital.

He was hurting bad by then, and was given prescription drugs to ease the pain. Billy spent four days in the hospital, and agreed to undergo more chemotherapy treatments. He went back to the hospital on September 27th. First, the doctors tried to build Billy's strength with transfusions and vitamins. Then they started the chemo.

This was all very bad timing, as far as Billy was concerned, because the "Thinkin' Zebra" EP wasn't quite done. He'd listen to the unfinished tapes in his hospital bed, scribble down notes, and send them back to the studio for producers Billy Triplett and Steve Branson. He wasn't happy with his vocal tracks on "Feels So Nice (Love)," and he wanted to re-record that song, with his sister Ellen singing background.

"No way, Billy, I can't do it," she protested. She still lived in Seattle, and she was just in Portland to support her big brother. She'd stay at the hospital, she'd bring him anything he wanted, but she couldn't sing. In her mind, she ran through all her excuses. "I'm too shy. My throat's sore. I can't sing that part." When she opened her mouth, "OK, I'll do it," came out.

Billy wanted to oversee this project personally, so he checked out of the hospital.

"He was so sick," Astrid says. "The studio was way on the west side of Portland (in Hillsboro, actually, about 10 miles west of downtown Portland). Ellen and I had to guide him there. I couldn't believe he could even sit up."

Billy and Ellen sang, and it worked out perfectly, just like he told her it would. Then he checked back into the hospital. He checked out on October 18th, after three weeks of chemotherapy treatments.

Karen woke up at 6 a.m. October 24th, with Billy shivering beside her in bed. Karen stuck a thermometer in his mouth. 106 degrees.

She started to panic. "Should I call an ambulance?" she asked Billy.

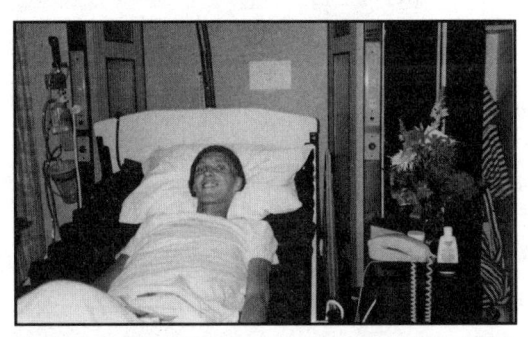

"No," he told her. "Just take me to the hospital. Quick."

Billy was in septic shock. He had a dangerously high fever, and a bacterial infection, a complication of the chemo.

From October 24th, 1985, to February 24th, 1986, Billy spent most of his time in a hospital bed.
(Courtesy of Karen Sage)

"What's going to kill him first," Karen wondered, "the chemo or the cancer?"

Astrid was advised to call Ellen in Seattle, pronto. "We don't think he's going to make it," one of the doctors told her. While Karen, Astrid and her husband Jack, and Lenny and Ilme waited in agony, Billy was in the intensive care unit, hooked up to several machines. He was on a respirator, and pumped full of drugs so he wouldn't fight that. A catheter was inserted into his chest, another tube into his stomach. The doctors were trying to replace fluids his body had lost, but his lungs filled up with water. His arms were swollen. Veins had collapsed. His eyes were taped shut. One intestine was blocked with a newly discovered cancerous tumor.

Ellen arrived from Seattle. She got a phone call in the hospital from her husband, Steve Pearson. Ellen's favorite cat had died. Ilme, who was a floral designer, made a beautiful wreath, then Ilme and Ellen drove to the Burnside Bridge and tossed it into the Willamette River. Back at the hospital, friends and family had started a vigil in the waiting room. Karen remembers that the doctors and nurses who came out to speak to them that day didn't sugar coat anything. "We don't think he's going to make it," became the standard line.

But Billy did make it, at least he was still with them when October 24th turned into October 25th. On a day that started so bleak, that was good news. A miracle, in fact.

Billy spent the next 10 days in the intensive care unit. Only Karen and family members were allowed to see him, never more than two at a time. They took turns massaging his hands and feet, telling him it was going to be OK, that he was going to get better. He heard them, but he couldn't respond. Dr. Kimberley thought to himself that Billy looked like a spaceman, with his hair gone, his belly swollen and tubes running into his body from all angles.

Finally, on the 10th day, Billy's condition improved. Astrid knew Billy was feeling better when he demanded to be taken from the intensive care unit and placed in a regular private room, so his family would know how well he was doing. "We have our Billy back," she told Jack, as Billy was being wheeled down to his new room.

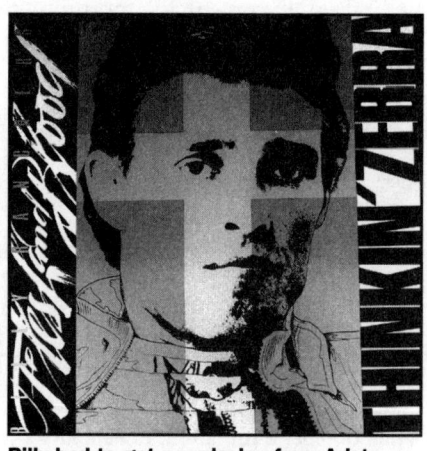

Billy had to get permission from Arista Records to make "Thinkin' Zebra." The Flesh and Blood five-song EP was released while Billy was in the hospital.

It was obvious Billy was going to be there for a while, so everyone did their best to make him comfortable. His friend Fritz Johnson brought a VCR and tapes. Billy and Karen watched a lot of movies in his room. "The Emerald Forest" and "Gremlins" were two of Billy's favorites. He also had a tape of the 1985 World Series, and he'd watch The Three

Stooges until he laughed so hard it hurt. Hundreds of cards poured in for Billy from fans, and friends, wishing him well, and offering support.

Billy listened to a lot of reggae music, although he was frustrated by his lack of creative inspiration. He wasn't in the mood to write any songs. He was looking forward to getting out of the hospital, though, when he was sure the energy and passion for writing and playing music would return.

Fall turned to winter, and Billy was still cooped up in his hospital room. Thanksgiving came and went. Bed sores were a problem from being there for such a long time, so Astrid ordered a special bed with air pockets that cost $130 a night.

Astrid and Karen joked that the new cancer wing being built at Good Samaritan should be called the Rancher wing, since Astrid's money and the insurance was probably paying for it.

The good news was that the chemo seemed to be doing some good. Tumors on lymph nodes near his stomach, and one on his liver, had shrunk. The level of cancer in his blood was down. And Billy was still positive. He granted interviews in his room. There were times, sick and weak from a chemo treatment, he had to stop talking for a minute to throw up. *OK, sorry about that. Next question?*

The copper coils had arrived from Sweden, and Billy made Astrid and Karen bring them to the hospital. One was placed in the corner of Billy's room. The gadget was a series of copper coils in a circle, and each day, Billy would step into the middle of the coil, and hold it up to his waist.

"Dr. Kimberley thought it kept him going," Astrid says. "It seemed to stimulate his brain waves."

Billy liked to get up and move around when he could, walking the halls, or playing a game of pool with Karen. On the night of November 15th, drugged up with sleeping medication, he got up from his bed and began sleep walking, sending IVs and tubes flying. His legs gave out, and he fell to the floor, cutting his mouth and nose.

"The nurses came in and said, 'Oh, we're sorry, we forgot to put his rails up,' " Karen remembers.

All his hair was gone, but he kept his head covered with a cap Astrid had knitted in blue and yellow Swedish colors. Karen and Ellen had spent much of their time in the hospital being taught by Astrid to knit. They all made scarves and caps for Billy. The cap Astrid knitted matched the poster hanging in Billy's room for the "Thinkin' Zebra" EP. Like the album cover, it was a picture of Billy over an image that could have been a Swedish flag, deep blue with a yellow cross that ran down the middle of Billy's face.

"Thinkin' Zebra" was released shortly before Billy was allowed to leave the hospital on December 22nd, 59 days after he'd been admitted. Fritz Johnson and Mo Stevenson, Billy Hults and Jim Crawford had all invested in the project, and Stephen Kimberley threw a party at his home that raised $700 to help get the album printed.

Ten days after it was released, "Thinkin Zebra" had sold more than 1,000 copies. The songs "Oh God" and "Please Don't" were being played by Seattle, Portland and Eugene radio stations. But Flesh and Blood was finished. Mary Reynolds was singing with a Portland group called The Esquires. Any thoughts Billy might have had about keeping the band together were dismissed because of Lenny's drinking.

"He gave up on Flesh and Blood," Lenny says. "Actually, he gave up on me would be more accurate. I was drinking pretty heavy again."

Billy was far too weak to play his guitar, his arms and hands numb from the chemotherapy, and he wasn't inspired to write any songs. But he was able, for short periods of time, to do some drawing. He was given sketch pads for Christmas. The bad news was, he was going to have to use them back at the hospital. Billy spent Christmas Eve with Karen at her parents' house in Lake Oswego. He was admitted to Good Samaritan again on December 28th, and released on December 29th. But he went right back in on December 30th for a couple more days, suffering from withdrawl symptoms. Billy had been pumped so full of painkillers the past couple of months, he'd become addicted.

"They thought he was going to die, so they just kept giving him drugs," Karen says. "He'd have DTs. He'd have to go back in for a fix, basically. He'd usually be real anemic, too, so he'd get a blood transfusion, and more painkillers. He'd always tell me, 'I'm sick again, I've got to go back to the hospital.' The doctors would tell him, 'You're addicted to this. You don't need it anymore.' I thought they were very unsympathetic. Well, excuse me, he did live, and now he's addicted. I remember them telling me, 'There's counseling for this type of problem.' I said, 'Wait a minute, this is your fault.' He finally kind of got off that by himself."

After being released on New Year's Day, 1986, Billy had to go back in on January 6th, this time with an infection. Karen and Astrid had to wear masks to visit him. He received blood transfusions, a constant injection of nourishment, drugs and more chemo. This stay lasted until January 18th.

He was back for a couple days of bloodwork and therapy January 29th to 31st. On February 13th, he was back for more chemo, staying five days this time. Whenver he was at the hospital he also used the copper coils.

Billy had spent most of the past five months at Good Samaritan, which gives a guy plenty of time to think. Billy's evolution toward being a more spiritual, and thoughtful person, began after the recurrence of cancer in Los Angeles, and was evident in the songs he wrote for Flesh and Blood. But he was continuing to change, to see things differently. Being a rock star, playing at La Bamba seemed like a million years ago.

"When Billy became so ill, his concern for other people grew," Astrid says. "He was concerned about wars, starvation, Indians, everything. There wasn't anything he didn't think he could fix."

Bart Danielson, Billy's photographer friend, remembers that Billy "wanted everything to be nice, everybody to be happy. He was so gentle. There was a lot of crap going on in the world, and he couldn't understand that."

While he was in the hospital, Billy wrote a letter to President Ronald Reagan, proposing an end to the famine in Ethiopia. His solution was simple. He asked Reagan to pledge to give money that would have gone into the development of one nuclear warhead to Ethiopian famine relief, instead. And to get the same commitment from Russian leader Mikhail Gorbachev. The two countries would wipe out famine in Ethiopia, and there would be two less missiles to worry about.

"That's the kind of stuff Billy thought of," Danielson says. "He didn't know why they wouldn't listen to him."

On February 21st, Billy checked into the hospital to have some bloodwork and tests done. On February 24th, the doctors had the results. The news was not good. The chemo wasn't working anymore. The cancer had spread from his back to his kidneys and liver. He'd lost almost 60 pounds, down to a skin and bones 120. The doctors told him he could continue chemotherapy treatments, but there wasn't much hope.

Karen was working that day at her part-time job at a clothes store in downtown Portland. Billy called her at the store, from the hospital.

"Well, we just talked to the doctors, and they told me I have three months to live."

It took Karen a while to know what to say. "The doctors have said things like this before," she managed. "There were nights they said you weren't going to make it to the next morning. They were wrong about that."

Karen and Billy had never really talked about death, certainly never in such absolute terms. It was always in the back of Karen's mind, but she thought to have actually said it would have been to admit defeat.

This news shouldn't have come as a big shock to Karen. She knew that Billy was slipping, and that the chemotherapy treatments weren't helping. But still, there's really no way to prepare for "I have three months to live."

30 Beating the Death Sentence

It was April 6th, and there was a constant ringing in Billy's ears, his hands and feet were numb, and walking wasn't something he could take for granted anymore. Still, he looked good, considering, and he sure didn't feel like someone who had used up a good share of the three months the doctors said he had to live.

Starting the day he walked out of Good Samaritan on February 24th, when it was decided that chemotherapy was no longer an option, Billy committed himself to the holistic methods he had tried the previous summer without much success. It was all that was left. He tried acupuncture treatments. He was eating a healthy diet, taking vitamins and herbs, and he wasn't partying. He went for walks when he could. And he was still pulling the copper coils around his body. There had been no miracle cure, but at least he felt up to getting on stage for the first time since he'd played with Flesh and Blood the previous summer.

The occasion was a $50 a plate benefit dinner for Billy at Aldo's, a Portland restaurant. After the meal, Billy and a few of his friends played a five-song set.

Billy sat on a stool in the middle of the stage. He wore a dark shirt, buttoned all the way to the top, a white tie, and his favorite coat, a snazzy red, green and yellow number with tails. All the clothes, and the hot lights on stage were making Billy sweat under his wig. He didn't really need to wear the wig anymore. He had hair, but it was short.

"This evening is really special. I'm honored," Billy began. "I want to thank everyone, but I'm not going to name names, because I believe everything is channeled through Jesus Christ. Not to come across as a born again Christian, but when you start to dig down into what life is all about, a person changes. And I've changed a lot."

Then he introduced the first song, "Who'd Ever Thought This Could Happen to Me." Lenny opened with a laidback reggae guitar line. The rest of the lineup was Dave Stricker on bass, Pete Jorgusen playing his zebra-striped drum set, and, on keyboards, Attilio Panissidi III, a local rock 'n' roll writer who had played on the "Thinkin' Zebra" EP.

Until five years ago,
I was just like you
... Until that day
the doctors would say
so straightforwardly,
I had cancer

The next song was called "I Don't Know Why I Love You, But I Do."

"Hey Lenny," Billy said, turning in his stool toward his brother, "I don't know why I love you, but I do." At the end of that song, Billy called another old friend, Jon DuFresne, to join him on stage. The next song was called "Treasures." For DuFresne, it was fun to play with Billy again, certainly more enjoyable than the aborted recording session in LA and the last Unreal Gods shows had been.

"This show wasn't rehearsed at all," DuFresne says. "The pressure was off, and you could just have a good time. Actually, after the band broke up, my relationship with Billy improved. And by this time, it was great. We'd hang out together, and Billy wasn't as crazy as he'd been at the end of the Unreal Gods. I remember thinking, 'Oh yeah, this is the guy I met five years ago, this is the guy I remember. Glad to see you're back, Billy.' It was really sad to see him with this incredible thing, the cancer, hanging over him, but it was good to see him being his old self again."

At the end of "Treasures," Billy was handed a napkin, with a note scribbled down.

"Somebody has requested a David Bowie song. 'Heroes.' "

The somebody was Trinket Allport, a musician and friend of Billy's.

Before the song, Billy reached down to a table in front of the stage and took a glass of champagne. He needed both hands to hold it. Squeezing it with both palms, he lifted it to his lips and took a sip. "This one goes out to Trinket," he said, and the band launched into the Bowie tune.

Midway through the song, Billy stood up to dance. The supportive crowd cheered as Billy shuffled his white tennis shoes back and forth. At the end of the song, Billy plopped down on the stool.

"I need five seconds to catch my breath," he said. "I feel great, though. This is the most energy I've had in six months."

Then he introduced the final song, "Far Above the Clouds."

"I've tried to understand God, get closer to God," Billy said. "I never imagined I was going to need so much help. When the Unreal Gods played in Portland, I had no idea anything would ever get in my way, or in the way of the band. But I'm a very different person now."

He dedicated the last song to Karen and Astrid. When the last note had faded away, Billy got off his stool. "That was wonderful," he said, as friends and family cheered. "Now if I can just walk."

Karen moved home to finish school at Portland State so she could be closer to Billy while he was fighting cancer.
(Courtesy of Karen Sage)

Billy was given a choice: He could use the money that was raised at the Aldo's benefit to cover medical expenses. Or he could take Karen to Hawaii. No one said it was a difficult choice. Billy and Karen made plans to fly to Maui. First there was one more benefit show, this one at the Pine Street Theater on April 15th, Karen's 24th birthday.

Karen was looking forward to the trip to Hawaii, but she was worried, too. "What if he dies in Hawaii?" she asked herself. "What

206

On September 1st, 1986, Billy and Karen were engaged to be married. The date was set: April 25th, 1987.
(Courtesy of Karen Sage)

would I do?"

Billy and Karen stayed at Sugar Beach, just outside of Kihei on the island of Maui. There were good times. They'd put their chairs at the edge of the ocean, and read to each other. They relaxed, and talked, for hours. Billy loved snorkeling. His body was free to float on the water, and he was entertained by the thousands of colorful fish below him. It was about the most physical exertion he could handle. He had severe nerve damage in his hands and feet, a result of the heavy doses of chemotherapy the past two years. Some days were better than others, but walking was always a chore, and Billy's fingers were numb, and almost useless.

"We sat on the beach, and we came to some really frustrating realizations that Billy couldn't be active any more," Karen says. "That was really tough."

Billy and Karen's friends Fritz Johnson and Mo Stevenson were scheduled to join them in Maui. On May 21st, the day before Mo was to arrive, Billy decided to do some body surfing, which Karen found amusing, given the fact she had to help him dress and tie his shoes. But he strapped on a life preserver and waded out into the surf. After bobbing up and down for a few minutes, he'd had enough, and Karen had to drag him to shore.

Billy's muscles, atrophied after months of chemotherapy and little exercise, couldn't take the pounding. He hurt from head to toe when he got out of the water. The muscles in his chest felt like they were ripping apart.

"Billy, are you OK?" Karen asked. "What do you want me to do?"

"I'm all right," he said, struggling to catch his breath.

Billy lay awake all night, too sore to sleep. The next morning, after picking up Mo at the airport in Kahului, Billy was still struggling. He had trouble getting in and out of the rental car, and his breathing was labored.

"Billy, we're taking you to the hospital," Mo said. Karen agreed that Billy needed to see a doctor.

"OK, but only if you promise not to leave me there," he told them. "I didn't come to Hawaii to stay in a hospital."

They promised they wouldn't leave him overnight.

Billy was examined by Dr. Charles Mitchell. Karen and Mo talked nervously in the waiting room while doctors and nurses ran tests on Billy.

Finally, Dr. Mitchell gave them the bad news.

"Karen," he said, "there's internal bleeding, and his blood counts are not good. We'd like him to stay overnight."

"I'm not spending the night here," Billy reminded Karen.

"I know, babe."

Karen and Mo helped Billy up, and they walked down a hallway, toward the door.

One of the nurses came chasing after them. "Wait, you can't leave yet."

"Oh yeah?" Karen said. "Well, we're leaving. Thanks for your help."

Karen called the doctors back in Portland, and reported the blood levels from the tests done at the hospital in Maui. "Actually, that's pretty good for Billy," Karen was told. "And don't let him body surf any more."

There were times in Hawaii that depression got the best of Billy. He was frustrated because he couldn't make his fingers work, and he ached. There were times there was nothing to do but put his head in Karen's lap and cry.

Having Fritz around helped. Billy and Fritz had become like brothers, though they were an unlikely pair, Billy the kid from a working class northeast Portland neighborhood, and Fritz, the rich entrepreneur.

"It didn't seem that they had anything in common," Karen says. "They just really hit it off. Fritz was a true friend of Billy's."

Unfortunately for Fritz, he wasn't getting along as well with his girlfriend, Mo. One day, as Billy and Karen sat in their chairs on the beach, they could hear Fritz and Mo screaming at each other back in the hotel room.

They were also joined by Dave Stricker and his wife, Laura. After a couple of weeks, Billy and Karen's Maui vacation was over, and it was time to head back to Portland. Billy's health hadn't improved any, but it hadn't gotten any worse, either, despite the body surfing incident. At least he had a nice tan, and had gained some weight back. He looked good. And he'd outlived the three-month death sentence the doctors had given him in February.

Back home, Billy moved into the bottom half of a duplex with Karen in the Corbett district, not far at all from Malchick Manor and the Unreal Gods house. Billy was the best man at Glen and Amy Baggerly's wedding in June. Glen had been a baseball teammate at Mount Hood Community College, before Billy ever picked up a guitar. He remained a close friend and fishing buddy.

Billy looked awfully healthy and happy, Astrid thought, for someone who was supposedly on borrowed time. Billy, Karen, Astrid and Jack made a trip to Jim West's cabin on the Sandy River to do some fishing. Billy hooked a beautiful salmon, then gave his pole to Jack, so he could reel it in. The fish made a nice meal back at Astrid's house.

Billy and Karen spent a lot of time that summer at Mo's home in Hood River. Mo lived in a huge, wooden house on a hill. It wasn't Maui, but it was about the best place Billy knew to get away from everything and relax.

Mo enjoyed helping Karen take care of Billy, giving him a place to stay, someone to talk to. She'd make chocolate chip cookies that Billy would literally eat until he got sick. And Mo was undergoing a spiritual awakening of her own, and wanted to share that with Billy.

"I had just met an Indian man who taught me the basics of what it's all about, truth and love," she says. "Billy was singing the same song. He really was a teacher to a lot of people. It wasn't so much Christian as it was spiritual. He wasn't preaching Jesus Christ. But he got to the basics."

Billy wasn't going to church, but the messages he delivered in his post-Unreal Gods songs, and the comments he'd made at the benefit shows that spring at Aldo's and the Pine Street Theater indicated he thought of himself as a Christian.

He considered the fact that he'd made it through the summer, and was starting to feel better, nothing short of a miracle. He felt so good, in fact, he proposed marriage to Karen on September 1st. She accepted, and a date was set: April 25th, 1987.

About time, thought Annie Farmer, Billy's old friend. "I always thought Karen was perfect for him. She was the balance in Billy's life, and he worshipped the ground she walked on. He loved her, with all his heart and soul."

Billy and Karen had no doubt there would be a wedding.

"The cancer seemed to be in remission," Karen says. "We were optimistic. Maybe we were a little blind, but he was doing fine. He was healthy, he wasn't partying. His mental attitude was good. It was miraculous."

That's the way it looked to Mo, too.

"We all thought he was on the way to a recovery," she says. "I believe in herbs. I've heard miracle stories. He was doing so well."

Mo planted 2,000 tulips in her huge yard. They'd be ready next April for the rehearsal dinner at her house.

31 Another Way to Play

Shortly after Billy and Karen were engaged, Billy's health took a turn for the worse. It was fall now, and each of the past two autumns had brought a new crisis, so why should this one be any different? It was in the fall of '84 that Billy learned the cancer had returned, after three years in remission. Billy spent nearly all of the last three months of '85 in the hospital. Now, Billy was battling the effects of the aggressive chemotherapy treatments that had ended in February. Just walking was painful. His arms and hands were numb, and there was a constant ringing in his ears. Billy moved in slow motion.

Physically, he was a mess. But Billy's creative impulses were back. He had a head full of songs he wanted to write and perform, but he could barely hold a guitar, let alone play one. In fact, he'd given away all his guitars to other musicians, all except one, a light blue Fender Stratocaster he kept for the memories, and for inspiration.

Attilio Panissidi III — sometime rock journalist, sometime musician, usually known just by his first name — worked with Billy during the recording of the Flesh and Blood EP, and had become a good friend. He was working on a solo routine, calling himself Art Carnage, using synthesizers, sequencers, drum machines and assorted electronic gadgets to create a wall of techno pop sound. He figured Billy could continue to make music, even if he couldn't play his guitar anymore.

Attilio knew Billy's arms, hands and fingers ached, but he knew Billy could play a drum machine. Attilio's idea was to show him how the drum machine worked — it was easy enough, requiring only the striking of buttons and pads to make different sounds — then work with him, or let Billy use it by himself. Anything to free Billy from his physical constraints and let him play his music again.

Billy was like a kid at Christmas, but this was better than any toy he'd ever had. He couldn't believe the sounds he could make with Attilio's drum machine.

"I've got to have one," he told Attilio. The next day he did, a brand new KORG ddd-1. He handed Attilio the thick instruction booklet.

"Read this and come back tomorrow to show me how to work it."

With his new drum machine, Billy was ready to form another band. Attilio advised him against that, telling him it was more trouble than it was worth. "Just do it yourself," he told Billy. "You don't need a band."

But Billy longed for the interaction of other musicians. He could write the songs, using his drum machine to figure out the basic rhythms, but he wanted to record the songs, and he wanted to play them live. And he was going to need help from some old friends.

Billy had been working with Hundread Percent, a reggae band fronted by Houston Bolles. Just a few years earlier, Houston had been watching Billy and the Unreal Gods at all-ages shows and writing about it for his Lincoln High School newspaper.

Houston, a guitar player, singer and songwriter, formed the Harsh Lads in 1983, while he was a senior in high school. That band broke up in '86, and three members of Lenny's band, the Pipsqueaks — drummer Pete Jorgusen, guitarist Franklin Stewart and keyboard player David Diaz — joined Houston and bass player Dave Held. They still called themselves the Harsh Lads for a short time, until Billy got involved, and told them they needed a new name.

"We were in this basement, rehearsing one day, and Billy sat us down and said, 'We're not leaving here until you guys come up with a name,'" Houston says. "Hundread Percent was a song we did, so it just kind of came out."

Billy had a plan. He wanted to form a band (despite Attilio's objections). Then he wanted to play shows around Portland. Attilio's Art

Carnage would open, Billy and his band would play second, then Hundread Percent would close. The show would be called The Concrete Jungle, named for a Bob Marley song that Billy and his band would play.

Billy chose reggae for two reasons. First, it fit best with the spiritual lyrics he was writing. And he knew it would require less effort on stage than his hectic Unreal Gods routine. So Billy set about forming his band, and tutoring Houston Bolles. Houston was an eager student, soaking up everything Billy said.

"Sing where you're comfortable," Billy always told Houston. "Find your range. If a song doesn't work in one key, move it around. Keep it simple."

"I wasn't real developed as a songwriter yet," Houston says. "I'd written a song, and I asked him, 'Billy, this song only has two verses, does it have to have a third?' He just cracked up and said, 'Well, if you've got a third verse that's great. If you don't, don't worry about it.'"

Billy never worried about it, that's for sure. All Billy ever needed for a song, especially back in the early Unreal Gods days, was a nice hook and a few silly words.

Houston, still just 20 years old, was no Billy Rancher on stage, and he knew it. He remembered Billy performing at Lung Fung and La Bamba during the Unreal Gods' glory days. He remembered how crazy, how frenzied a scene that was. He remembered how the crowd hung on every word, every movement of Billy's. And he wanted to know how to do it.

"Treat the crowd like they're in your living room," Billy told Houston. "Look at them. Make them feel at home."

Houston took Billy's advice to heart.

"When a guy comes out in leopard skin pajamas, you've got to listen to what he has to say," Houston says. "He taught me a lot about how to perform."

Houston was energized by Billy's enthusiasm. Billy was writing new songs, working with Hundread Percent, and getting his Concrete Jungle show ready. Lenny, Dave Stricker, Attilio, and horn players Tom and Jim Cheek were recruited. Billy had talked with Jon DuFresne, who had moved to Los Angeles, and Jon agreed to come up and play at some of the shows.

Billy and Karen lived in the little duplex in the Corbett neighborhood, and Houston was there a couple days a week, listening to songs Billy was writing.

"It was really hard for him not to be able to play his guitar any more," Houston says. "He'd have ideas for songs, and he'd want me to play guitar parts to see how they would sound. He was going like crazy. One of the funniest things was he was keeping a notebook that was nothing but song titles, like 300 of them. He would just throw words together, move them around, mix them up to come up with stuff he liked."

But it was more than just song titles. There were lyrics and music to go with many of them. Billy was cranking out songs, and he wanted to record them.

Houston called on David Zimmerman, a musician and audio wizard who had played in one of the first incarnations of the Harsh Lads.

"Billy wanted someone who could help him record, so I called Zimmerman," Houston says. "I said, 'You know Billy Rancher, you know what he's doing. This guy is creating some great stuff and he needs help. Call him up.' "

Zimmerman called Billy, and agreed to help him with the recordings. Billy never seemed to have a problem finding people willing to assist.

"Billy was kind of like a politician," Attilio says. "He had an unusual way of putting out an energy that got people to want to donate their energies to his project. Maybe he knew he couldn't do it all alone. He needed a lot of people's help. You're either blessed with the ability to draw people, or you're not. Billy was."

"It was almost like everyone was waiting on him," Dave Stricker says. "He'd have an idea, and we'd just do it. When you have a real band, everybody's throwing ideas in. This was more like, he'd have an idea and everyone would do it. A lot was getting done real fast."

Houston: "He created things. That was his talent, really. He was a catalyst. Things were always fun around Billy."

Billy had his new drum machine, several songs already written, and talented musicians who were ready to help. "Billy just rented some gear and said, 'I've got to do this. I'm going to write songs, I've got ideas already,' " Attilio says. "He just plunged ahead."

Billy and Karen's bedroom was turned into a recording studio. Different musicians came by every day. Billy began work on a tape he was going to call Mr. Groove.

"We just started recording," Attilio says. "He'd have little snatches of songs worked out in his head. We'd figure out what the beat was, put the keyboards in, bring in people he wanted to play other parts. It was just great. He'd really matured, turned into a whole different kind of guy."

It was a nonstop parade of musicians, in and out, all day long.

"The first time I went there, there was just this ghetto blaster they were recording with," Houston remembers. "The next time I went over, they were playing tapes of what they'd done and I said, 'You guys did that here?' They had been recording this in this little room, and it sounded incredible."

There were times David Zimmerman and Attilio had to beg Billy to stop. They'd had enough for one day. But not Billy. He was relentless in his effort to record all the songs he was writing.

Astrid remembers trying to talk Billy into slowing down.

"He just would not stop," she recalls. "I don't know why he didn't just give up."

It could have been that Billy knew he was running out of time. One of the songs Billy was recording was called "Chemotherapy," a song he had written with Lenny that spring, sitting by the pool in Astrid's backyard. "It just came together really fast," Lenny says. Astrid thought the song would be too painful for Billy to perform, too real. But Billy had always written songs about what was going on in his life, and now, that was cancer.

Billy performed the song in April at the benefit show at Aldo's, introducing it as "Who'd Ever Thought This Could Happen to Me."

Until three years ago, I was just like you
Looking for fun ... the romancer
Until that day, my doctor's office would say
So straightforwardly, I had cancer

But I'm getting better every day
Taking strength from my master
So know it's a game, a game for me and you
Making a triumph from a disaster

Chemotherapy, look what you've done to me now
I don't feel so good
I don't feel so good

I don't feel so good
I don't feel so good

Billy had recruited Tim Tubb, a trombone player in a popular Portland band called the Crazy Eights, to play a solo on "Chemotherapy." The Crazy Eights were recording albums by now, and touring nationally, and were arguably Portland's hottest band. But a few years earlier, they'd played their first show opening for Billy Rancher and the Unreal Gods. Tim Tubb was happy to help Billy any way he could. No matter how painful it might be.

The night before, at a Crazy Eights gig, Tim had to use a nickel mouthpiece because his gold mouthpiece had been stolen. When he came over to Billy's duplex, his lips were ugly and swollen from using the different mouthpiece. He could barely play, but he got through his part, with Billy and David Zimmerman recording. "That was good, but let's do it again," Billy told him. "Make it sad, make it sad as it can be." And Tim played, and played, and played, until it sounded sad enough to suit Billy. Then he left, presumably to go home and ice his lips.

Houston was a regular at the duplex. And he often served as chauffeur, on the rare occasions Billy left, to go to a record store, or to Astrid's house, or just to get out of the duplex.

"Billy really liked to ride in my VW bus, because it was easy for him to get into," Houston says. "He didn't have to fold himself up to get in. He'd ride in the front seat. One time I turned the wrong way down a one-way street. I can still hear him screaming, 'Houston!' I'm thinking, 'Great, the guy's survived cancer, and I kill him in a car wreck.' "

Some days were better than others for Billy.

"He had a lot of hope he was going to make it through," Attilio says. "He was working himself real hard. By the end of the sessions, he would wrap up in his copper coil. There were some days where he was really shitty."

Billy's battle with cancer had certainly affected his music. The words he was writing were either autobiographical stories about cancer, or love, so real they hurt, or messages about social causes Billy had taken up.

From "The Big Picture":

I used to cry about the problems at hand,
'bout money and pain, leading a band

*And then when cancer materialized
I thought that my own strength would keep me alive
But all of the sudden, from nowhere he came
A perfect stranger, he came up to me*

*And now the big picture, the big picture
is coming in loud and clear
on the television in my soul
Yes, the big picture, the big picture
is coming in loud and clear
on the television in my soul*

*We used to walk in our favorite park
then play in the city, till way after dark
And think about choke brain
just living it high
Squandering love, we'd shout at the sky
but those days were unreal
those days turned black
the nights were painful, and hard to stop*

*But in the big picture, the big picture
there's no fear, only love
In the big picture, the big picture
no fear of dying, only love*

The 15-song Mr. Groove cassette included songs about apartheid, war and God.

Billy was taking a more active interest in the message his music could deliver. Before, he had been a rock 'n' roll star, living that life to the fullest. Then he became more religious, more spiritual.

Attilio: "I saw him grow so much, and it was just amazing to see. You could tell it in the music that came out of Mr. Groove. He had matured. Instead of writing about go go boots, he was writing about world peace and brotherhood."

"He'd found God," Houston Bolles says. "It didn't seem out of character to me at all. It seemed like he was taking advantage of every minute he had. When you know someone like that, how can you find fault with any of their actions, how can you not enjoy being around them, not crave talking to them, savoring all of that? He became a very giving person, a much more sensitive person."

It was important to Billy to finish the Mr. Groove tape, to leave something behind. He wasn't admitting to anyone that he didn't expect to be around much longer. But Billy's actions suggested he knew his time was almost up.

"Billy really wanted that music to be heard," Houston says. "He believed so strongly in those songs. He was dubbing off copies as fast as he could. He really wanted it heard, but not for commercial reasons."

Attilio: "He was really desperate to get as much on tape as he could for posterity."

Between recording, and preparing to play live shows, Billy was working with Jan Baross, an independent Portland filmmaker, on a documentary on his life.

At one point, while he was still working on Mr. Groove, Billy decided to take a break and throw a little party in his duplex/recording studio. Billy had a few drinks, and was particularly animated that night. He put an old Brian Eno record on the stereo and cranked it up loud enough that Karen was afraid the cops would show up.

"Billy, be quiet, the neighbors are going to get us kicked out of here," she told him. "We've still got to live here."

"Fuck 'em, we're partying," Billy said, grabbing Karen and giving her a kiss.

Billy was celebrating. He had a tape almost recorded, he had live shows planned, and he and Karen were getting married next April 25th. If he made it that far.

"I kind of realized there wasn't much time left," says Dave Stricker, who had been with Billy since the Malchicks, and was working with him now on Mr. Groove and the Concrete Jungle show. "It was hard to think about that when you were trying to work with him. Everybody knew he was going to die. I think he did, too."

32 "They Can't Say the Ranch Never Tried"

Despite his deteriorating physical condition, Billy talked more about dying in his song lyrics than he did in real life. It wasn't a topic he was ready to disccuss, not yet at least. Still, his actions spoke of a person trying to tidy up his life. His Concrete Jungle show and the Mr. Groove recordings would take care of the music. Now he had a few personal relationships to deal with.

Billy loved fishing, but he hadn't gone much in the past year or so because of his failing health. But he talked Glen Baggerly and Joe Dreiling into one last fishing trip, on the Nestucca River near the Oregon coast. His doctors told him not to go. It was late fall, and too cold for Billy to be comfortable. But Billy didn't really see the harm in it. He felt like shit, what was the difference if he felt like shit at home in bed or if he felt like shit standing on the banks of the Nestucca River, reeling in a nice steelhead?

Billy stepped gingerly from the car. Billy, Glen and Joe grabbed their poles, and walked down to a nice hole and tossed their lines into the river. Ten minutes went by, no bites.

"OK, fuck it, I'm done," Billy said, reeling in. "That's all I wanted to do, just throw my line in the water one more time."

They drove back to the house where they were planning to stay. The people who owned the house were friends, and fans, of Billy's. They talked, and sipped hot tea. Billy was tired, and he excused himself to lay down on a couch. A few minutes later, he looked up at Glen. "Man, I've never felt this fucking bad in my life," Billy said.

Glen knelt down beside his friend. "What's the matter?"

"Fuck, I don't know, I'm just ... "

Glen hadn't seen this before. Billy had been dealing with cancer on and off for five years, and had never complained to Glen about the way he felt.

"Just take me home," Billy said quietly.

It was a somber exit. Everyone in the house knew Billy was hurting. Glen and Joe carried Billy to Glen's car, and carefully put him into the front seat, reclining the seat to try to make Billy comfortable. Billy was the only one who wasn't crying.

Glen drove home as Billy tried to rest. He was in too much pain to sleep. Billy cheered up when "Brown Sugar" by the Rolling Stones came on the radio. He turned it up loud and listened. The song took him back to the Malchicks days, back to playing with Lenny at the Long Goodbye, trying to make enough money to buy some beer. What happy, simple times those were.

Billy was the best man at the wedding of his old college baseball buddy, Glen Baggerly.
(Courtesy of Karen Sage)

As they closed in on Portland, Glen and Billy talked. Really talked. About life, and death, and happiness.

"Ranch, give me some advice," Glen said, turning to look quickly at Billy. "What do you say to anyone who wants to make it?"

Billy wasn't sure what Glen meant by making it. In music? In life? Career? Relationships? Then he realized it didn't matter, the answer was the same.

"You know, you hear it all your life, but I'll tell you, no matter what you do, if you want it bad enough, no matter what it is, you never, never, never give up."

Then Billy had to pause, worn out from the simple task of articulating that thought. He looked at Glen and smiled a tired smile.

"You know what, Bags? They can't say the Ranch never tried."

"No they can't, Billy. No they can't."

Billy closed his eyes and went to sleep. Glen Baggerly wiped away tears as he finished the drive to Portland.

Billy had taken another fishing trip earlier that fall, this one with Lenny. There were two things Billy wanted Lenny to understand. One, Lenny had to quit drinking. And two, no matter how many fights they'd had, no matter what had been said, he loved Lenny.

"I could see it in his eyes. I could tell that he wasn't going to be around much longer," Lenny says. "I couldn't even be around him, because I knew that what he was going to talk to me about was so heavy that I wouldn't be able to handle it. But then he planned this fishing trip, and I had to do that. He was adamant about having things in order."

Lenny was having a tough time. He was drinking a lot. Eight years earlier he'd lost his dad, and now he was afraid he was going to lose his brother. And the worst thing was that Billy and Lenny hadn't soothed enough bad feelings that they could confide in each other.

It bothered Lenny that Billy still wouldn't totally open up to him. He heard the songs Billy was writing, and he knew what was going through his mind. He imagined Billy was talking to Karen, and Astrid, and Glen Baggerly and Dave Stricker, everybody but him. *God, why won't he talk to me?*

"I think he just wanted to show how strong he was. He always had to be the big brother, never let me see any weakness," Lenny says. "But he could have shown me that, I'd have understood. I'd have still loved him. He opened up to people who weren't as close to him as me, and that was really frustrating to me. Also, he thought I was always critical of his music, but that wasn't it at all, it just wasn't my bag. He thought it was a jealousy problem. God knows he criticized my music. Of course, all that was right on, you know, 'Tune up before you go out there.' But until that last fishing trip, he was always like he was performing around me, never just totally honest."

Billy and Lenny did their best to make amends on the trip, but Lenny still got the usual speech from Billy. "You're a shell of a man. You've got to quit drinking." Lenny knew Billy was right, but he also knew he wasn't ready to quit. Still, he appreciated that Billy had made an effort to get closer to him, to talk to him, even if it did come with a lecture.

Billy was also doing his best to make peace with all the Unreal Gods. Stricker had been a true friend to Billy since the Malchicks, and was playing with him on the Mr. Groove recordings and in the Concrete Jungle shows.

Billy Flaxel was in Los Angeles, singing in a heavy metal band called Creature. He hadn't parted best friends with Billy Rancher for a couple of reasons. For starters, he didn't win any good will by walking off the Starry Night stage, then returning when Billy Rancher sat down behind the drums during what turned out to be, for obvious reasons, the Unreal Gods' last show. And there were hurt feelings over Billy's messy business dealings. Dr. John Flaxel had been a large financial backer during the early days of the Unreal Gods, then had been basically cast aside when Alf's brothers and William Gladstone got involved in producing and managing the band. But when you're dealing with cancer, those look like petty concerns.

Billy Rancher called Flaxel and asked him if he could come up and play in some of the shows. Billy Flaxel told Billy he wanted to, but couldn't get out of commitments in LA.

"I told him, 'I hear you're kicking ass,'" Flaxel says. "He said he was doing OK. He told me he believed in me, and wanted the best for me. That was about it."

Jon DuFresne, who had moved to LA during the summer of '86, received a phone call and a Mr. Groove tape from Billy.

"Hey man, come up and play some shows with me," Billy told Jon. "And listen to the tape and be ready to put down some guitar parts over some of the songs."

Jon came to Portland and worked with Billy in his bedroom, recording guitar parts Billy was going to add to Mr. Groove. As Jon played, Billy laid down on his bed, too weak often to even sit up. He would listen, and make suggestions as Jon strummed and picked away. Just like the old days, Jon thought. *Billy can't even get off the bed, and here he is, telling me how to play.* There was a time that would have bothered Jon.

Billy took his Mr. Groove act to the Key Largo stage, but he was too weak to stand.
(Courtesy of Karen Sage)

But he'd gotten over that last spring when he came to Portland to play with Billy in the benefit shows at Aldo's and the Pine Street Theater. Billy, despite his illness, seemed then more like the guy Jon had met back in 1981 than at the bitter unraveling of the Unreal Gods.

Now, during the few days Jon spent with Billy, any bad feelings that remained were washed away, replaced by happy memories. That really had been a hell of a first summer with the Unreal Gods, the best time of Jon's life. "A total rock 'n' roll fantasy," he told Billy, as they sat in Billy's bedroom studio, swapping stories about the good old days.

Jon remembered a post-Unreal Gods car trip he'd taken with Billy, along the Columbia River Gorge. They'd had a long, rambling talk, at first about music, then about cancer, and finally, about God. It seemed to Jon that it was the first time Billy had considered the subject.

"It seemed like he was contemplating this like he'd never talked about it before," Jon says. "He was kind of moralistic about it, of course. Like anything Billy does, he was totally into it, and seeing it in real black and white terms. I'm sure it was a real solace to him."

One subject that was not discussed was death.

"We never talked about dying," Jon says. "Not then, not ever. That would have been like admitting defeat, and I never heard Billy admit defeat."

The only Unreal God who wasn't invited to take part was Alf Ryder. Apparently, there are some wounds even a life-threatening disease won't erase.

As Billy continued to record Mr. Groove, he had assigned Karen the chore of organizing all of his recorded music. She sorted through hundreds of tapes, listening to them to see what songs were on them, then labeling the tapes.

"There were boxes and boxes of tapes and song ideas," Karen says. "At this time, it was so important to him to get everything categorized and organized. 'Make sure you don't lose anything,' he told me. I was trying to write down what was on every tape. I remember this was just so important to him. We had to do this."

33 The Show Must Go On

Billy called on his friend Steve Hettum, and told him to set up some shows.

"Let's do it up, just like the old days," Billy said.

Steve knew Billy had been working on the Mr. Groove tape, and had written several new songs. But when he saw Billy, he wasn't sure he should be playing live. Billy's weight was down to 130 pounds. "Billy, are you sure you can do this?" Steve asked.

"Just call the clubs and make the dates. I'll be there," he said.

The first shows were scheduled for October 24th and 25th, Friday and Saturday nights, at Tony DeMicoli's Key Largo club. A Halloween show was set for October 31st at Lung Fung. Then it was the Pine Street Theater on November 8th, and the Last Hurrah on November 21st and 22nd.

Steve thought Billy was stretching his luck. "We can't get a big crowd all of these nights," he told Billy. And the truth was, he wasn't sure if Billy would be around to play all of them. But Billy insisted, and there was no way Steve could turn him down. He'd always been there for Billy, and this certainly was no time to argue.

On October 24th, a long, black limousine pulled up to the curb outside 2756 NE Fremont Drive, Astrid and Jack's house.

"Time to go," Billy announced. Billy and Karen, and Astrid and Jack, who had just returned from a vacation in Sweden, piled into the limo and headed downtown to the Key Largo.

"Mom," Billy said, taking Astrid's hand, "the cancer is back. They've found more tumors." Billy had a slight smile on his face, and Astrid thought it was strange how matter-of-factly he had delivered the news.

Astrid told Billy she wanted him to move back home. He was still living with Karen in the duplex, and musicians were still coming and going, finishing up the Mr. Groove recordings. Astrid told Billy she was going to take a leave of absence from her job as hostess at the airport restaurant to take care of him. Billy said he would move back home after the Key Largo shows.

"This time I had a feeling Billy might not be with us much longer, so I wanted to devote every possible moment to him," Astrid says.

"Welcome back, Billy Rancher." After Tony DeMicoli's introduction, Billy stepped onto the Key Largo stage, stumbling once, then taking his seat in a director's chair that had "Mr. Groove" inscribed on the backrest. It was after midnight by the time Billy took the stage. The dance floor was packed, and Billy and his band began playing several of the best songs from the Mr. Groove tape, "Cool Fire Lady," "Here Comes Mr. Groove," "Gotta Stop Apartheid," and "Chemotherapy."

Billy stood occasionally, but spent most of the time sitting in his chair. When he wasn't singing, he'd turn to his drum machine, and punch in commands. Lenny played guitar, Dave Stricker was on bass, Attilio played keyboards, Tom and Jim Cheek were blowing their horns and Trinket Allport played drums. Actually, Trinket was on stage to look like she was playing drums. Billy's machine was taking care of most of the work, but he didn't think it looked right not to have a drummer on stage, so there was Trinket.

"She loved Billy so much, she'd have done anything for him," Houston Bolles says.

People were dancing, and having fun, but this was different than a Billy Rancher and the Unreal Gods show. Billy had something to say this time, and he was saying it in his songs. Against a reggae beat, Billy was preaching about love, and peace, and understanding. The songs are about one cause or another, or deeply personal messages about dealing with cancer, and death. In "The Big Picture," it's clear that Billy is aware of the changes he's making.

> *So I got my paintbrush and I started to draw*
> *I thought my cause was the noblest cause*
> *I thought about power, and reaching for fame*
> *But greed is an island where no life sustains*
> *Now the day has come when all my friends can see*
> *A different painting that flows from me*
>
> *And in the big picture, the big picture*
> *No hate or jealousy*
> *Only rock and roll*
>
> *And in the big picture, the big picture*
> *I spend my time thinking 'bout love*
> *playing that rock and roll*

"He had a very fatalistic thing," Two Louies publisher Buck Munger says. "He had an attitude of, 'If you knew you were dead, you'd hear things, too, so listen to what I'm saying.' "

Tony DeMicoli was simply giving him a forum to do it, even though there were some who felt Billy was too sick to play. "It was sad, but I always made sure he wanted to do it," DeMicoli says. "I made sure it was Billy's wish to play. He found comfort in playing, being able to express a lot of his feelings in his songs. It was just a great vehicle to get his message across to people."

Buck Munger was one who thought the message could be conveyed just as easily on his recordings.

"I didn't like to see him playing shows," Munger says. "He was propped up in a chair. I didn't encourage him to do that. I didn't like him doing it, I didn't think he should be doing it, and I thought Tony DeMicoli was an asshole for providing him a space to do it."

Of course Tony DeMicoli wasn't the only one, and the truth is, the club owners were friends of Billy's, and were simply doing what they thought would make Billy happy. It was understood that this was Billy's last chance. And everyone understood that Billy was never happier than when he was on a stage, singing.

The shows at Key Largo each drew big crowds. Billy's fans enjoyed the music, and Billy enjoyed the intimate experience of sharing his words with them.

Billy did move back home with Astrid and Jack. Karen kept the duplex, but spent most of her time at Astrid's house with Billy. Her parents had recently moved from Lake Oswego to Arizona, and the Ranchers had always accepted her as part of the family, anyway. Billy read a newspaper story about a man who had rid himself of cancer by walking, so he decided to give that a try. He went for long, slow walks with Astrid, even struggling up Rocky Butte — "the little mountain," he called it — behind Astrid's house. Walking at all was extremely painful, and difficult, but each day, Billy would walk around the northeast Portland neighborhood, exhausting himself. A friend, Jonetta Walter, came by two or three times a week to give Billy massages.

The Concrete Jungle show kept rolling, playing Lung Fung on Halloween, then Pine Street the next week. Each show drew a few hundred people. Hettum was right. The shows weren't getting the same kind of promotion the first two at Key Largo had, and therefore weren't attracting the same size of crowds. And the shows began to have a macabre feel to them. Billy was getting sicker. At the Pine Street show on November 8th, he curled up on the stage floor to rest as the band made its way through an excruciating version of "Lenny's Blues."

Tony DeMicoli welcomed Billy to play at Key Largo. Seven years earlier, he'd given the Malchicks their start at the Long Goodbye.
(Courtesy of Karen Sage)

"On one hand, it was so fucking beautiful, it was like playing Woodstock or something," Attilio said. "There was a great feeling in the crowd and on stage, but his endurance was becoming less and less. There were times he'd just lay down on the stage in pain, while we grooved on."

Steve Clarke, a musician and writer for Two Louies, got a call from Buck Munger at about noon on Wednesday, November 12th. Get down to High Tech Recorders, Buck told him, Billy was going to record. Clarke called The Incredible John Davis, who had time booked that afternoon at the east Portland studio. The Incredible told Steve that he had donated his studio time to Billy, and that Billy had a song he wanted to get out. Steve was welcome, if he wanted to play.

If Astrid had her way, Billy wouldn't have made it to the studio.

"We have to cancel this, you're not feeling good," she told him.

"No mom, I have to, all those musicians are down there," Billy said.

"What song are you going to play?" Astrid asked.

"Don't worry, I'll make something up."

Actually, Billy had a song that he had just finished, and that he wanted the world to hear. The studio was filling up with musicians by the time Billy arrived. He laid down on a green couch, resting his head on a yellow blanket that had been folded into a pillow. Astrid sat at the end of the couch. When all the musicians were there, Billy began teaching them "Make Love Not War," a "We Are the World" type of anthem. After about 45 minutes, the players — Clarke and Jeff Alviani of the popular Portland band Cool'R on synthesizers, John Davis on guitar, Gregg Stockert on accordian and Jan Celt of the Esquires on bass — had their parts figured out and were ready to record. Actually, they had to be ready. Astrid was pushing to hurry the session along, worried about Billy's strength.

John Lindahl was manning the control board, and David Zimmerman, who had helped Billy record Mr. Groove, was programming the drum machine. David Jester had cameras, lights and video equipment spread all over the studio to record the occasion. Two Louies photographer David Wilds was snapping pictures. Billy's sister Ellen was there, having agreed to sing background vocals.

The band played along to a drum machine pattern, and Billy sang, still lying on the couch. He held the microphone with his right hand and the lyrics in front of his face with his left. During breaks he let his thin left arm fall across his forehead, and closed his eyes. He sat up occasionally, to take a drink of water from a bottle, but was far too weak, and groggy from painkillers, to stand. The instrumental parts and Billy's vocal were done in one take. Same with the background vocals. Then John Davis had his young daughter Julie and another young girl, Jasmine Stoner, sing along with Billy's vocal. Then the whole thing was mixed, mastered, finished. The entire process took three hours. What they had when they were done was far from perfect, but it was all they were going to get — Billy's eight-and-a-half-minute Christmas wish for the world.

Billy's voice was hoarse, his singing strained, but it was from the heart. The chorus:

> *Make love not war*
> *Make yourself some friends*
> *Make love not war*
> *Let us live again*
> *Make love not war*
> *I wanna be your friend*
> *Make love not war*
> *Touch me, touch me, like a brand new friend*

John Davis handed Steve Hettum a master tape of the song and told him to make sure people heard it. Copies were given to local radio stations, but it was decided the song couldn't be sold commercially. As if he didn't have enough problems, the IRS told Billy he owed back taxes from the Unreal Gods days. Not a lot, a few thousand dollars, but enough that Billy and Astrid were working with an accountant to try to sort it all out, and had made a couple of trips to the IRS office to discuss the situation. A few payments had been made, extensions granted. Still, the unhappy prospect of having any money Billy made taken away by the government loomed, so none of Billy's music was being sold, for now at least. In addition to this tape, there were about 300 copies of Mr. Groove in circulation.

Billy had to be helped out of the studio. He was exhausted, but he was proud of "Make Love Not War."

David Jester was back in his office after recording the session when John Davis burst through the door, bawling like a baby. "It was a sad day, but we all felt like we'd been part of something special," Jester says. "He had so much music inside and he felt like he could change the world with his music. And he believed in it so strongly that you believed it, too."

"Make Love Not War" was typical of the sentiments found in Billy's songs.

"He just had a natural tendency to care about people," says Stephen Kimberley, a Portland doctor, musician and good friend of Billy's. "He was a natural born leader. He was willing to look at important issues in life. He had the ability to look beyond himself."

The "Make Love Not War" recording was another example of the

Portland music community's willingness to help Billy. "There were always a bunch of guys waiting to get up on the stage and kick ass if Billy needed them," Buck Munger says. "There were a lot of people who believed in him."

The one person who wasn't with him anymore was the one Billy wanted there the most — Lenny. Billy and Lenny had always had a volatile relationship, and it had been strained by the breakup of Flesh and Blood a year earlier. Lenny agreed to play in the Concrete Jungle shows, but he'd lost interest, in the shows and in the circus surrounding Billy.

"It got to be cool to be involved with Billy," he says. "I got so turned off by that. It's like the focus of what he was trying to say was lost through all the hype. The thing that bothers me to this day about our relationship is that people think I didn't care, that I was nonchalant about Billy. But I was just that way. I didn't do any interviews, I didn't want to talk about it. Then there were all these shows. People I barely knew were jamming with Billy. It totally destroyed any confidence I had in the press, or in these benefits, because people were making money off these."

Lenny sensed people like Tony DeMicoli questioning his loyalty to Billy, wondering about his attitude. But this was a tough time for Lenny, too, and he dealt with it by withdrawing.

"At that point, I didn't give a shit about much anyway," Lenny says. "It's really sad. Me and Billy had a relationship unlike any two brothers. There were just so many people around Billy at that time, that it was hard for me to get close to him. But Billy knew I loved him."

Lenny dropped out of the Concrete Jungle show, or Billy dropped him out. Jon DuFresne was recruited from Los Angeles to fill in. Billy wanted Jon to play with him at the shows scheduled for November 21st and 22nd at the Last Hurrah, and to record some guitar tracks to be added to the Mr. Groove tape. Billy's condition was worsening each day. He was losing weight, he could barely eat, and sleeping, which is what he really wanted to do, was nearly impossible because he was in so much pain.

But he had one last hope. Billy had heard of a doctor, a cancer specialist named Glenn Warner, who was in charge of a treatment program at Francis Cabrini Hospital in Seattle. Billy wanted desperately to see Dr. Warner. Astrid was afraid Billy was in for a disappointment, not to mention an unbearably painful car trip, but she was willing to believe there might be one more miracle, so she arranged a trip to Seattle.

Billy couldn't fly, because he wouldn't be able to sit up that long. And Astrid had a fear of driving on freeways, so it was decided that Karen would drive. On November 17th, Astrid and Karen guided Billy into Karen's Honda. They reclined the front passenger seat and cradled Billy's body with pillows in an attempt to make him comfortable for the three-hour drive to Seattle.

The cancer program at Cabrini is a lifestyle treatment routine in which the patients live together at the hospital. Dr. Warner had agreed to talk to Billy, and to run a series of tests to determine if he was a candidate for the program. Astrid and Karen were given a room next to Billy's. Astrid woke up the first morning they were there to find Billy poking her with a stethoscope. "Well, I'm afraid you're not doing too well, mom," Billy reported.

Neither was Billy. After three days at the hospital, he was told there was no reason for him to stay. "Of course there was nothing any doctor could do," Astrid says. On November 20th, Astrid, Karen and Billy began a long, quiet drive back to Portland.

As they headed home in silence, Billy decided he wanted some chicken. The hot, greasy stuff you get at convenience stores. Karen pulled off the freeway and searched for an AM-PM, a 7-Eleven, any place that would have that chicken. No luck. She didn't take every freeway exit between Seattle and Portland, but it sure seemed that way. She ventured onto any road that offered the hope of fried chicken. Finally, they found some. Karen, Astrid and Billy all had a good laugh as Billy gobbled down his chicken. They needed something to laugh about.

Two nights later, Karen and Astrid sat with Billy in the dressing room at the Last Hurrah, pleading with him not to go on stage.

"You're not going to play tonight, Billy," Astrid told him.

Houston Bolles, whose band Hundread Percent closed the shows, told Billy he didn't have to go on. "Billy, you don't have to play tonight, we've got it."

"I have to play," he said. "This might be my last one."

Cheryl Hodgson, the lawyer who bailed Billy and the Unreal Gods out of the $25 million lawsuit filed by William Gladstone, was also there. The call came that it was time to go on, and Cheryl and Karen helped Billy off the couch and walked him through the kitchen toward the stage. He couldn't make it that far. "I've got to rest for a minute," he said, and he laid down in the middle of the kitchen. About then, Peter Mott, who ran the Last Hurrah with his brother Michael, came through the kitchen doors.

"Oh my God, is he OK? Should I call an ambulance? Is he going to be OK?"

Billy looked up and said, "Hey man, I'm just resting. I'm cool."

He stayed there for another five minutes, then got up and walked onto the stage.

There was a good-sized crowd that night, including a drunken rugby team from Canada. Billy sat on his chair, singing his Mr. Groove songs and playing his drum machine. The lineup of the band was basically the same as it had been throughout the Concrete Jungle shows, except that Jon DuFresne was playing guitar, not Lenny. Jon was glad to have the chance to play with Billy again.

Billy wearing his rasta wig.
(Courtesy of Karen Sage)

"It was such a fun experience, it was like reliving the old days," he says. "There were a lot of people there, it was a fun show. But Billy was definitely in a lot of pain. He'd play a few songs, then go off to the side of the stage and lay down for a few minutes. You could tell it had taken a lot out of him. But then he'd get back up, and go back out to the stage. And he was great when he was on stage. That was a really cool experience. I thought, 'OK, things have come full circle.' It was kind of like when we first met. He didn't expect anything from me, I didn't expect anything from him, but we knew what we could do together. Musically, it was fun, and it was fun to talk to Billy. But it was also kind of weird playing with him in the kind of shape he was in."

Dave Stricker knew the show at the Last Hurrah would be the last time he played with Billy.

"The shows were incredible," he says. "Every show we did, whether it was packed or not, every person in the audience was focused on Billy. But the show at the Last Hurrah, I knew he was going to die then, because he thanked me for playing with him all those years, and said he had a great time. It was kind of spooky."

After the final song was played that night, as Billy walked off the stage, he saw another old friend, Annie Farmer.

"Annie, come with me," Billy said. They walked slowly into the dressing room. Billy walked into a bathroom to throw up, then walked back out into the dressing room. He was alone with Annie. He laid his head on her lap, and they talked.

"Annie, I think I'm ready to go. It's just too much for me."

Annie started to cry, then slowly caressed and stroked Billy's head with her hand. "I know, sweetheart."

After the show, Astrid had strict instructions for Steve Hettum. "Steve, no more," she told him. "No matter what Billy tells you, don't let him schedule any more shows."

"At the time, I didn't think he looked sick," Karen says. "But now I watch it, and I say, 'Oh my God, how did people let him get on stage?' But that's what he wanted to do."

34 "I've Talked to God"

Glen Baggerly couldn't believe his eyes. He was leaving Good Samaritan Hospital on the chilly morning of November 24th with his wife Amy, who had just suffered a miscarriage. In the hallway, he saw Billy Rancher, looking as thin and as sick as he'd ever seen him, being wheeled slowly to his room.

"Glen, it's got me again," Billy said.

It looked like Billy was out of miracles. He was rushed to the hospital with a very high fever, shaking, and hurting from head to toe. All the doctors could do was pump him full of painkillers. The only real comfort to Billy came from being surrounded by his family and friends. Astrid, Karen and Ellen were at the hospital 24 hours a day. Jack visited often, which made Billy happy. Billy wanted to know that Astrid was going to be OK when he was gone, and the more he saw Jack, the more convinced he was that Jack would take care of his mom. Lenny visited, although he wasn't at the hospital as much as the rest of the family.

Flowers and gifts poured in for Billy. Friends and fans came by to see Billy, some not understanding how serious his condition was. Those who did know found it difficult to deal with. Billy had beaten this so many times, but it didn't look like he would this time.

Nobody said it out loud, but everyone was prepared for Billy to die. "We'd all seen him suffer so much," Ellen says. "He was very weak. You didn't want to think it, because he had done the impossible before."

This was a difficult time for Ellen, who was still in Seattle. She and her husband, Steve Pearson, had moved in with Pat Connors, another member of Steve's band, the Heats. On Labor Day, Ellen came home to find Steve with another woman. "I realized I was out, and she was in."

A week later, Steve told Ellen, "You should probably look for another place to live." Not so fast, Pat said. They were living in his father's house. "Don't worry," he told Ellen, "you're not going to have to move out. Steve's moving. And he's never bringing that woman into this house."

So Ellen stayed and Steve went. Ellen took time off from her job and came down to Portland when Billy checked into the hospital. She talked with Karen, and Astrid, and visited with Billy when he was up to it. Billy managed to cheer her up, telling her that she could go with him and Karen on a trip to Europe. Ellen didn't share much about her breakup, knowing that everyone had enough to worry about now with Billy.

Then Billy got a surprise visitor — Steve Pearson.

"Get the fuck out of here," Lenny said, slapping Pearson when he saw him at the hospital. "There's nobody here that wants to see you."

"He had kind of been an idol of mine, but he turned out to be a creep," Lenny says. "I thought he had a lot of nerve to show up at the hospital. I lost it. I had a lot of hatred for that guy because of what he'd done to Ellen. He's lucky I didn't kill him."

Ellen was afraid that was exactly what Lenny was going to do.

"Lenny really wanted to murder him, right there," she says.

Lenny's outburst aside, most of Billy's family and friends were holding up pretty well.

"Astrid and Karen and Ellen were all very calm," says Mo Stevenson. "I think we'd all been there before, thinking we were going to lose him. We just didn't want him to suffer any more."

In September, Mo had left for Mount Everest. One of her girlfriends was marrying a Sherpa at the base camp of the mountain, and needed Mo to be the maid of honor. At 17,000 feet. She was out of town for more than two months. When she got back, Billy was in the hospital. A few days later, Mo had 25 friends and relatives at her house in Hood River for Thanksgiving. She got sick, and spent the entire day vomiting. She had a cousin drive her into Portland, to Good Samaritan, where she was given a room a floor above Billy. She had contracted hepatitis on her Everest adventure.

On Friday, November 28th, Mo had a feeling it was time to say goodbye to Billy, so she walked downstairs with Fritz Johnson to see Billy. His breathing made Mo think of a sea turtle, which, when flipped over on its back, takes one breath a minute. Billy was making gurgling noises as he drew each breath, his lungs filling up with fluid.

"Billy, don't stay here for us," Mo told him. "It's OK to let go."

Cheryl Hodgson dropped by to talk with Billy, and gave him the same message. What she got in return was an inspirational speech from Billy. Cheryl had recently decided to try to make a go of it by representing musicians. She was managing Portland rocker Dan Reed, and finding out what a nasty business rock 'n' roll can be.

Billy met with Cheryl in a lounge outside his room, laying down on a couch. "It was a very difficult time in my life," she says. "But I left there, and there was something in that conversation that he said that inspired me to go on, to believe in myself."

It was funny, all these people with different problems, and they were being cheered up by Billy, who didn't know if he'd be around to talk to them tomorrow.

Old friends continued to drop by and visit. Steve Hettum. Stephen Kimberley. Pete Jorgusen came by with his mother. He kissed Billy on the cheek while he was sleeping. "I love you Billy," Pete told him. "See ya later."

Glen Baggerly returned to the hospital to see Billy. "It's not supposed to be this way," Glen told him, tears streaming down his cheeks.

"I'm ready, man. I've met God, I've talked to God. I'm ready," Billy assured him.

"Why don't you just go? Just let go."

"Don't worry, I'm going," Billy said. "He's waiting for me."

Billy told Glen he had only one regret.

"If I had it to do all over again, I'd take my chances with the cancer, let the cancer kill me," he said. "Look what the chemotherapy has done to me. What could be more frustrating for me than not being able to move, not be able to play my guitar?"

Glen held Billy's hand. It felt rubbery, he thought.

"Man, I'd rather die than take the chemo."

Billy was trying to convince himself it was OK to let go, but he'd been fighting the cancer for so long, it was a hard habit to break.

"He was undying in his spirit," Lenny says. "Billy was a fighter. In a lot of ways, he was living to fight against cancer. It was his last big gig. It was incredible the way he had that spirit. Like he was saying, 'See, I can fight this.' Like the fight was what was important."

Bart Danielson was another frequent visitor.

"He was really hurting," he says. "He told me, 'Scoutski, I just want you to know I love you.' I knew this was the final point. But he never said die. All the way through, with the chemo, and the copper coils, and everything else he tried, he never said die. He was just a major competitor, and this was his last battle."

"Karen and I, and my mom, had seen him suffer so much," Ellen says. "He was very weak. You don't want to think it. ... but I just didn't want him to hurt any more."

Jon DuFresne worked with Billy the night before he was brought to the hospital, recording guitar licks that Billy wanted to put on the Mr. Groove tape. He kept working on it, with David Zimmerman, while Billy was in the hospital, reporting to Billy every few days to let him know how it was going. On Friday, Jon talked to Billy on the phone.

"OK, we're done, it's finished," Jon told him.

"That's great," Billy said. "Jon, thanks for everything."

Jon noticed that he sounded bright, alert. "OK, well, I'm going back home to LA tomorrow. It was great seeing you again, Billy."

"You too, man."

On Saturday, Jon called again before he left, to say goodbye. This time, Billy was incoherent. He sounded drugged up, Jon thought.

By Sunday, his sixth day in the hospital, Billy was sleeping a lot. His breathing was getting slower, more labored. He asked Astrid if Jack was going to visit him, it was very important that he talk to him. Yes, Jack was coming, Astrid said. Seeing Jack seemed to make Billy rest easier. Billy thanked Jack for loving his mom, and made him promise to take care of her. It was as if he wanted to make sure he hadn't chased Jack off, Astrid thought. After Jack left the room, Astrid sat next to Billy and massaged his hands.

"Good night Mom," Billy said, turning his head to look at Astrid.

"Mom ... "

"Yes Billy?" Astrid whispered, leaning closer to Billy. He looked up at her and smiled. "I'm sorry."

Then Billy closed his eyes and drifted off.

35 The End of Billy's Rocky Road

For two days, Astrid stayed in Billy's room, talking to Billy as he lay in a coma. She read from books and magazines she found in waiting rooms. She talked to her son about everything he'd accomplished, all the fun they'd had, all the joy he had given her.

She told Billy how happy she had been when he was born, how his birth had turned an old rascal like Joe Rancher into a softie. She talked for hours about what a happy, funny kid he had been, how he rode bikes and made up games with Lenny and Ellen as they grew up in Alaska, what a good baseball player he was, how much she enjoyed his games at Madison High School and Mount Hood Community College.

Astrid told Billy that she could still remember how thrilled he had been when he bought his first guitar, and how passionate he was when he had told her that he was going to be a musician. She talked about Karen, how sweet Karen had been to Billy, how much she and Billy loved each other.

Billy couldn't share Astrid's laughter, or tears, but Astrid was sure he could hear her. She wanted to make sure Billy knew he wasn't alone, that, as she had always been, she was there for him now.

Then, on Tuesday morning, December 2nd, Astrid told Billy it was

OK to let go. He was fighting so hard, she thought.

"It's all right, Billy," she whispered. "I'm sorry you hurt so bad. It's OK to go now. We'll be all right."

A few minutes later, the room got quiet. Billy wasn't breathing any more. At 9:15 a.m., his body finally gave out on him. Astrid picked up a carnation John Davis had left in the room the day before, and laid it on his chest. Astrid thought she could make out a faint smile on Billy's face.

Ellen, who was sleeping with Karen in a waiting room down the hall from Billy, woke up when the sun shined through a window, filling the makeshift bedroom with its bright light. She knew as soon as she sat up that Billy wasn't with her any more. A nurse came into the room and told Ellen and Karen that Billy was dead.

Ellen and Karen joined Astrid in Billy's room. They hugged each other, and cried.

A hospital chaplain came into the room, and asked if the family wished to donate any body parts.

"What could he possibly have left that anyone would want?" Karen asked. She thought it would have been funny, if it weren't so sad.

Other friends and family, who had been at Good Samaritan overnight, were told of Billy's death. The official cause was liver failure, due to lymphatic cancer. Billy's body just quit working. The hospital received several hundred phone calls that day, after Billy's death had been announced, from fans and friends hoping to console Astrid and Karen, and just to let someone know how much they would miss Billy.

Billy's funeral was at 1 p.m. Saturday, and more than 300 people crowded into St. Mary's Catholic Cathedral in Portland. Lenny, Fritz Johnson, Tony DeMicoli, Glen Baggerly, Stephen Kimberley, Bart Danielson and Rick Jones, a Portland actor who shared Billy's concern about apartheid, were the pallbearers.

Two of Billy's songs were were played over loudspeakers.

From "My Life":

My life is a picture book
I know it's worth a second look
My songs have a thousand hooks
but the message changes every day

My life is a comedy
My life is a tragedy

If Shakespeare was alive today
I wonder what kind of things he would say

From "The Big Picture":

And in the big picture, the big picture
The fear of dying is only life

Lenny had been through the ritual of burying someone he loved before, his father, and he didn't like it.

"I was totally oblivious that day, totally gone," he says. "I didn't talk to anybody. I didn't want to. I didn't feel like I should be there. To me, Billy and I had already separated after that last fishing trip. I'd made my peace with Billy. I don't know why I felt that way, but I didn't have anything to say to anybody. I felt kind of like a stranger. It was a very strange day. I think it was a relief for a lot of people, for my mom and Karen."

Annie Farmer had just returned from New Orleans, where she had been for the funeral of her best friend. Like Lenny, and like most of the people at Billy's funeral, she didn't have much to say.

"I was in an absolute state of shock. I was completely numb," she says. "I was so emotionally upset, I just sat by myself and didn't talk to anyone. I said goodbye to him as the casket went by. It was one of the hardest things I've ever done."

As Karen sat through the service, memories of the past six years raced through her mind. It didn't seem like that long ago that she had met Billy at the midnight movie, but so much had happened since that night. Lenny pointed out a mural on the cathedral wall, a painting of a young boy. "Oh my God, look, it's Billy," he told her. Karen was mesmerized by the boy's face. It was Billy, she thought.

Steve Hettum, who had known Billy since the Malchicks days, who had been the Unreal Gods' first manager, and who had remained such a loyal, and good friend to Billy, offered a eulogy:

"In a world of subcompacts and mini cars, Billy was a '57 Cadillac. He had the power of a V8 engine, wall-to-wall carpeting and power windows. That was what the Malchicks were all about. When we ask ourselves why Billy had to die, I'd like to think that God needed another engine. We could all learn from the saintly way Billy lived his life while battling cancer. I hope you all leave here with not so much a heavy heart, but a happy heart, because of the joy his music gave to all of us. Billy would have wanted it that way."

Stephen Kimberley was next:

"Let us all take a second look at the life of Billy Rancher. He once said, 'The minute you think you know all there is about life is when it's over.' He wished that people would stop fighting and hating each other, and love each other instead. Through the power of his music, he wanted people to put aside their differences and work together. He wanted above all for people to be happy and to long not for what they did not have, but to long for what they did have."

Tony DeMicoli said that afternoon, "Billy always had a way of bringing people together, but this was not a day I was looking forward to."

There were obituaries, of course, in The Oregonian newspaper, in The Rocket, the Seattle magazine that had featured Billy on its first color cover back in 1983, and on the local television newscasts. But none were more fitting than Buck Munger's in Two Louies.

Buck wrote:

"Billy's long struggle with cancer ended on December 2, when he died. It was a beautiful day, the sky a deep winter blue, the kind of a day on which an angel might float away to heaven. Those of us whose lives were touched by Billy will not soon forget him.

"Bill came over to my house, last September, to do an interview. I hadn't seen him in many months. In that time, a great change had come over him. For the past four years, Billy fought a valiant fight against his illness. And every time he recuperated, even slightly, from a bout with cancer, the guy was back out there with a band. Billy's intrepid bravery was always apparent. But the change I noticed in September was of a much higher, finer nature. Billy had reached peace with himself and his life. He knew that he was in contact with a force far more vital and rich than those of money or power or fame: the pure white light of the universal spirit. Billy realized that his true purpose lay in conveying a message of love to his fellow human beings.

"Anyone who talked with Billy in the past four months knows that this was no act. For only in confronting the absolute inevitability of his own death did Billy find a true reason to be alive. Were all of us to follow his lead, indeed, this world would be one of peace, love and harmony.

"This was a real human being."

Billy and a homeless man in downtown Portland, during the Unreal Gods years.
(Bart Danielson)

A wake was held at the Last Hurrah, the club owned by Peter and Michael Mott. Billy's last show had been there, on November 22nd, just 10 days before he died.

Houston Bolles turned 21 years old on the day of Billy's death. He'd learned everything he knew about music, about writing songs and performing them, from Billy. "I just remember this incredibly sad feeling at the wake," he says. "I remember sitting there, looking at Karen, wondering how she was even standing."

The private burial was at Lincoln Memorial Park Cemetery, on a hill above Bart Danielson's house on Mount Scott where Billy had lived for a short time. Astrid wanted to bury Billy with his father, a World War II veteran, but was told that Billy was too old, that only young children could be laid to rest alongside fathers or mothers in military cemeteries.

Billy's grave is marked by a flat, gray rectangular stone. Written on the marble top, in white lettering:

Billy Rancher
1957-1986

Billy's likeness, from the chest up, is etched into the marble, with musical notes stretching across the gravestone. Under the musical notes are these words:

I'm Walking Down a Rocky Road For You

The grave is often covered with guitar picks, left by Lenny, Dave Stricker, Houston Bolles, Chuck Retondo or others who have played with Billy, or just wanted him to know that they heard what he had to say.

Billy Rancher will never be forgotten by anyone who knew him, or saw him play. He left behind music that sounds as good today as it did when he played it in Portland's clubs. "Boom Chuck Rock Now!" and the "Thinkin' Zebra" EP by Flesh and Blood show up in used record stores, and there are tapes of other studio sessions and live performances by the Malchicks, the Unreal Gods, Flesh and Blood and Mr. Groove in circulation. Billy was recorded on video, first by David Jester, and then by Jan Baross, who filmed a documentary shown on KOIN-TV in the spring of 1987.

Billy left his music. He left his image. He left memories of sublime performances and the best times anyone ever had. And every spring, Mo Stevenson's tulips bloom as a reminder, beautiful and bright, and full of life. Just like Billy.

ABOUT THE AUTHOR

Bill Reader is an assistant sports editor at The News Tribune in Tacoma, Washington. He lives in University Place with his wife Stephanie and their cats – Tribune and Baby.
This is his first book.

Order an autographed copy of
"Rocky Road/The Legendary Life and Times of Billy Rancher"
by mail.

Please send _____ copies to:

Name: _____

Address: _____

City: _____ State: _____ Zip Code: _____

Send a check, money order or cashier's check to:

**No Fate Publishing
3800A Bridgeport Way West
Suite 492
University Place, WA 98466**

The check, money order or cashier's check should be made out to No Fate Publishing for $12.00 for each book, plus $2.00 shipping and handling. Washington residents add 8.0 percent tax (96 cents) per book.

For information about Billy Rancher's music on CD contact:

Locals Only
Portland, OR
(503) 227-5000

To purchase "Pure Billy" and other Billy Rancher videos, call or write:

David Jester
Pro Video Productions
1816 NW Kearney St.
Portland, OR 97209
(800) 324-9669